The
Secret
Of
JOB

and

The
Great Irony

By

D.W. Clement

Table of Contents

SecretofJob.com

iv

Who wrote the Book of Job and when? Scholars can debate this all they'd like. What we do know is that it is right in the middle of the Word of God, and that the Lord has kept it there, with the help of thousands of scribes, down through time.

And it is indeed there for a purpose.

In The Secret of Job, I speak often of the "Word". When you see this, I am writing about the Lords Words to us, in the Bible and by His Holy Spirit.

I have generally used the King James Version for the passages and references in this book, though I have simplified the Old English at times so as to make it easier and more understandable for the reader.

Preface

How many times have you opened up the Word of God and wanted to go directly to the Book of Job?

If you are like most of us, pretty much never.

How many times have you heard Job taught, and had that abandoned sinking feeling, when those bringing the message would either begin or end with "Well, God is God, and He does whatever He wants, whenever He wants, even if it is painful..."

There was always a magnanimous, painfully pious countenance when someone would begin, and you knew it was going to be about Job. "We will never know why God does what He does, and in His infinite Wisdom He does these things, and we'll just have to learn how to accept it and go on..."

How many times have you wondered about the lessons and teachings and vague understanding on the subject of Job? Did it sometimes feel like those teaching were reaching too far for an explanation, or not far enough? Haven't you known in your inner being that something was missing? Or that something was not quite right with the various almost cloaked opaque explanations?

Why did the teachings seem so far removed from the rest of the Bible? Even though it is right in the middle of God's Word, directly in front of Psalms, it always seemed that the things that were said about it were so completely detached from Who God was and is. Every apologetic, every teaching, every sermon I heard concerning Job removed what I understood to be true about God, and in its place inserted a complete "unknowing" of Who the Lord is, and in the end always reiterating that we would never be able to know God, until maybe one day in the "bye and bye..."

How many times have we avoided the uneasy fear that all that happened to Job, seemingly out of nowhere, might happen to us?

All of this was not the God I knew. Jesus clearly taught otherwise, and He was the very character of the Father.

The God I knew sent His own Son, to show us of Him, that He might be with us, and that we might be with Him; Emmanuel - God with us. I knew by experience that He answers by His Holy Spirit, and He shows us so many things when we spend time with Him. Why would He separate Himself and distance Himself, as what was being taught? What part of the Word of God explained why He would do such a thing?

It just didn't fit.

Up to this point, I really didn't want to read the Book of Job. Bad things happened to Job. Really bad things. And there was apparently no answer. No help. No solution.

So one day I asked the question.

"Lord, what is the story with Job? Why is it even in the Book? I really don't want to read it. I know there must be something to it, or it wouldn't be in your Word. The interpretations I've heard don't agree at all with who You are. So please show me about Job."

The Lord likes our questions, and I think He especially likes the big ones. And apparently I was ready to hear the answer.

Then, the Holy Spirit, in that inner Knowing, that still gentle voice, said,

'Read it again...'

"It is the glory of God to conceal a thing:

but the honor of kings is to search out a matter."

Proverbs 25:2

~~~~~

"What you hear in the ear, proclaim upon the housetops."

Mat 10:27

The Secret
of
Job

Everyone Loves a Secret

*"To you it is given to know
the mysteries of the kingdom of God..."(1)*

Everyone loves a secret.

Secrets are hidden things which, when told or discovered, come to be known, come to the light and become evident.

The Lord has hidden many amazing things in His Word. I believe He has done this in the hope that we will assert ourselves, ask the questions, and find the answers. And then we'll get to reap the reward of finding the thing out, to realize the joy in the revealing of it, even by the Holy Spirit from the Lord to us personally. It is certainly great reward.

And everyone loves a mystery.

The thing about a mystery – the anticipation, the curiosity, the thrill, the enjoyment, the revealing – is the fact that the answers lie just below the surface,,, and they've been there all along. It's just taken someone, or a group of someone's, to take the time to seek and find the thing out.

Detectives do it every day. They don't take anything for granted, and apply all manner of tests to the mystery, ask many questions, and eventually, and sometimes with a little help, discover the answers from the clues.

Again, the marvelous thing about it is that the answers have been there the whole time. It's just a matter of searching the thing out.

How awful is a mystery that has no solution, no ending. A person would never read it, or as in our very visual and visceral society, never watch it. There would be no pleasure, no satisfaction from it, only a vague emptiness at having no result, having no real conclusion. Nothing would be gained, nothing would be revealed, and nothing would be known.

1

What I knew about the Book of Job had this same feeling for me.

Of all the sermons, teachings, and 'learned' explanations I'd heard, the answers had the same conclusion. It was still a mystery without a solution, without an ending, without even a thread of cumulative clues as to what it was about and why it was even in the Book.

The Lord loves our questions, and again, I believe especially the big ones. He loves when we search diligently to find out more, more about His creation and just as importantly, more about Him.

There are so many amazing and beautiful mysteries in the Word of God just waiting to be revealed, to be discovered, to be found, and to be rejoiced in.

Right in the middle of the Bible there is a secret, a hidden mystery.

That mystery is the Secret of Job.

The Past

"Beware lest any man spoil you through philosophy and vain deceit, after the tradition of men, after the rudiments of the world, and not after Christ."(1)

The past teachings of Job would tell us that God isn't reachable or understandable. How much stock have we put in what we've been told about the things said by Job and by his friends all of these years? How much of our personal theology has been affected by these handed down and passed along thoughts and teachings of Job? How ingrained are they in our concept of God, that we can't go to Him, and that He hands out good and evil on a regular basis? What has been the negative impact of all of these explanations on our Christianity over all of these generations and even centuries?

Old school theories of Job have continually left us with no answers except for, "Have Patience in Misery for However Long it Takes." Not only do we not gain any more answers or know any more about who God is, we, by way of the old explanations, seem to be left with more questions, and may possibly be inclined to look no further, as "God is God, and does whatever He wants." We are left to dwell on our own, having to live with a seemingly random uncaring and unknowable good/bad Deity.

The resulting considerations of these former teachings seem to only generate and perpetuate a "God wants us only to know that He is Great, that's all we need, and we better know this or else" mentality.

I would also contend that these old school answers to Job not only may serve to keep us away from God, and suggest that we should keep a distance out of fear (as Job did), but they also may allow for an easy excuse to avoid seeking God in the first place.

Not only can these old explanations be fairly pervasive inhibitors to having a deep relationship with the Lord, they may also be, and/or may become, a considerable obstacle to fulfilling our Great Commission.

The reality and the truth about Job is that God is right here, right now, and He wants us to know <u>all</u> about Him, and His Son, and His Spirit.

Do we go to God? Do we know the Holy Spirit well enough to know how to go to God? Are we learning any more about Who God is, Who Jesus is and all He came to bring to us, and who the Holy Spirit of God is, the Spirit of God who Jesus made available to us when He died on that cross? Do we know about this Comforter He sent to show us all things?

God is our strength and our fortress and our strong tower.

Do we believe it? Do we know it? Do we go there?

Did Job go there?

May we endeavor to search for all that Jesus came and died to bring us, and that we would know Him, and know the Father, and know the Holy Spirit in a much more full and more profound way; that we would know that it is the Lords will to give to us and to show us of Himself and His will in our lives, that we would know all that He has given to us, and that all the things can be made manifest, or can happen in our lives, that we, and others, may receive all that He is and has, and that *our* joy would be full.

So let's now take a new look at the Book of Job.

My hope is that you will see Job, and our own nature, and our marvelous Father, His Son, and His Spirit in a new, and more tangible, and more glorious way.

So What *is* the Purpose of Job?

*"For whatever things were written before were written for our learning,
that we, through the patience and comfort of the Scriptures,
might have hope."*(1)

Let us begin by considering that many of the events written in the Old Testament were dramatic in nature in order to get the readers (or listeners) attention to something that the Lord God wanted to communicate to His people.

These happenings only occurred once, and were written and passed on to show us or to reveal to us something.

The Book of Job is a great example.

God knows that extreme conditions or events teach us things. They stick with us.

The Word of God is filled with people who were in various situations which were presented to us as either a test, or were set as an example for us and others. These events don't happen continually, and/or with such great magnitude, but they are there as examples for our benefit. Here, briefly, are a few...

➤ Abraham and Isaac. Does God require us to put our sons on a pyre on a regular basis? Ah, No. The Lord was showing us what Faith was. Trust God.

➤ Lots wife turning to a pillar of salt? Haven't seen too many salt people lately. Don't look back at the things that were evil or discouraging in your past. Press forward and onward, "toward the High calling" in your life.

➤ Noah. How many times has the earth flooded completely? Actually, never again. Rainbows. Trust the Father and listen to, and for, Him.

➤ Jonah was swallowed by a big fish and spit back out. Yuk. Doesn't happen too much. Better to just go ahead and do what the Lord puts in your heart to do.

➤ Part any seas lately, Moses? Follow the guidance of the Lord and He will do amazing things. He wants us to be free too. Sans serpents, locusts and frogs....

➤ How about Joseph? Who was the last person you knew who was sold into slavery by his brothers, and then became Vice King? Do your best, and God will use you for great things.

➤ Shadrack, Mischak, and Abednego. Trust God, and serve Him. It's worth it, no matter how hot it gets.

➤ Daniels trials. God first. Always.

➤ Joshua and Caleb. "Not the Wilderness again, we're supposed to be over there." Know that God is with you, even in the unknown ahead.

➤ Joshua and the walls of Jericho. Just do it. Have patience and listen to the Lord.

➤ David with Goliath. Giants anyone? They're everywhere. But Our God is so much greater.

➤ How about Gideon. Way outnumbered? Know the Greatest power on earth, the Power of God, is with you.

All of these situations were one-time events which happened with an intended result. And by the way, all of them overcame and succeeded in the end.

These extreme events were either meant as a test, or as an example to us. Or both.

Job is both.

God has certainly put Job in the Word of God for a reason. There is an intended result in the Book of Job which will help us realize who God is, and will help us with our walk in Him. Just as the Father, the Son (Jesus, the Word), and Holy Spirit are multidimensional and omni-dimensional, so also is the Book of Job.

The beginning of the Book of Job starts with a clear insight into the workings of good and evil. Nowhere else in the Old Testament do we have such a clear description of the goings on in the spirit realm as in the first two chapters of Job.

Jobs reactions to all that happened in his life reveal much about him, and his relationship with God.

Job is indeed persecuted, not by who we think, but from a rarely considered, unexpected source.

And in the end, Job's amazing revelation from the Lord holds the answers to one of the great mysteries, to how and why we can truly worship God.

The purpose of the story of Job is to show us more about ourselves, and about the Father. To show us things that we, for any number of reasons, may never have seen before.

God wants us to know, in our lives, and in this generation,,,

the Truth about Job.

Part I

God

(and Satan)

There was a Man in the Land of Uz,,,,

"There was a man in the land of Uz, whose name was Job;
and that man was perfect and upright,
one that feared God and shunned evil..."(1)

Well, what do we have so far?

We have the man Job, who is perfect and upright, he fears God, and eschews, or shuns, or even hates, evil.

Before we get started, let's look at some definitions of what we're about to explore. Let's begin by considering the meaning of the phrase "feared God" in the above verse. The Hebrew definition of the word "fear" used here is "yare" (pronounced "yaw'-ray"), which is 'to revere', and similar to yirah ("yir-aw") which means 'reverence'. As a side note, I find it very interesting that this word "yare" is pronounced similarly to "Yahweh", one of the primary and most holy names of God.

I would like to point out something else here about our use of this "yare" word "fear". Jesus showed us so many things in His short time here on earth. One very important clarification Jesus made for us in the New Testament concerning this word for 'fear' comes when Jesus quotes Deuteronomy 6 in the Old Testament.

> *"Thou shall **fear** (yare) the Lord thy God, and serve Him..."(2).*

In Matthew, when Jesus directly quotes this verse, he purposely changes the word fear and makes a very important distinction when He says,

> *"Thou shall **worship** the Lord thy God, and Him only*
> *shall you serve."(3).*

Think about this. The ramifications of this clarification are enormous.

Now, anytime we see the word "fear" in its "yare" or "yirah" form as it relates to God, we can replace it with the more understandable and reverential word "worship."

This may help us in our perceptions of His Word and help us in how we relate to the Father, as I believe Jesus intended it to.

A little further on we will talk about another Hebrew word for fear; "pachad", which means to be startled or afraid, as used in other verses in Job.

Let's continue. What does Job being "perfect and upright" mean? Does this infer that Job could do no wrong?

The Word says *"All have sinned and come short of the glory of God."(4)*

"All" means everyone. Job was not exempt from this. None of us are. What is being said here is that Job has a pure heart toward God and was honest before Him. It doesn't mean that he was actually a perfect man and infallible, but it means that his heart, his focus, was pure and honest toward and before his God.

So Job is focused and honest and has a strong reverence toward the Lord.

One of the first traits we see of Job is him worshiping and giving sacrifices to God for his children.

> *"And his sons went and feasted in their houses, everyone his day; and called for their three sisters to eat and to drink with them.*
> *And it was so, when the days of their feasting were over, that Job sent and sanctified them, and rose up early in the morning, and offered burnt offerings according to how many of them there were: for Job said, It may be that my sons have sinned, and cursed God in their hearts. And Job did this continually."(5)*

During the days of feasting his sons and daughters would eat and drink heartily together. Job was always concerned about the possibility that they all may have done something wrong while engaged in these activities, so he would make burnt offerings continually to God in case they had sinned or cursed God in their hearts.

Just in case...

While reading this, I was curious as to why this particular trait of Job's was one of only a few characterizations given to us of Job, and why it was presented here. The answers will become apparent later on as we delve further into Job.

We often mistake Job's actions, in giving sacrifices for his children just in case they had done anything wrong, as being perfect.

What did God consider as "perfect" before Him? Was the performance of these sacrifices by Job what was found as perfect, or was it Job honoring God in his life that was considered perfect? There is a difference, and I would suggest that it was the latter. We will look at this later on as well.

Note something here. Job is coming to God with everything in his life at this point. Continually, even with things that actually may or may not be happening.

In looking at Job further we see that Job is that He is very, very wealthy.

> *"His substance was also so... that this man was the greatest of all men in the east."(6)*

He had much substance, and was the richest man in the land.

We also see that Job was always teaching and helping others, and encouraging others around him.

> *"Behold, you have instructed many, and you have strengthened the weak hands. Your words have upheld him that was falling, and you have strengthened those with feeble knees."(7)*

So Job was upright, an encourager, and had a pure heart before God.

The first impression we generally decide to apply to Job is that he had these wonderful traits, was perfect before God,,, and therefore couldn't do anything wrong.

The Adversary

"Now there was a day when the sons of God
came to present themselves before the LORD,
and Satan came also among them."(1)

The story then breaks off to the sons of God coming before God one day.

Here enters Satan.

We see in the Book of Job that Satan is able to walk among the sons of God, and that at this time he is able to talk with God.

Much can and has been written about Satan. Without getting too involved here, Satan, or Lucifer, is considered to be an original angel, who through his own pride considered himself equal to or greater than God. Satan then rebelled against God, and was cast out of heaven to earth.

Jesus speaks of this event in Luke:

"I beheld Satan as lightning fall from heaven..."(2)

There is considerable mention of Satan and devils in the New Testament, along with their portrayals and influences. The Word also describes Satan as the "adversary," or the "enemy". Jesus had many encounters and dealings with him and with them in His time here on earth.

I like what CS Lewis had to say about Satan and devils in his Preface to The Screwtape Letters.

"There are two equal and opposite errors into which our race can fall about devils.
One is to disbelieve in their existence.
The other is to believe, and to feel an excessive and unhealthy interest in them."(3)

12

We are making a mistake if we don't believe they exist, and we also err if we feel they have more power than they do and if we begin to have an excessive interest in them.

I once heard a good description of devils as being just wee little objects, all gnarled and slovenly, without any real power, with only the ability to suggest ideas into the thoughts of men.

We see a representation of this enemy in Genesis, when the serpent cunningly talked Eve into eating the fruit from the tree of the knowledge of good and evil.

"And the woman said, the serpent beguiled me, and I did eat."(4)

Beguile means to deceive. I do believe that the enemy can at times present unhealthy and even evil thoughts into our minds and into our thought patterns. These thoughts are meant to distract us from what is good and right and true. The enemy tries to deceive us and move us away from what is good and right and true.

These thoughts are harmless if we don't pursue them, and the only way they can actually affect us is if we act upon them. Only then is it possible to hurt ourselves and others. The actions can be physical actions, or with our words, which many times can be more powerful and hurtful than any physical act.

Because of God's protections in our lives, the enemy can only suggest thoughts and introduce us to wrong or deceiving ideas, but cannot force us to act on them. We fail only when we are tempted and follow through on those thoughts.

The answer to this is to bring into captivity, or bring under control all thoughts by realizing and being renewed in our minds as to what is good and right and true; to the things of the Lord. This helps us and gives us strength to **not** act on the diversionary suggestions and tactics of the enemy, keeping us from potentially harming ourselves and others.

Another observation of Satan is when Jesus describes him as a thief when He says, *"The thief comes only to kill, steal and destroy..."(5)* and again when He says that the devil is the father of lies, and *"there is no truth in him."(6)*

So Satan is a thief and a liar.

Keep in mind, in the bigger picture, that In Jesus' Name the enemy must flee. Also know that the Lord is far more powerful than Satan or his adversaries. By far.

> *"If you believe that there is one God; you do well: the devils*
> *also believe, and tremble."(7)*

Another description of the enemy is that he is an accuser of the brethren, and an accuser of the truth (in people) which oppose him.

> *"For the accuser of the brethren is cast down, which accused them*
> *before our God, day and night."(8)*

As a side note, it is interesting to see the level of accusation being used against others trying to do good in our society today. Where might these accusations really be coming from?

The next verse talks about Satan as a "roaring lion".

> *"Be sober, be vigilant; because your adversary the devil,*
> *as a roaring lion, walks about, seeking whom he may consume..."(9)*

In life, the enemy will roar loudly at times, especially when accusing the brethren (us or others) and will by this try to take our minds off the truth.

Consider this; has the roar of a lion ever hurt anyone? Scared some maybe, but the roaring has never physically hurt anyone.

So we see that the enemy has a habit of lying, and of sometimes roaring, and he certainly tries to put us into fear, trying to take us away from what is good, and divert us from the strength of faith and trust.

In putting these descriptions together, we see that the enemy can be loud, that he lies, and that he sometimes lies loudly.

Or, if you'd like,,, he roars lies.

The adversary is easily defeated in Jesus Name, but we need to understand and recognize that he is indeed out there trying to influence us, and take away the good things that God has for us.

The Challenge

*"And the LORD said unto Satan, have you considered my servant Job,
that there is none like him in the earth..."(1)*

Then the Lord asks Satan where he has come from, and Satan answers,

"From going to and fro in the earth, and from walking up and down in it."(2)

So here Satan is, walking about in the earth, and shows up as the sons of
God came to present themselves before the Lord.

God again directs his words toward Satan and begins to praise His
servant Job.

> *"Have you considered my servant Job, that there is none like him
> in the earth, an upright and blameless man, who fears God and
> shuns evil?"(3)*

At this point Satan gives a marvelous insight into the protections that
the Lord has set up on Jobs behalf.

> *"Does Job fear (yare-worship) You for nothing?"* Satan says.
> *"Haven't You established protection all around him, around his house,
> and all around everything he has? You've blessed the work of his hands,
> and all that he has continues to increase."(4)*

Satan could do nothing to Job while God had His covering of protection
around him. The Lord, by His grace, and out of His love, has the same
protections around us as well, whether or not we choose to believe it.

Let's stop here and consider what might be the case if God weren't with
us, and didn't have his protections around us.

Since *"God is Love"(5)*, if God were not with us, there would be no love on
earth in any form whatsoever. Imagine what it would be like without
any kindness or goodness or truth or trust in the world. If the Lord were
to ever take Himself away from us, there would be no protection, no
love, no honesty, no caring, and no goodness, whatsoever. There would

only be the opposite, all the time; a continuous chaos of evil, hatred, lies, greed and sorrow. Can we imagine that?

Even though there is an adversary and evil in the world today, it would be a completely different place than the grace, caring, trust and kindness that we are accustomed to, even moment by moment, if God weren't with us.

In His grace, God has a covering of protection around all of us, and one day we will know the extent and all we have and have had from our Father.

Satan then continues on and presents a challenge to God.

> *"Destroy all that Job has, and he will curse You to Your face."(6)*

Satan's goal is to get Job to curse God openly. He is saying that if God removes His protections from him, that Job will turn around and curse God to His face. Satan desires this to happen, and it is because of this desire he presents his challenge.

So God, considering Satan, and considering the man Job and all of his great traits and how he is "perfect" before Him, accepts the challenge.

> *"Okay, all that he has is in your power, only don't touch him."(7)*

God is saying, "I will lift my protections. You now have authority over him, just don't harm him physically."

God is taking this challenge and removing His protections of Job in order to prove something. The Lord, in His amazing wisdom, not only has the intention of proving a point to Satan about Job, but is also intending to show us some amazing things as well.

Again, as a reminder, the Book of Job has been given to us for a purpose, as a lesson and an example.

So then, as a figure of speech, all hell breaks loose around Job. Satan has his way and the Sabeans take the livestock and kill the servants.

Fire from heaven (by Satan's hand) burns up the sheep, and kills more servants. Chaldeans take the camels and kill even more servants. A great wind shows up and blows the eldest son's house down on top of his sons and daughters, killing them all.

Satan uses the powers he has been given to kill steal and destroy in Job's life. Keep in mind where this hurt and destruction have actually come from. God has lifted His covering from Job, but what happens has been initiated, actuated, and all delivered and performed by Satan.

As a result of this challenge, Satan uses the full authority given to him, using Sabeans, Chaldeans, and even the weather to afflict Job.

Job's response to all of these events is to tear his cloak, shave his head and fall to the ground and worship God. He then responds with one of the most iconic phrases of all time.

> "Naked I came from my mother's womb, naked I shall return,
> The Lord gave, and the Lord has taken away,
> Blessed be the name of the Lord."(8)

This is Job's initial reaction to it all, and we see Job directly attributing these events directly to God. God did allow it, but the attacks were purely caused and delivered by Satan.

The Word then says,

> "In all this, Job sinned not, nor charged God foolishly."(9)

Despite all that has happened, in Jobs reactions he has not sinned, or stepped out of line, or, as Satan desired, cursed God to His face.

The story continues when there was another day when the sons of God showed up before the Lord, and again Satan is there.

And the Lord once again extols Job. He asks if Satan has taken notice of Job, who is still perfect and upright, and blameless before Him. Job still hasn't sinned and has not cursed God to His face. God then adds,

> *"And he still holds fast to his integrity, although you moved Me*
> *against him to (allow you to) destroy him, although he has done*
> *nothing wrong."(10)*

At this point, Job has done nothing wrong.

As Satan considers this, he then suggests that all Jobs family, servants and livelihood really didn't matter enough, but if Job's person, his skin and bone, if his physical being is touched, then he will indeed turn on his God and curse God openly.

God once again considers the challenge and considers Job, and once again agrees to the new challenge, and allows Satan to have power over Job, now with the only caveat being that Satan could not take Jobs life, could not kill him.

Satan then puts boils on Job from head to foot.

Job couldn't believe it. Now, on top of his children and much of his wealth being destroyed, he was now also plagued with physical ailments and afflictions.

As it all sinks in, Job's wife makes a suggestion that Job abandon his integrity and his beliefs, curse God, and die. His wife is suggesting that Job just give up.

He then answers her,

> *"Shall we receive good at the hand of God, and shall we not receive*
> *evil?"(11)*

Job then resigns himself to it all, and ties all the good things God has given them in the past, with all of the evil which has just befallen him by Satan.

Again we see Job expressing his belief that God has caused all of this evil and attributing all of the things being done to him directly and solely to God.

Yes, God has allowed it, but keep in mind once again that it is Satan who has actually caused all of the evil and affliction of Job.

So why did God do this? Why did God allow this? Was it only for the challenge by Satan? Or was it just because God is God?

Or may all of this have taken place in order to reveal to Job, and to us, a far greater and more important set of truths and lessons...

So Job still does not curse God to His face.

> *"In all this Job did not sin with his lips."*(12)

Job may be initially blaming God, but he has not cursed Him.

Note that this is the last we see or hear of Satan in the Book of Job. Satan has done his thing and is now gone.

Job now mourns and contemplates his misfortune, and as he is doing so, three of his friends head for Job's house (Job still has his home) to "mourn and comfort him."

> *"And when they lifted up their eyes afar off, and when they didn't recognize him, they lifted up their voice, and wept; and they tore their robes, and sprinkled dust upon their heads toward heaven."*(13)

When they got to Job and saw him, they didn't even recognize him as he had shaved his head and was covered with boils.

Here was Job, in this awful condition, sitting in silence.

> *"So they sat down with him upon the ground seven days and seven nights, and none spoke a word unto him: for they saw that his grief was very great."*(14)

Once again keep in mind that this is a one-time event, dramatic in nature, in order to show and/or teach us a thing or things.

All for a reason...

Job's Integrity

"...a perfect and upright man, one that fears God and eschews evil and still he holds fast to his integrity..."(1)

The one thing that remained with Job, the one thing that he held on to through-out this ordeal was his integrity.

Webster's Dictionary defines "integrity" as "honesty and sincerity".

Job was a completely honest and sincere person. Job could not lie and could not curse God. He honestly and sincerely honored God. He had integrity within himself and with God, and he wouldn't give it up for anything.

God likes it when we hold fast to our integrity. He likes it when we strongly hold on to our belief in Him, and on to things that are good and right and true, that are in and of Him.

I think that we are often challenged in this way at times in our own lives. In this world full of easy distraction, and lack of integrity, it is easy to just say "well, so and so did it," and give up to the temptation and/or the easy way out. Job's wife suggested that very thing to him.

But Job held fast to what he knew to be the truth.

This is, by the way, a good way to discern the 'character' of a person.

Do they stand fast in their beliefs, even when it might not be popular and very much against the flow to do so? Though many times it may not be the easy or popular route, there is great strength and great reward in doing so.

So Job wouldn't quit, and wouldn't lie, and wouldn't believe a lie.

What we'll see later on is that he had to defend his integrity to the greatest extent with, of all people, his friends who continuously accuse him of doing something wrong, of sinning so egregiously that he deserved all of these afflictions.

But Job hadn't sinned, and he knew it.

Another of Webster's definitions of integrity is "wholeness, or completeness."

I'd like to suggest that when we decide to do something that we know is wrong, or make a decision to compromise to whatever degree, large or small, the decision takes away from our wholeness and completeness. It diminishes our integrity, and ourselves to a certain degree. Even if it is just a small wrong, it can cause a change in any number of our behavior sets, because we know the truth inside.

Because of this even subconscious awareness, doing what you know is wrong can affect behavior patterns, actions and outcomes. Insecurities and/or defense mechanisms can engage which may cause any manner of out of character behavior, if even slight, which can manifest and alter outcomes in many different ways.

So any lack of integrity, no matter to what degree, can cause harm to ourselves and to those around us. This can, in varying degrees, have a ripple effect which can, and often does have far reaching consequences.

The Lord wants us to be whole and complete, honest and sincere.

Job had this integrity, and God liked it.

Part II

Job

Job

"After this Job opened his mouth, and cursed his day..."(1)

Okay, so here we are. Satan was given authority, and attacked Job with numerous afflictions. He attacked Jobs family, his wealth and his flesh, but has not been allowed to kill him. Satan has caused it all, as God had given him permission.

Because we know that God is good, we can know that all this is happening for a purpose that is good.

And maybe even great.

Satan is now gone and completely out of the picture. We find that Job has been sitting and grieving now for seven long days in silence. A whole week, night and day. That's a long time. His friends have been there with him, but haven't said a word because of his grief. With all of the things that have happened to him, certainly deep grieving was to be expected. He had just lost many dear and important parts of his life, unexpectedly, and apparently without reason.

In that first seven days, in all this time in silence, Job has done a lot of thinking. He has mourned his family and his riches. He has lived with his physical ailments. He has certainly been questioning why this has happened to him. He also at the same time began to formulate some conclusions, and from these conclusions came responses. Whether right or wrong, he has made decisions about what has happened and what his responses will be.

At the end of these seven days, after all the things that have now happened in his life, and after considering all of it in silence during this time, Job has determined his course of action, and he finally speaks.

> *"Let the day perish wherein I was born, and the night in which*
> *it was said, 'there is a man child conceived.'*
> *Let that day be darkness; let not God regard it from above,*
> *neither let the light shine upon it.*

Let darkness and the shadow of death stain it; let a cloud dwell upon it; let the blackness of the day terrify it.
As for that night, let darkness seize upon it; let it not be joined unto the days of the year, let it not come into the number of the months. Lo, let that night be solitary, let no joyful voice come into it.
Let them curse it that curse the day, who are ready to raise up their mourning. Let the stars of the twilight be dark; let it look for light, but have none; neither let it see the dawning of the day:
Because it shut not up the doors of my mother's womb, nor hid sorrow from my eyes."(2)

Job doesn't curse God, but he completely curses his life, and everything about it.

"Let the day perish wherein I was born."(3)

Job is regretting his life in its entirety.

After considering all that has befallen him, Job has decided that his course of action is going to be...

...to dwell completely in his loss, to mourn fervently, and to completely and deeply regret his whole life.

He has decided to react to it all by cursing everything about his life, by completely disengaging from everything he believed, and as we'll see, including even from his God.

I would like to point out here that, as we'll look at later on, the Lord may have been expecting a very different reaction from Job, from someone who was completely whole and upright and worshipful of and before Him.

To his credit, and throughout all of this, Job didn't curse God.

It seems to me though that _not_ cursing God would be one of the very basic and most fundamental of behaviors if you were determined to be upright before Him. "Not blaspheming" your Lord would be considered to be minimum at best, and certainly not the highest of goals to be achieved.

As we will look at later on, there are many other reactions and behaviors which might also be possible, no matter the situation, from someone who truly trusts and honors God.

So Job goes on and on and on, dwelling in his misery and cursing his days.

> *"Why didn't I die from my mother's womb?"*
> *"Why is light given to him that is in misery, and life to him who is bitter in soul; who longs for death, but it doesn't come?"(4)*

In Chapter 3 Job says,

> *"For the thing which I greatly feared is come upon me, and that which I was afraid of is come to me."(5)*

Here we find the other Hebrew word for fear, "pachad." This "pachad" fear means to be startled or afraid (fear) or to dread.

Some theological explanations and teachings suggest that it was because of his (pachad) fear that all of these things came upon Job. That this all happened because of his fears.

I believe that this particular explanation by and of itself as the cause of Job's afflictions falls well short of an answer to it all, as we all would be in dire straits if any amount of fear could cause such misery. Job had a certain amount of faith in God, and this explanation would suggest that anyone who has any fear has no faith and is susceptible to any number of horrible circumstances.

As we will see, this pachad type of fear may indeed have had something to do with prolonging his misery and his suffering, but it was not the cause of it all.

We have all been given a measure of faith, and it is up to us to use it. If we do not use it we are not necessarily susceptible to bad things in our lives, but we may suffer in not having the things that we might have had, if we were to fully use our faith and to exercise and grow in it.

So Job has decided to go very deeply into misery, and is expressing it fully.

> *"Oh that my grief were thoroughly weighed, and my calamity laid in the balances together! For now it would be heavier than the sand of the sea: therefore my words are swallowed up.*
> *For the arrows of the Almighty are within me, the poison of which drink up my spirit: the terrors of God do set themselves in array against me."*(6)

Is what Job is saying really true?

We will see later on that God has not done any of these things. There are no poison arrows, and God has never set any terrors up for him.

Job continues to pine and commiserate and mourn about all the misery and all of his afflictions for the next 35 chapters.

While Job still does not curse God, he continues to express his innocence from sinning, and believes to the end that his suffering is unjustified because he hasn't sinned, so there is no reason for God to punish him.

It is interesting to note that Satan is never mentioned by Job or his friends as the possible cause of Job's troubles. Though they didn't actually know the source of these afflictions, and God never reveals this to them, Job and his friends by their words attribute all of it to God.

Job especially speaks at great length about what he feels God has done to him.

> *"He (the Lord) has fenced up my way that I cannot pass,*
> *and He has set darkness in my paths. He has stripped me of my glory, and taken the crown from my head.*
> *He has destroyed me on every side, and I am gone: and my hope He has removed like a tree. He has also kindled His wrath against me, and He counts me as one of his enemies."*(7)

Again, is this true? We'll see that God never counts Job as one of his enemies, and that these words of Job, along with his actions and his reactions, may be the result of the decisions he himself has made.

Job has decided to react to it all by being wholly sorrowful, languishing, and remaining in his misery.

As a side note, there may be many readers who, at some point will want me to add the clarification that Jobs condition did not continue for years and years, as it may seem, but may have only lasted for a matter of weeks or months.

I'm okay with that, but even if it were only for a matter of hours or days, anyone who has been in painfully sorrowful circumstances knows that time completely removes itself, and is never rationally seen as a factor under and/or during such events. In those conditions, time seems to be torturingly eternal, we feel that we will be forever in that state, and we are not able to realize the inevitable truth that our set of circumstances, at some point, will change; that this situation too will pass.

I'd like to make another brief observation of our human condition here. I have always thought that there is a certain part of our nature which is able to reside in sorrow. It is usually a deep place in our being where we can dwell for a period of time, where our soul can dwell, and we may even find a degree of comfort in abiding there for a time, if not for the circumstances that have brought us to that place.

It just doesn't benefit us at all to stay there.

So Job continues to speak extensively about his misery.

> "My soul is weary of my life; I will leave my complaint upon myself; I will speak in the bitterness of my soul."(8)

Job also speaks the truth about the greatness of God.

> "He (God) is wise in heart, and mighty in strength: who has hardened himself against Him, and prospered? Who removes the mountains, and they know not: who overturns them in His anger.
>
> Who shakes the earth out of her place, and the pillars of it tremble. Who commands the sun, and it rises not; and seals up the stars. Who alone spreads out the heavens, and treads upon the waves of the sea.

Who made Arcturus, Orion, and Pleiades, and the chambers of the south.
Who does great things past finding out; and wonders without
number."(9)

It seems Job comforts himself with these words, but then continues in his woeful misery, and pining in his sorrow, all the time applying the cause of it all to God.

That is, until Chapter 38, when things abruptly change.

Part III

Eliphaz
Bildad
Zophar
and
Elihu

Eliphaz, Bildad, Zophar and Elihu

"Now when Job's three friends heard of all this evil that was come upon him, they came each one from his own place; for they had made an appointment together to come to mourn with him and to comfort him."(1)

In the beginning, when Jobs friends heard that Job was going through these calamities and that he was going through some very tough times, they decided to go to him and be with him in his time of need.

Doesn't this happen today? Isn't it our nature to be with someone during the hard times in order to be there to comfort and mourn with them?

In this particular case, Jobs friends start out with these good intentions to help and comfort Job out of compassion, but along the way they appear to have developed some other motives.

They all believed that bad things come solely from God in response to, and as punishment for, sin. Because of this belief each friend concluded fairly quickly along the way, that Job must have really messed up and sinned badly and must be continuing to sin somehow. Why else would this be happening to him?

After attending a bemoaning Job for seven days, after sitting in silence with him as he is in complete and deep misery, they are ready to try to "help" Job as a part of their comforting by also showing him the error of his ways, to help him stop "sinning" in order that he may return to Gods favor and to health.

So now, after this initial seven days of silence, they are ready...

> *"If we attempt to commune with you, will you be grieved?*
> *But who can hold himself back from speaking?"(2)*

"Job, will you be upset if we have a word with you? Who could possibly keep quiet about the reason all of this is happening to you?"

31

They have something to say.

> *"Job, you have instructed many. You've strengthened the weak hands. Your words have upheld him that was falling, and you have strengthened the feeble knees.*
> *But now it comes upon you and you faint. It touches you and you are troubled."*(3)

Job's friends truly believe that Job is doing something wrong to have caused all of these afflictions, and they begin to suggest that God has put all this on him because of the error of his ways, otherwise he would be healed and removed from his misery.

Do we also think this way at times? Do we think that God punishes us? What we will see is that though it may be in our own human nature to punish, it is not God's nature.

Also, do we also think that if we could somehow be "perfect" before God that our lives would somehow be made right, and that we would always be healthy, healed and whole?

Though we may have a desire for perfection within us, it is inherent in this world that there is no human perfection (other than Christ), and it is also inherent in this life that at some point or points there will be difficult situations, trials and tribulation.

What we will also look at is the question of how we deal with our very human trials and with the adversity that comes along with it.

So after seven days of silence, Jobs friends then fairly quickly move into how Job must be doing something terribly wrong before God, and they continue to attribute the suspected wrong to his present condition....

> *"Whoever perished, being innocent? Or what righteous person was ever killed unexpectedly? Even as I have seen, they that plow iniquity sow wickedness and also reap the same."*
> *"By the blast of God they perish, and by the breath of His nostrils, they are consumed."*(4)

Each one of his friends, as part of their argument, mix talking about the sin that Job must be doing with how great God is, and that God doesn't allow sin to happen without consequence.

Eliphaz then suggests to Job,

> "If I were you, Job, I would seek God, and unto God would I commit my cause:
> Who does great things and unsearchable; marvelous things without number: Who gives rain upon the earth, and sends waters upon the fields: He sets up on high those that be low; that those which mourn may be exalted to safety. He disappoints the devices of the crafty, so that their hands cannot perform their enterprise.
> He takes the wise in their own craftiness: and the counsel of the contrary is carried headlong. They meet with darkness in the daytime, and grope in the noonday as in the night.
> He saves the poor from the sword, from their mouth, and from the hand of the mighty. So the poor has hope, and iniquity is stopped.
> Behold, happy is the man whom God corrects: therefore don't despise the chastening of the Almighty."(5)

These verses are all great attributes of the Lord. The problem with this argument is that God is not chastening Job for anything.

Note here that Eliphaz is suggesting that Job should seek God about it.

Let's clarify something at this point. Job has not sinned. At the time of his afflictions at the hand of Satan, he is still considered by God to be a "perfect and upright man, one that fears God and eschews evil, and he still holds fast to his integrity." God said that Job has done nothing wrong and has not sinned, which shows us that 'sinning' is not the issue or cause of his afflictions.

So Job defends himself to them and refutes the accusations of Eliphaz.

> "How forcible are right words! But what does your arguing prove?
> Do you imagine to disapprove of words, and the speeches of one that is desperate, which are as wind?
> Yea, you overwhelm the now fatherless, and you dig a pit for your friend.
> Now be content and look upon me; for it is evident to you if I lie."(6)

Then one of his other friends, Bildad the Shuhite, begins to speak.

> "How long will you speak these things? and how long will the words of
> your mouth be like a strong wind?
> Does God pervert judgment? Or does the Almighty pervert justice?
> If your children have sinned against Him, and He has cast them away
> for their transgression; If you would seek unto God, and make your
> supplication to the Almighty; If you were pure and upright; surely now
> he would awake for you, and make your life prosperous."(7)

If you were innocent, Job, God surely would show up and fix it all.

Notice that Bildad also suggests that Job should go to God.

I would suggest that Job looks up to Bildad, as he agrees with him about
God's attributes and then ties his misery to all that has been said. Job
talks about what he would say to God, yet he is only talking to Bildad.

Zophar the Naamathite then has his turn.

> "Should your lies make men hold their peace? And when you mock,
> will no man make you ashamed?
> For you have said, my doctrine is pure, and I am clean in your eyes.
> But oh that God would speak, and open his lips against you; that He
> would show you the secrets of wisdom, that they are greater than you
> can see!
> Know, Job, that God exacts of you less than your iniquity deserves!"(8)

You've really messed up, Job, and you're lying about it. We don't know
how, but you must be doing something really wrong in order to have all
these things happen to you, and we think that God is probably
punishing you much less than you actually deserve.

These three "friends" continue to increasingly accuse Job for several
more rounds, or several more "cycles" of conversation and debate. This
goes on for many chapters, with Job's friends accusing, and with Job
continuing to rebuff them, growing more and more agitated and defiant,
defending himself more and more from their accusations and
persecutions.

> *"Miserable comforters are you all.*
> *Shall vain words have an end?*
> *What emboldens you that you answer me in that way?*
> *I also could speak as you do: if your soul were in my soul's place,*
> *I could heap up words against you, and shake my head at you, too."(9)*

Interwoven into each of their debates and accusations they continue to add their versions about the greatness of God, as if to prove their case.

Then the youngest one, Elihu, who has entered the group, takes his turn.

> *"Listen to this, Job: stand still, and consider the wondrous works of God.*
> *Do you know when God disposed them, and caused the light of His cloud to shine?*
> *Do you know the balancing of the clouds, the wondrous works of Him which is perfect in knowledge? How your garments are warm, when He quiets the earth by the south wind?*
> *Have you with Him spread out the sky, which is strong, and as a molten looking glass?*
> *Teach us what we shall say unto Him; for we cannot order our speech by reason of darkness. Shall it be told Him that I speak? If a man speaks, surely he shall be swallowed up.*
> *And now men see not the bright light which is in the clouds: but the wind passes, and cleanses them. Fair weather comes out of the north: with God is terrible majesty..."(10)*

Elihu suggests that Job may possibly be righteous, but that he is certainly not perfect and cannot possibly understand the things of God.

At this point Job doesn't respond as God, Who has been listening to this discourse the whole time, has finally heard enough.

Let me interject here that God hears everything we say.

> *"But I say unto you, that every idle word that men shall speak,*
> *they shall give account of those words in the day of judgment..."(11)*

The Lord is always listening, and it would benefit us greatly to realize our own words are very important,,, and are always heard.

The Lord has been listening to all that Job and his friends have said, and He has heard enough to know that nothing is going to change at this point. Job was still going to continue to complain in his misery, his friends were still going to persecute Job, and all of them are continuing to put the blame on God.

It was time for God to step in and set it all straight. The challenge was over.

God then shows up in a whirlwind and abruptly ends Elihu's speech.

> *"Who is this that darkens counsel by words without knowledge?"(12)*

God is talking to Job and his friends, but mostly to his four friends.

"Who is giving bad advice without having any understanding?"

"Who are these that don't know what they're talking about?"

What we will find in the end is that God is revealing to Job's friends that their personal perspectives about Job, and about the Lord Himself, are very wrong.

Iyyob – Persecuted One

"Miserable comforters are you all; shall your vain words have an end?"(1)
"How long will you vex my soul and break me in pieces with your words?"(2)

Here's a hint to one of the truths and secrets of Job.

Job is not persecuted by God.

It's worth saying again. Job is *not* persecuted by God.

Let's look at the Hebrew name for Job. It turns out this meaning is quite profound. In Hebrew, the name "Job" is interpreted "Iyyob", which means "persecution".

Webster's definition of "persecution" is "to afflict constantly so as to distress, as for religion, race, etc..." Another definition is "persistent annoyance or harassment."

The popular online site Wikipedia defines it as "the systematic mistreatment of an individual or group by another individual or group."

A broader definition of 'persecution' would be "to constantly afflict with accusation as to forcefully change a person's thoughts and/or behavior."

So let's ask the question, "Is God persecuting Job?"

As we saw earlier, the Lord praised and bragged on Job twice for being upright and for being perfect, or having a "perfect" heart before Him. He held Job highly in that regard.

Does this sound like someone who would be persecuting or afflicting Job, especially because of his "race or religion"?

And where is God during all of this?

At first, He allowed Satan room to move, but did God initiate any distress or attacks on Job?

Did He put fear on or in Job? Does He consider Job His enemy?

Is He punishing Job for anything?

No, no, no, and no.

God has remained removed from the whole ordeal. He is within hearing range, as is His nature, until a request is made, or, as in this case, if a request is not made, until an interruption and entrance is warranted and inevitable to accomplish an intended result.

God remains silent the whole time, until the end of the Book.

How about Satan? Is Satan persecuting Job? Does Satan afflict Job continuously? In the first two chapters of Job (of 42), Satan is allowed power from God and attacks Job attempting to destroy Job's faith in the Father. Satan afflicts Job two times, first by destroying his children and much of what Job has, and then after that, by afflicting Job's health. But then Satan is not heard of again.

This could possibly be considered a form of persecution, as it was done to distress and destroy Job's religion and/or faith, but Satan's physical attacks of Job were done all at once, and even though the results of the two incidents lingered for some time, the attacks themselves did not persist and were not of a continuous nature. This differs from the general meaning of persecution, which describes it as a continuous, repetitive and systematic mistreatment. Satan attacked Job in the first 2 chapters with the intent to do harm, to cause injury to Job's property, family, and to Job's person. Then Satan is gone.

As the story of Job shows, the characters and dialog reveal that Job was indeed continuously persecuted, but not by God. And although Satan started his distress by two physical attacks, Job is not being continually persecuted by Satan.

When we look more closely at the Book of Job, the "persistent annoyance" and "continuous accusations" and "mistreatment" "as to distress" and to "change behavior" of the person Job in fact actually comes from, as we saw briefly in the last chapter,,,

Job's friends.

Here are a few of the other things his 'friends' said to Job.

Zophar:
> "...Should a man full of talk be justified? Should your lies make men hold their peace? And when you mock, will no man make you ashamed? For you have said, "My doctrine is pure, and I am clean in your eyes". But oh that God would speak, and open his lips against you..."(3)

Bildad:
> "If you were pure and upright; surely now He would awake for you..."(4)

Eliphaz:
> "Is not your wickedness great? And your iniquities infinite?"(5)

Over and over we see that Job's friends were accusing him of sin or wrongdoing, and continually trying to change his behavior. They go on to verbally harass him for 35 chapters, for almost all of the Book of Job, accusing and even berating him for something he did not do.

Here are Job's own words describing their ongoing accusations:

> "Miserable comforters are you all; shall your vain words have an end?"(6)

> "How long will you vex my soul and break me in pieces with your words?"(7)

> "Are there not mockers here beside me? And can't I see their continued provocation?"(8)

> "But you are all forgers of lies, you are physicians of no value. O that you would altogether hold your peace!"(9)

> "Why do you persecute me, as God has, and are not satisfied with my flesh?"(10)

We see that Job's "friends" were certainly "afflicting constantly so as to distress..." and provoking "persistent annoyance or harassment." And Job was indeed distressed by it.

Was this just light friendly banter and/or off the cuff remarks?

It doesn't appear to be, as the intensity of the discourse grows greater and greater as the dialog continues.

Although Job also accuses God of persecuting him in the last verse, we see that God in actuality isn't persecuting Job at all.

In the end, as we'll see, God strongly admonishes that Job's friends were completely wrong, both about Job, and also about Him.

But again I get ahead of myself.

This overview of Job as Iyyob in itself is not the Secret of Job, but it does shed light on the dynamics of all that was going on in and around him. It is all very revealing about the attitudes, events, and characters and characterizations of those involved in the Book of Job.

Job is persecuted by his "friends" throughout almost all of their time together. Until God shows up and sets it all straight.

For those of you who like symbolism in your spiritual diet, let's take a look at Iyyob, the Persecuted One, from a different perspective.

Who else do we know who was persecuted by men for something they didn't do? Who else was persecuted, and then suffered by the hands of His own people, to the point of dying on a cross for all of mankind?

Every Book in the Old Testament has some form of foreshadowing of the Messiah, of the Christ, of Jesus. The Book of Job is no exception. The persecution of Job, of Iyyob, is certainly a type and shadow, a marvelous foreshadowing, of Jesus, and the persecution He suffered at the hands of men, of his very own people.

Jesus was persecuted greatly, without cause, for things He didn't do, and then was crucified.

By the very people He came to save.

Part IV

God

God

"Then the LORD answered Job out of the whirlwind, and said,
who is this that darkens counsel by words without knowledge?
Gird up now thy loins like a man;
for I will ask you, and you will answer me."(1)

Up until now, events have transpired and Job and his friends have been discussing every scenario and every possible explanation they can think of surrounding Job's afflictions. Job is woefully commiserating; his friends are accusing, and all of them arguing and lecturing about God.

Then God, Who has been listening to this fairly chaotic discourse the whole time, finally intercedes.

Here we find probably the most impressive, and to many the most magnificent passages in the Bible. The Lord God Almighty Himself shows up, and out of a whirlwind demands that Job listen to, and answer, Him.

"Where were you when I laid the foundations of the earth? Declare it,
if you have understanding. Who has laid the measures of it, if you know?
Or who has stretched the line upon it?
Where are the foundations fastened? Or who laid the corner stone of it;
When the morning stars sang together, and all the sons of God shouted
for joy?
Or who shut up the sea with doors, when it broke open, as if it had
issued out of the womb? When I made the cloud the garment of it,
and wrapped it in thick darkness..."(2)

God now begins to proclaim all that He has created. He continues in this manner for some time.

"Have you entered into the springs of the sea? Or have you walked in the
search of the depths?
Have the gates of death been opened unto you? Or have you seen the
doors of the shadow of death?
Have you perceived the breadth of the earth?
Answer if you know it at all."(3)

As I was reading, and as God went on, I couldn't help but ask the question, "Why is God going to such great lengths to proclaim His greatness?" Job and his friends have all along been expressing the attributes and the majesty of God, and now God comes on the scene and continues in greater detail to expound on all that He has done.

> "Who has made a place for the overflowing of waters, or a way for the lightning and thunder; To cause it to rain on the earth, where no man is; on the wilderness, wherein there is no man; To satisfy the desolate and waste ground; and to cause the bud of the tender herb to spring forth? Does rain have a father? Who hath created a way for drops of dew?"(4)

Why God is saying these things just did not make any sense. His greatness and magnificence were on display, and had certainly been expounded upon, but there didn't seem to be any reason at all for Him to be proclaiming all of these acts to Job, even and especially after all Job had gone through.

Is God just showing Job that Job doesn't know everything, when both knew that Job didn't? Is God giving a more perfect account of Himself, to show a greater picture of all He has done, in order that Job would be more informed? Or, as is possibly inferred by past teachings of Job, does God have a super-sized egotistical nature, and could not help but take the opportunity to relay to Job of all He had done, and how much greater He is than Job?

This was not like the God I knew, and not like Jesus, who came to show us the character of God. This ego explanation has been given credence in the past as one of the only plausible explanations of this powerful speech to Job. But why?

God is greater and more magnificent than we can ever know. But is this the point of it all? Does God telling Job He is Great over and over in such a profound way somehow bring us to the answer and conclusion of Job, as has been previously taught? Is this the end of the dilemma? Is it the resolution to some unknown question? Is this the lesson, that "God is Great" and that's that? That "God is great and we're not"?

Or, is the Lord actually showing Job, and us, something entirely different and of far greater importance...

> *"Do you know the ordinances of heaven?*
> *Can you set the dominion of it in the earth? Can you lift up your voice*
> *to the clouds, that abundance of waters may cover you? Can you send*
> *lightning that they may go, and say unto you, here we are?*
> *Who has put wisdom in the inward parts of man?*
> *Or who has given understanding to the heart?"(5)*

Job and his friends had just finished 36 chapters in which, among other things, they were telling each other of the greatness and wisdom of God and of how God created everything and knows everything.

So why is the Almighty God reiterating this? Again, was it just to give a more perfect account of Who He was, and/or just to expound upon His greatness?

This just didn't fit. This wasn't an answer, and didn't solve or accomplish anything.

One more time God tells Job:

> *"Gird up your loins like a man: I will ask of you,*
> *and you will answer Me.*
> *Will you also disannul My judgment?*
> *Will you condemn Me, that you may be righteous?"(6)*

Though Job never sinned, God was likely chastening him at this time a bit for Jobs suggestions that God had actually done all of this to him.

"Are you telling Me that My judgment is wrong and that I'm wrong for what I do? Are you blaming Me in order that you might justify yourself?"

Job had assumed that God had personally inflicted all of his hardships, and though God knew otherwise, that Satan had inflicted it, He does not directly tell Job. Again, why? Just so that the Almighty could give a speech?

"Do you have an arm like God? Or can you thunder with a voice like Him? Clothe yourself now with majesty and excellency; and array yourself with glory and beauty. Cast abroad the rage of your wrath: and behold every one that is proud, and abase him. Look on every one that is proud, and bring him low; and tread down the wicked in their place. Hide them in the dust together; and bind their faces in secret."(7)

Or might there be something else more important here that God is trying to get across to Job…

The Secret of Job hinges on two verses found in the Book of Job. This next verse is the first of the two. God says in Job 40:14:

"Then will I also confess to you that your own right hand can save you."(8)

As I considered what God was saying, The Holy Spirit, in that still, inner Knowing, began to reveal a greater understanding of all that was being said here.

God is saying to Job, "If **you** could do *all these things* that I've done, and *all* that I have been reminding you of, then I would tell you that **_you_** could save yourself."

And then the words jumped off the page…

God was saying to Job that if Job could do all these things, then he could save himself.

"But Job, you *didn't* do all these great things, so you can't save yourself,,,"

But **I can.**

The Lord is telling Job that He did all these great things, and He is the One who can save him and bring him out of all this.

"*I* am the One who can save you. *I* am the One who can heal you. *I* am the One who can deliver you, and set you free. *I* am the One who can bring life back to you. *I* am the One who can bring you peace and even joy again. *I* am the One who can do all these things!"

Here it was. Simply put, God was saying that Job couldn't save himself, but it was He, the Lord of All, Who had created and moved in all of those great things, and that it was He, his Almighty God who could save Job and heal him!

The reason God had shown Job all those great and wonderful things that He had done and created was not to boast or prove Himself again to Job.

It was to give Job the understanding that it was He, his God, his Creator, his Strong Tower, his Lord Who could heal and save and deliver him.

Part V

God
and
Job

God and Job

*"Hear, I beseech You, and I will speak:
I will ask of You, and declare it to me."(1)*

At this point God pauses in His dialog just long enough for Job to digest what He has just said. If Job could do all these things, then he could heal and deliver himself. Job couldn't. But God could.

This that the Holy Spirit was showing me, and the realization of what God was saying, was initially incredibly profound, but then the implications of it all began to grow larger and began to reveal even more.

It then came to me that from the start of Job's ordeal, and during this entire time, during all of Job's events and trials, during all of his suffering and misery, and throughout the whole 38 chapters of Job's afflictions, there was one thing that Job had not done.

And it was huge.

In all of this, in all of his events and circumstances, in all that he went through,,,

Job never once went to God.

In all of this, in all of Job's trials, in all of his 'suffering', in all of his afflictions, in all of his misery, in all the time with his friends, and even when they had suggested he do it,,,

I read through the Book of Job over and over.

Job never went to God with any of it.

Not even once.

48

The Father then continues in His soliloquy in a different direction and from another perspective. He has been describing all that He had done, and now starts describing what He is doing and can do, in real time, in the present.

> "Behold now behemoth, which I made with thee; he eats grass as an ox. Lo now, his strength is in his loins, and his force is in the navel of his belly. He moves his tail like a cedar: the sinews of his stones are wrapped together. His bones are as strong pieces of brass; his bones are like bars of iron. He is the chief of the ways of God: He that made him can make His sword to approach him."(2)

> "Can you draw out the whale with a hook? Or his tongue with a line which you let down? Can you put a hook into his nose? Or bore his jaw through with a thorn?
> Will he make many supplications to you? Will he speak soft words to you? Will he make a covenant with you? Will you take him for a servant forever?"(3)

Job has now been hearing from God Himself, and has been considering all of these things. As God finishes this second soliloquy, Job puts it all together.

He finally "gets it".

Job now understands completely what God is saying, he now realizes all that God can do, and how these great and mighty things apply directly to and about him.

Job then says,

> "I know that You can do everything, and that no thought can be withheld from You.
> Who is he that hides counsel without knowledge? I have said things that I didn't understand; things too great for me, which I didn't know."(4)

Job is not just guessing here about something he might have missed from God. He's not just paraphrasing the Lord, biding time, waiting for God to give him the real answer.

Iob – Repentant One

"I abhor myself, and repent in dust and ashes."[1]

Scholars suggest that that the name "Job" may also have come from the Arabic word "Iob", which means "to come back, or to repent". From this name "Iob" is derived the most commonly considered characterization attributed to or bestowed upon Job; as the "Repentant One".

After God's soliloquy and Job's revelation Job says,

> *"I have always heard of You, but now I understand what You're saying for myself."[2]*

Then, as a result of his whole new understanding, he immediately and profoundly says,

> *"I abhor myself, and repent in dust and ashes."[3]*

Job's reaction to these realizations was to immediately and fervently humble himself and repent.

As I considered Job's reaction, another question which seemed to never have an answer came to mind.

If Job was perfect before God, and did not curse God despite all he went through, what did he do that he had to be repentant for at the end?

What was he deeply regretting?

Traditional teachings and explanations suggest that Job must not have understood the greatness of God until God came on the scene to show him. These customary teachings dictate that even though Job and his friends had just spent a good part of 35 chapters talking about how great God was, Job didn't really understand the fullness of God somehow and needed to repent for that.

This explanation did not make any sense to me, and even seemed to contradict itself while never giving anything close to a clear or reasonable answer.

Is Job repenting for not knowing how great God was?

Do any of us?

Is he repenting for having to be reprimanded, but not really knowing why?

In former teachings here again was an explanation without an answer, without a reason, without a solution. Job may not have known God in his entirety, but Job knew of the greatness of God better than anyone else at the time. God bragged on him about that, so it didn't make much sense that he had to repent for it.

Was Job repenting for not realizing that God was God, and he was not?

Again, this seemed to be another one of these Job, 'non-answer' explanations that has been passed down through time. Does the explanation that God has to make a distinction between Himself and ourselves give us a clearer understanding of Who He is and what He wants of us? Don't we pretty well know that difference already?

As we said before, was Job just really sorry that he didn't know God well enough? Did Job somehow feel he was required to show some sort of expression of humility from it all?

Was God just making this whole thing up so He could reprimand Job, just because He's God...?

The Word says that *"it is impossible for God to lie"(4)*, so such a grand deception would not be possible.

Job also hadn't done anything wrong, so that could not have been why he was repenting and regretful either.

So the question remained. "Why was Job asking forgiveness? What was he repenting for?"

The answer lies in the realization of the greatness of what had just been revealed to him by God.

Job is deeply repenting is because he has now fully realized that up to this point in all he has gone through, in all his misery, he has not gone to his beloved God at all, not once, with any of it. It must have been absolutely crushing to Job to realize that he had not gone to his Lord with any of this.

He is instantly and profoundly regretting how he has reacted to it all from the very beginning. From the depths of his being Job is earnestly repenting for all of his actions and reactions from the moment his afflictions broke loose upon him.

He is deeply regretting the route he has taken, with all of his misery and commiseration, along with all of the contemplation, pontificating and arguing. He regrets that he never once looked with faith toward the God he loved and revered, and that he had not once gone to God for help or even comfort with any of his traumatic difficulties and adversity.

He is also repenting for purposely and deliberately hiding from the God he loved, the God he worshipped, and the Lord Whom he maintained his integrity for.

He is repenting for not continuing to worship his God after these things happened.

He is repenting for making the decision to wholeheartedly pine and mourn, to curse his life, to avidly complain and live in his misery, and for at times being angry and defiant.

He is repenting for directly and indirectly accusing God of all of it, and for having all along assumed that the Lord had done these things to him, including all his fear and torment, which he also now realizes God hadn't done.

He is repenting for not remaining in his good character when it all happened and He is repenting for not seeing the truth in his actions and reactions. He is repenting for not seeking God, and for not going to God for help, for his shelter, for refuge and comfort and for healing.

This is a very deep and great regret that Job has. He would take it all back if he could. He had missed the opportunity to live what he believed, even before others, about going to God, praying for his friends, and being thankful for his life. He had wallowed in misery and had blatantly blamed his very own Lord and amazing God.

Job is repenting because he completely missed it.

He messed up. He blew it. He'd completely ignored and abandoned the One Who could save him. He is regretting not realizing and not knowing who God was, and is, and what The Lord could do and wanted to do for him.

But along with this realization and all that he had been through came an amazing new understanding. It was a great new revelation about being able to come directly to God. He now had a personal experience and revealed understanding about God, that he can ask of his Lord anything and that God would answer him.

Despite all that Job had done wrong, he now realized a much deeper and greater understanding of the Majesty and Greatness of God, and now has a greater understanding of Who his God really is.

"...and now I repent for not understanding, for not really hearing or seeing You before..."

Now, it all makes perfect sense.

In the end, Job was indeed The Repentant One.

But for things that were very, very different than what we have been taught, for generations.

God Directs

*"And the Lord turned the captivity of Job, when he prayed for his friends:
Also, the Lord gave Job twice as much as he had before."(1)*

At this point God gives firm direction to Job's friends.

> *"And after the Lord had spoken these words unto Job, the Lord said to
> Eliphaz the Temanite, My wrath and anger is kindled against you, and
> against your two friends: for you have not spoken of Me the thing that is
> right, as my servant Job (now) has.
> Now take seven bulls and seven rams, and go to my servant Job,
> and offer a burnt offering for yourselves; and Job will pray for you:
> for his prayer I will accept: lest I deal with you after your folly, because
> you have <u>not</u> spoken of me the things which are right..."(2)*

> *"So Eliphaz the Temanite and Bildad the Shuhite and Zophar the
> Naamathite went, and did according to what the LORD commanded
> them to do..."(3)*

This first verse is very important for two reasons.

First, God is strongly saying to Jobs friends, "You have not spoken the
truth about Me..."

God was angry to the point of wrath with Job's friends because all along
they expressed many things about Him, and many of those things were
completely wrong.

He was angry because their personal assumptions and perspectives
were <u>so</u> wrong the whole time about Him, and about His Nature, and
about Who He really was.

God then firmly directs the friends to go to Job to be prayed for, and
tells them again why.

"...because you have <u>not</u> spoken of (about) Me the things which are
right..."

We need to understand in greater depth Who the Lord is, so that we can speak those things that are right in, and about, Him.

The second important part of the verse is that God is directing them to go to Job and have Job pray for them.

It is at this point, when his friends go to Job, and for the first time since the very beginning of the Book of Job, we see Job actually seeking and asking something of God. He now prays to the Lord, and certainly in a new way for his friends.

The Lord then receives and accepts both Job and his prayer.

> *"And the Lord turned the captivity of Job, when he prayed for his friends: also, the Lord gave Job twice as much as he had before."(4)*

After he does this God gives Job twice as much as he had before. Keep in mind that before all this Job was the wealthiest man in the east, so what God now was giving him wasn't just a marginal amount. It was massive.

> *"Then came there unto him all his brethren, and all his sisters, and all they that had been of his acquaintance before, and did eat bread with him in his house: and they bemoaned him, and comforted him over all the adversity that the LORD had brought upon him: every man also gave him a piece of money, and everyone an earring of gold."(5)*

His family and acquaintances didn't understand all that had happened.

But Job now did.

Great things happen when you receive understanding from the Lord.

> *"So the Lord blessed the latter end of Job more than his beginning: for he had fourteen thousand sheep, and six thousand camels, and a thousand yoke of oxen, and a thousand she asses. He had also seven sons and three daughters.... And in all the land were no women found so fair as the daughters of Job: and their father gave them inheritance among their brothers."(6)*

"After this Job lived a hundred and forty years, and saw his sons, and his sons' sons, even four generations."(7)

"So Job died, being old and full of days."(8)

So Job ended up living a long, and full, and grateful, and fruitful, and very blessed, life.

God's
Expectation

God's Expectation of Job

"Surely I would speak to the Almighty, and I desire to reason with God..."(1)

Throughout all that has happened to him and through all that happens afterward, though he "would speak to the Almighty", Job refrains from going to, or speaking to, God.

Even his friends suggest that he go to God, but he does not.

I believe that God, especially in the beginning, had very different expectations of Job and his actions and reactions to his adversity than what Job actually did.

The one characteristic of Job that we see in the beginning of the Book of Job is that he is always going to God with everything. He goes to God even when he thinks his children may *possibly* have done something wrong, whether they had or not. We are shown that he is continually honoring the Father and waiting before his God.

When Satan shows up before the Lord, God goes on and on to Satan about how perfect and upright Job is before Him, more than any in the earth.

> *"Have you considered my servant Job? How he is perfect and upright before Me?"*(2)

God is speaking very highly of Job here.

Wouldn't such words from God suggest a strong confidence in Job, and a certain earnest conviction toward and about him?

Looking at Job's life actions to this point, wouldn't God have been able to fairly easily presume that Job would also come directly to Him when something very real was happening to him, when there was a true need and not only a potential one? That he would come to Him as fervently as he did all the time otherwise?

Because of God's praise of Job, Satan suggests a challenge to this assumption, and further implies that if anything bad would happen to Job, he would curse God to his face instead of going to Him.

Doesn't God's conversation with Satan suggest that a particular response from Job was anticipated, or expected? Because of Job's lifelong actions up to this point, wouldn't God have been able to be fairly confident that Job would come to Him, no matter what, and especially if Satan would cause any harm in his life? Wouldn't God have been able to anticipate that Job would not only **not** curse Him, but that Job would also come to Him, his God, immediately with everything?

In fact, couldn't much more than just not cursing Him be expected, especially of someone perfect and upright before the Lord? Mightn't God have been able to anticipate that Job would come to Him as his fortress, his shield and his refuge, to come to his God for help in time of need? That Job would come to His powerful God for peace, comfort and even for healing?

How was God going to win Satan's challenge?

How would the challenge be satisfied and indeed won?

Didn't the answer to the challenge require a certain response and reaction by Job to whatever Satan would do to him?

Could God have anticipated that Job would come to Him at least to worship, and to at least possibly ask why all this was happening?

The answer to all of these questions is Yes.

So, to quote a cliché, this should have been a pretty 'safe bet' for God.

So God then accepts the challenge from Satan.

A little foreshadowing here - God also knows at this point all that He will be showing Job, his friends, and us.

So after the challenge is agreed to, Satan is given the ability, applies his new found powers, and directly afflicts Jobs wealth and his family.

Job doesn't curse God, and still at first continues to worship Him, but he is devastated and disheartened.

After this first round of abuses, God again justifies Job in stating that Job was still "perfect" and upright before Him and had "held fast" to his integrity despite what had happened.

As a side note, many teachings suggest that by Job holding on to his integrity here and throughout the ordeal, that this is the final answer to what we are supposed to learn from the Book of Job.

But is this the end of the story?

No, it's just the beginning...

The second challenge is accepted, and Satan again uses his temporary powers to afflict Job, this time physically to his person.

After this second round of Satan's abuses, things change. Though Job never curses God, we don't hear about him worshipping any more, and Job seems to now turn to absolute misery. And while still talking about God's greatness, he also indulges in blaming Him for it all too.

Gods accepted challenge with Satan may have initially considered Job's reactions.

How did Job react? Did Job react along the lines of God's possible expectations? What was Job's decided response to these adverse events in his life?

"After this opened Job his mouth and cursed his day."(3)

Job's Choice

"Have pity upon me, have pity upon me, O my friends;
for the hand of God has touched me"(1)

During his afflictions and for seven days of silent grief afterwards, Job had arrived at several conclusions and made a number of decisions.

First of all, he had concluded that God had done all this to him, directly, by His Almighty hand.

Wrong conclusion #1.

Let's make sure we understand this. God did not physically do these things to Job and his family. The adversary, the enemy Satan did. God allowed it for this event, even possibly knowing what Job's reactions would be, and that it would eventually become a great volume of lessons for us as we'll see, but it was solely Satan who initiated it and was the very cause of Job's afflictions.

Does Job even consider that it might not have come directly from the hand of God? No. Job has decided that it is all God. This has much to do with his decisions and reactions.

After reaching wrong conclusion #1, and based upon the above determinations, he then decides on how he is going to respond to all that has happened to him. The thing was done, and there he was.

Should he go to God for help? In his mind if God had caused it all, there wasn't any reason that God would help him.

Should he keep worshipping God? Why, if the Lord is going to do this?

Should he be thankful for all he has left? He might, but that's not the direction he chooses. Instead, he chooses to focus intently and intensely on all he's lost.

Of all of the actions and reactions he could possibly have had, he makes the decision that his response is going to be to dwell in misery and to mourn, and to do so fully and completely.

> "Therefore, I will not refrain my mouth;
> I will speak in the anguish of my spirit;
> I will complain in the bitterness of my soul."(2)

Job now begins to speak very bitter things, which was unlike him, as even one of Job's friends had pointed out.

> "Behold, you have instructed many, and you have strengthened the weak hands.
> Your words have upheld him that was falling, and you have strengthened the feeble knees..."(3)

We will talk more about this later on, but Job's extreme mourning, and misery, and despair, and anguish, which continues for many chapters, repeatedly steers him away and even blinds him from seeking and seeing the truth of who the Lord really is, and was, in his life.

Does that happen with us at times? Do we decide to continue in our misery or in other directions and not go to God?

We have choices all the time on how we react to situations in our lives, and we have many opportunities, even daily, to come to Him.

Do we?

Relationship

"Come to me, all of you who labor and are heavy with burdens, and I will give you rest."(1)

Earlier I mentioned that God may have had different expectations and considerations of Job's reactions and direction than what actually occurred. As soon as these afflictions started, I believe He considered that Job might look to Him, to his God and Protector and to his Refuge, for help and answers for it all and to be healed.

Job might have questioned these events for a time, but then he had the opportunity to come to God and to his Strong Tower, and to his Deliverer as all of these things happened around him. Then, by bringing to the Lord his troubles and inquiring of God about what was occurring, God would have had the opportunity to show up in a big way on Job's behalf.

If Job had done this and gone to the Lord with it all, God would have been able to remind Satan once again of how altogether upright and perfect Job was before Him, as shown by his actions of trusting his loving Father and seeking Him. God would have then been proved more than correct in Satan's challenge, and Job would have been healed and restored at that time.

But that didn't happen.

In all that he went through, by Job's own choice, he never goes to God. Even those around him suggest that he do so, but he does not. He, by his own will, chooses not to.

By the way, our will is very important. We will see this later on.

In the beginning of the Book of Job we see that Job worshipped and gave offerings to God, especially in the days of feasting when he would offer up numerous burnt offerings just in case his children had sinned.

> *"And his sons went and feasted in their houses, and sent and
> called for their three sisters to eat and to drink with them.
> And it was so, when the days of their feasting were gone about, that Job
> sent and sanctified them, rose up early in the morning and offered burnt
> offerings according to the number of them all: for Job said, It may be that
> my sons have sinned, and cursed God in their hearts. Job did this
> continually."(2)*

As we looked at before, Job was constantly asking forgiveness for his
children just in case they did anything wrong. He seems to be overly
concerned about this, but it appears he wanted to do everything he
could to make sure that all was just right before his great and Almighty
God.

What kind of relationship might this be? What kind of a relationship
does Job really have with God?

Were these things done out of fear (pachad) and/or duty and/or
obligation?

Or were they done out of a great personal connection with the Lord?

When calamity struck, where did Job turn? As we've already seen, it
wasn't to God. Again, Job speaks to his friends about going to God, but in
fact he never does.

It seems that the only verse where Job comes close to communicating
with God, prior to God showing up in the whirlwind, is this next one, in
which Job's relationship with God is very much revealed and reflected
in his attitude and actions. This verse gives a fairly accurate picture of
Jobs relationship with God.

> *"Only don't do two things to me: then will I not hide myself from You.
> Withdraw Your hand far from me: and let not Your dread make me
> afraid.
> <u>Then</u> call me, and I will answer: or let me speak, and answer me."(3)*

First of all, the first verse shows that Job is indeed actually hiding from
God. He is admitting it when he says he won't do it anymore.

Secondly, Job says that in order for him to change this attitude and behavior, God has to do two things.

The irony is that the two things Job is asking for God to do, or stop doing, God is not doing at all!

First, God does not have His hand on him as Job suggests, and is not physically afflicting Job at any point.

Secondly, Job's fear, this "dread of God" that Job says God is causing, has been conceived and exacerbated in Job solely by Job himself. The Lord has had nothing to do with inflicting any sort of fear on Job whatsoever.

Job says, "If *You* will stop doing these two things to me, *then* You can call and I will open the door to have communication with You."

Is Job communicating with God here, or is he setting 'the conditions' for his communication with God?

It is most certainly the latter.

Job is setting his own conditions on what he wants to have happen before he will even consider any form of communication with his God.

Do we go to God in this way at times? Do we set conditions and our own limitations on when and how we will come to the Lord, or even when and how God can come to us?

And as Job possibly did to begin with, do we perform our Christian walk out of obligation or duty? Do we feel that if we show up every so often, and put money in the offering plate that God will have mercy on us and everything will turn out just fine?

Or do we spend time with the Lord and the Holy Spirit out of love and friendship and relationship with our great and powerful God, and know that we have our God with us always?

Do we do our 'God things' out of necessity, or do we walk our walk with faith and strength and determination, and with confidence and joy as David in Psalms did?

The Book of Job also shows that Job and his friends knew a lot about God and His greatness and they even discussed it at length. It is an integral and reoccurring theme in the story.

But even though Job knew of the greatness of God, did he have a great relationship with Him?

We too, in varying degrees, also know that God is great. But does just knowing this mean we have an excellent personal relationship with Him?

It's all about relationship.

What is the nature of your relationship with God?

The Lord wants us to have a great and amazing connection to and with Him. The new covenant that Jesus brought to us, and died for, and prepared for us has everything to do with relationship.

Not until the very end of the book, when Job realizes what he had done, does he finally ask God openly of it all, and that begins a new and greater relationship for him with the Father.

The verse that comes after our beginning chapter verse reads,

> "Receive Me, and learn of Me...
> and you will find rest unto your souls."(4)

You will learn so much more, and will begin to live in this relationship, this great friendship, as you learn and discover more about the Father, His Son, and about the Holy Spirit.

And your soul will find rest...

Job's Fear

"Let Him take his rod away from me, and let not His fear terrify me:
Then would I speak, and not fear Him..."(1)

First of all, there is no reason to believe that Job didn't have previous communication with God. Though it doesn't specifically say he did, it also doesn't say he was startled at the whirlwind, or that he fell on his face, or any of that when God showed up. And many in those days had talked with God, including Adam, Eve, Cain, Able, Noah, Abraham, Moses, and Joshua.

Job prayed and offered burnt offerings to the Lord continually. Yet after these afflictions began, we are not told if he continued in these offerings and sacrifices or not, and I would suggest that maybe even these had stopped.

It also is probably a valid assumption that Job initially had a fairly high degree of pachad (scared) type fear of the Lord prior to these events, as seen in offering burnt offerings 'just in case' his children had sinned.

This is also evidenced when he expressed the following about his afflictions;

> *"For the thing which I greatly <u>feared</u> is come upon me,*
> *and that of which I was <u>afraid</u> has come to me."(2)*

The word "feared" used here is again the Hebrew "pachad", to dread or to be scared, and the word "afraid" in this verse is the Hebrew "yagor", meaning to be afraid, or startled.

Let's take a closer look at Job's fear as it relates to his actions and reactions, which we touched on briefly earlier. The dynamics of it may help us see one of the reasons why Job refrained from going to God.

Let's look at "fear" as a stronghold in the New Testament.

> *"For the weapons of our warfare are not carnal, but mighty*
> *through God to the pulling down of strong holds;"(3)*

There are two characteristics of a stronghold, or a snare. The first is that we generally don't see it coming, and the second is that it is big enough to hold us, and/or prevent us from doing the things we intend to do.

The fears that Job had, with the root cause being in his own initial reasonings and conclusions about God, grew large enough to blind him and to hold him captive in and to it.

Our 'weapons' in the above verse are spiritual in nature and _mighty through God,_ and given to all of us to use in order to avoid strongholds, or pull them down all together,,,

We just need to know how to use them, and it all starts with knowing who our God truly is.

The next verse describes these strongholds or snares.

> "Casting down imaginations, reasonings, and every high thing
> that exalts itself against the knowledge of God, and bringing into
> captivity every thought to the obedience of Christ;"(4)

This verse says that strongholds can come from imaginations, or things we ourselves conceive of, which may not be true (by which fear becomes stronger), or by reasonings (which The Amplified Bible uses to better clarify how these strong holds come about), or by anything else that exalts itself, or makes itself seem larger than the knowledge of God, and/or about what we may individually know about God.

These imaginations and reasonings can become fearful thoughts, and are what we need to control, or "bring into captivity", through Christ.

We have to realize and remember that the Father, Son and the Holy Spirit are far greater than any of these strongholds, and that we have the power through, and in, the Lord to pull them down and remove them from our lives, which is all done by bringing our thoughts in line with the truth and into His truth and truths.

Fear is definitely one of these strongholds. It can appear greater than, and obscure, who God really is, and obscure His power within us.

When not controlled, fear can have many effects. It can prevent us from seeing God, and can also keep us from using the weapons, the tools and the gifts that He has given us to use against it, which are to be used for good in ours and others lives.

Job had a stronghold of pachad fear which prevented him from seeing God, and from seeing Who the Father really was.

As Job initially reasoned (in his 7 days of silence) that it must have been God who directly put all these things on him, his imaginations were enhanced and exaggerated by his preconceived notions, this reasoning and his pachad fear of God, which resulted in misery and emotion to such a level that he was unable to see God or go to God at all. The snare had him and he didn't know it, and he ended up allowing this fear and imagination to take over his life and to overwhelmingly control him.

Job allowed his (pachad) fear of God to completely and fully overrule his (yare) worship of God, and this had a significant effect on his reactions and his responses, to and with God.

Again, if Job had gone to the Lord, as I believe God was desiring, I believe the story would have had a very different outcome.

I believe God would have stepped in right then, and there would have been no continuous and excessive self-afflicted misery involved. Job's friends would have been reproved right away, and Job's health and wealth would have been restored at that time.

But then we would not have had any of the revelations and realizations and great lessons that we are seeing in the Book of Job!

So let's look a little bit more at the results and ramifications of Jobs stronghold of fear.

Job believes that God himself has done this to him.

If God did it, according to Job's conclusions, how can Job go to Him?

It wouldn't make any difference if he did. Why would God change His mind if His hand had done it?

As we just talked about, because of his particular conclusions, Job now fears (pachad) the Lord, and he allows this fear and subsequent fear filled emotions to have control in his life.

Does this also happen at times in our lives? Do we have a (pachad) fear of God, and don't go to God many times because this? Do we take on this same reasoning when it comes to "bad" things in our lives?

Do we avoid God or hide from Him in the hard times because we think He is doing these things to us or that we think He may be punishing us for something?

Or do we have a greater knowing and understanding about Who our God is through our relationship with Him? Do we know that He is far stronger than any of this and is indeed our strong tower, and that He is here with us and for us and within us on our behalf?

This is what God shows Job in the end of the Book of Job.

As we come to know the Lord God more and more, we will find a more meaningful and grateful and worshipful understanding of Who He is and what He does in our lives.

We will then be able to receive, and understand, and begin to possess, all of the things He freely gives us. We will learn and understand ways to handle adversity when it comes along, and ways to dwell in His power and His strength in all of our lives.

Think about it. Which of these two types of fear do you have in your life?

A 'pachad', or fearful fear of God?

Or do you have a 'yare', worshipful form of fear, knowing that His incredible greatness is with you, and within You?

Don't Blame God

*"If I had called, and He had answered me, I would not believe
that He had heard me, for He breaks me with the tempest,
and multiplies my wounds without cause..."(1)*

In the above verse Job clearly states that he doesn't believe that God will ever hear him, even if he were to ask and God were to answer. He is saying this because he thinks that God is "breaking" him and continuing to "multiply his wounds."

During his calamities and afterwards, Job and his friends continually infer that God's hand has done these things to him.

As we asked before, did Job ever consider or contemplate that there might be something else going on, and that all this evil may have come from another source and not from God? He may possibly have, but if so, he has dismissed it altogether.

We see that God is not "breaking" him or "multiplying his wounds." As we looked at earlier, The Lord is also not afflicting him and not causing Job to have this great fear.

It may help our understanding here for us to differentiate between Satan's actions and God's actions in the story of Job. Let's take a look at what things are of Satan, and what things are of God, and let's also look at what responses and actions can be attributed to Job.

First of all, it was Satan who suggested the challenge to God. It was Satan who desired and pushed for the destruction of Job, and it was Satan who brought all of the affliction and injury into Jobs life.

God allowed these events in the first two chapters, but with a purpose as we'll see.

After allowing Satan to cause these events, we find that both God and Satan are out of the picture, yet God remains in a place of listening.

At the very end of the book He returns, in a whirlwind, and shows all who are involved the truth. He shows Job a better way to have handled it all, and then He brings Job to a much better place in his life.

But I get ahead of myself.

As we've seen previously, Job made the decision to mourn, and much of the torment he experiences afterwards may be attributed to emotions as much or maybe even more than the actual physical afflictions themselves. His emotional condition worsens as he continues to dwell in fear and despair, and his friends compound it all with their continued accusations.

Job continues to blame God for everything, even for things that God has not done.

Let's once again stop and ask ourselves this question. Do we ever do this at times in our lives as well?

Do we ever subconsciously, or even consciously blame God for things that we don't understand or don't know about, and that may not be related to God at all?

I would suggest that the answer to this is most emphatically yes. We can have a tendency to immediately blame God when anything bad happens in our lives, and we also can have a tendency not to remember God when good things happen.

One of the first expressions of our human nature when bad things happen is to look for an answer or combination of answers which can satisfy our desire for a solution. This often results in hasty efforts to find a source on which to apply blame in what we may feel is an unfair and unfortunate event.

We find we can fairly easily affix the cause to someone or something we cannot see, and even on Someone who is All Powerful, and we can more easily do this if we feel, without knowing the truth of Who God is, that He also is able to do bad things to us.

Let me give you an example of this. Several years ago the brother of a friend of mine was drinking heavily one night. He staggered out onto a highway and was hit by a car causing very serious, life threatening injuries.

I travelled to be with the family and joined them in his intensive care hospital room. As we were there, while he lay unconscious on the hospital bed with major head/brain trauma and other serious bodily injuries, his dear sweet Christian mother voiced the question, "Why would God do this to him?"

I remember it so vividly to this day. Everything inside me wanted to tell her No!!! It wasn't God!!! I wanted to remind her of Who God was and that it was the Lord God Who would be involved in saving his life, that this was all caused by her son's poor decisions, and that God was the One who could and would bring him out of it, that it is God Who brings good out of bad.

I think I held back my thoughts at the time, but I have always remembered it clearly. The Lord, by His grace, indeed did bring the man out of it. He was healed completely, and is alive and well to this day.

It is God Who brings good to us out of bad things that happen.

Many times, the bad things or bad situations that happen to us are caused by our own poor judgment, or by others poor judgment, and by all of the questionable causal reasoning behind these poor decisions, which is more about the human condition and the nature of our existence and/or good and evil influences on each of us than it is about God's character.

I believe also that this product of our nature of blaming God can be derived from thinking that God does bad things to us and that He punishes us.

Why do we default to the thought that God can even do bad things to us?

Where do we get these thoughts from? Is it innate, or something that has been passed down and passed on by others? Or does it come from our own human nature of trying to justify our situations, or could it come from teachings and thoughts handed down for generations?

Could we think that God does bad things to us because we believe some of the conversations and opinions in Job, what Job and his friends said about God and even past teachings about the Book of Job?

Could we be wrongly considering the words of Job's friends when they said that God did these things to Job as punishment, and also wrongly considering that what God being blamed for by Job is true?

In the end of the Book of Job God strongly rebukes both Job and his friends, telling them they were very wrong about all of these things.

Could our believing that God inflicts bad things on us come from the physical acts of God which are found in the Old Testament?

In the Old Testament or Old Covenant, God used physical manifestations in order to direct his people or bring retribution upon the enemies of His people. These were events such as fires, earthquakes, floods and such which were considered to be God's wrath upon the earth and upon people who were in conflict with His chosen people, Israel. There were weather manifestations, brimstone and fire, locusts and frogs, and other exceptional physical events, done or seen as firm vengeance on those who opposed God's people.

The truth is that after Jesus' death, burial, and resurrection, we now live under a New Covenant with God, which Jesus brought to us from the Father as a result of His sacrifice on the cross. He died for us to have this.

Under this New Covenant, as represented by and seen in the New Testament, God now manifests His will to us by and through His Spirit and by His Word. He shows us truths and gives us direction and wisdom through His Holy Spirit, by *spiritual* manifestations, and no longer by physical ones.

Yet we may still derive many of our ideas today about God as it relates to punishment or retribution in physical form from these Old Testament events.

Okay, now let's ask the question; Did God punish Job for something, and an even bigger question, does God punish us?

This is a good opportunity for us to get this straight.

In the New Testament Paul says:

> "Prove all things; hold fast to that which is good."(2)

In the beginning of the Book of Job, Job had done nothing wrong. Job was upright and "perfect" before God as God states several times. We see that God is not mad with Job, and we don't see anywhere where God afflicts or inflicts any form of retribution or punishment on Job.

In their lengthy and well vocalized accusations, Job's _friends_ said that God was punishing him, and it was because Job had sinned. But God in the end strongly admonishes them about this, telling them that Job had not sinned and that their personal theology was completely wrong and not the truth at all.

And as for God punishing us with evil, the Word of God tells us that God cannot possibly do, or be, evil, and that it is completely and adamantly against His very own nature.

> "Every kingdom divided against itself is brought to desolation;
> and every city or house divided against itself shall not stand..."(3)

Jesus is showing here why the Father can't do both good and evil. This is both wisdom and logic. A house, or group of individuals divided against each other will not be able to stand, or continue and remain whole and intact.

Jesus came to show us the nature and the character of God. He showed us of the Father throughout the New Testament.

By His nature Jesus showed us that God not only is good, but that He also cannot be or do "evil."

Jesus reveals this to Phillip in a much more profoundly personal way.

> *"Have I been so long time with you,*
> *and yet you have not known me, Philip?*
> *He who has seen Me has seen the Father..."(4)*

"If you've seen Me, Phillip, you've seen the Father..."

Let's stop to consider this. Did Jesus ever put disease or sickness on anyone? Did Jesus ever punish anyone? Did He do any evil or anything "bad" to anyone at all?

No.

At one point his disciples even suggested such retribution, and asked Him if they could strike down a certain group of people with fire as a punishment. Jesus rebuked them and said,

> *"You don't know what manner of spirit you are of. For Christ is not*
> *come to destroy men's lives, but to save them."(5)*

This is also a good example of the Old Testament (Covenant) vs. New Testament (Covenant) we talked about earlier. Jesus' disciples were responding with Old Testament/Old Covenant thinking, which was all they knew at that time. Jesus was changing all that and bringing the New Covenant to them, now in spiritual form or manifestation, in which the Messiah had come, as He said, to save people and not to destroy them.

Here's another consideration. Did Jesus ever create any adversity in anyone's life in order to show them something?

No.

He did just the opposite. He healed and forgave and set free.

Jesus was God in the flesh. He was the character of God in human form. He is our example of who God is, and it is so very important to know Who God is in these things, and in our lives.

Jesus was the character of God.

God does not put evil on us. God doesn't cause evil things to happen, just so He can fix them and make Himself look good doing it. If He did, He would not only be highly egotistical but He would also be schizophrenic. God is neither schizophrenic, nor egotistical. God does not do both good and evil. He does and is only good.

The Word does say that the Lord corrects us at times, but the way He corrects is not by punishment.

> "My son, don't despise the chastening of the Lord, or faint when you are rebuked by Him: For whoever the Lord loves He chastens, and makes clean every son whom He receives. If you endure this chastening, God deals with you as with sons..."(6)

To chasten means to correct or direct. The Lord loves us and directs and corrects us by showing us a better way. He did this with Job which we'll see clearly later on.

God is the God of second (and third and fourth and fifth and many...) chances. In the end He showed Job what he had done wrong, and when Job responded and repented, He then showed him the path to get everything back, and much, much more.

What the Lord does in our lives is to bring good things out of bad. He even brings good out of things that may have been set in motion generations before us, either from actions by others, or from our own humanity, including our own or others bad decisions, and any or all of the above.

Along these same lines, we also need to understand that there are consequences to our actions and decisions. God has given us free will to choose, but we may have to live with the results of our actions.

Let's ask another question. Is Satan allowed to do evil things to us?

Both the short and the long answer is No.

This situation with Job was a one-time event, created solely for our instruction. We will look at why God allowed this to happen to Job in the Great Irony chapters, but for now, we need to realize that God does not allow Satan the use of these powers outside of the Book of Job.

Some of the physical manifestations and forces Satan was allowed to use with Job were weather related. The form of the "fire of God", which fell from heaven and consumed Jobs sheep and his servants, and the "great wind" from the wilderness that felled the eldest son's house killing all inside are examples.

From all of the evidence given in our lives, compound catastrophic weather events of such severity, variety, and magnitude do not happen all at once.

As we've talked about previously, the Lord has a hedge of protection around us and keeps the enemy from having any exceptional powers to harm us. Satan was allowed the authority to use an exceptional severity of these multiple powers only in the story of Job and nowhere else in the Word of God. Nor in our lives.

Let me interject something else here. If the enemy could manipulate the weather as to harm us in such catastrophic ways, wouldn't he be doing it everywhere all the time? Wouldn't he be continuously directing crazy and chaotic weather at us, *especially* if he knew that we would always be blaming God for it?

Of course he would.

After the events of Noah, God set the weather systems on the earth in motion. These conditions continue to this day. Hurricanes, tornadoes, rain and flooding happen individually as a response to, and as a result of, various weather patterns. They even can involve the sun and moon and other forces, which were set in motion long ago.

These weather systems are amazing and self-perpetuating by God's wisdom and plan.

There are many people who believe that when there is a catastrophic earth or weather event, God has somehow caused it in order to punish us or someone for something.

Could this be Old Testament thinking, as we talked about earlier in this chapter?

We now have advanced technology that gives us considerable information about the various severe and harmful forms and forces of weather, and in what geographic area each form is most common, and how they are produced. If we live in one of these areas, we certainly need to do our best to protect ourselves from these severe events.

Do you live in a place prone to tornados? Don't be surprised if there is one, and don't blame God if one shows up and wrecks everything. The existence of tornado sirens should be a pretty good clue. Do you live in an area that has any history of flooding? Don't blame God if it happens. Do you live where there are earthquakes, or where there are faults and the potential for earthquakes? Don't blame God if the ground starts moving. Plate tectonics.

I presently live in an area susceptible to hurricanes, and live there with the consideration that I may have to evacuate, but that I will also have a degree of advance warning and time to either prepare or to leave the area. Again, if you live in one of these places, don't blame God if one or more of these events happen.

I do believe the Lord can and does protect us from potentially dire weather and other dangerous situations at times by His power and through His Spirit. You hear stories all the time of how a person or persons were miraculously spared during severe weather or catastrophic events. I have experienced this protection concerning the weather, and have prayed successfully for bad weather to be removed from situations many times. One particular event experienced by a friend of mine vividly shows this grace of God in our lives.

Several years ago, this dear friend called me one afternoon and told me that she had felt a strong urge to anoint the outside of her house with oil. This was a very unusual thought, as our crowd and church were not prone to this type of thing, and though open to it, it was fairly out of the ordinary. She told me she had just finished doing it, and said that she had also felt the need to call me and tell me about it.

At this time, we both lived in an area on the coast of the Gulf of Mexico where waterspouts are not uncommon, especially in bad weather, and every once in a while, they would turn into tornados after coming on land.

The next day was a very stormy day. About that same hour in the late afternoon, she called me, out of breath, and obviously filled with adrenaline as she quickly recounted what had just happened to her moments before.

She said that she had been standing in her front yard when she heard a loud noise coming from behind her house. When she went to the side of the house to look, she saw a violent tornado heading her way! Shingles and sections of roofs were flying off other houses and the tornado funnel was coming straight toward her home and toward her. She said she didn't even have time to run inside when all of a sudden, as she watched, the tornado veered away from, and around her house, and then came back behind her and continued on in its path.

It had gone right around her and around her house without doing any damage to her or her home at all!

I know that the Lord protects us, especially if we're listening for/to Him, and He answers our prayers even before things happen.

The answer to whether God uses weather events against us is also No.

Sure, there are still earthquakes and flooding today, but none of which can be attributed to any sort of retribution by the Almighty. As we talked about before, that's Old Testament. The Lord now moves us by and through His Holy Spirit.

Let's talk about the physical afflictions of Job by Satan.

By the number and variety of weather events which took place at one time with Job, we can probably assume that there were a number of physical ailments which Satan afflicted Job with as well.

The same train of thought as the weather applies to the physical ailments put on Job by Satan. He only had this control for a short period of time in the first two chapters of Job.

In our lives as humans, for whatever reason, and however it got here, we live in a world where sickness, disease and death are a part of it, and affect all of humanity.

Do multiple severe afflictions happen to us at the same time? No.

Do miracles and healings happen? Yes. We hear about "miraculous" healings and they happen even more often than we know. As a matter of fact, they are happening all the time. I've been involved in many personally, and have prayed for and seen many different types of miracles, initiated by prayer, and accomplished by the Spirit of God.

Doctors and medical personnel often see these events and miracles, and can only acknowledge them, but are not able to explain them in any other way than by the "Great Physician".

Having seen and experiencing these things of God, both small and large "miracles" that are certainly beyond all human understanding, I can tell you first hand that our Lord moves in very tangible and glorious ways in our lives.

...In the Name and Power of Jesus Christ...

So does God use sickness against us?

No.

He loves us. He heals and spares us or is with us and comforts us in the various conditions that are inherent in our lives here on earth.

*"Do not err, my beloved brethren. Every good gift and every perfect gift is from above, and comes from the Father of lights...,
with Whom is no variableness, neither shadow of turning."(7)*

James in the New Testament says, "Don't get this wrong. Every good and perfect thing comes from the Father."

God gives good things. That's the plan. That's what He does.

The last verse also says that He doesn't ever change, or even waver from this. Not even a little bit. Not even a shadow. Ever.

God doesn't do bad things, or bring bad gifts...

He brings only good and perfect ones.

This is the nature of our God, and the nature of our New Covenant in and with our God.

All of this is way beyond our own human understanding until we start to gain an understanding of Who the Father really is, of Who the Holy Spirit really is, and the truth about all of the things Jesus our Christ came to show us and bring us, and the Lords powerful presence in our lives.

Adversity is also inherent in the world we live in. It's part of the deal.

Jesus said He would help us by sending the Comforter, the Spirit of God, to help us in dealing with this adversity. He doesn't bring the adversity in order to help us with adversity. It's easy to somehow believe this, but as we talked about before, this would be ridiculously manipulative and schizophrenic, and our God is none of these.

So if Satan doesn't have use of these excessive afflictions, then what role does the enemy play in our lives?

Jesus gives us a fairly accurate picture and perspective of our real world dynamics.

"And his disciples came to Jesus, saying; tell us the parable of the tares of the field.

Jesus said to them, He that sows the good seed is the Son of man; The field is the world; the good seed are the children of the kingdom, but the tares are the children of the wicked one; The enemy that sowed them is the devil; the harvest is the end of the world; and the reapers are the angels.

The tares are gathered and burned in the fire; so will it be in the end of this world.

The Son of man shall send forth his angels, and they shall gather out of his kingdom all things that offend, and them which do iniquity; And shall cast them into a furnace of fire: there shall be wailing and gnashing of teeth...

Whoever can hear this, let him hear."(8)

None of this portrays any external control of the elements or our physical health. We have enough adversity inherent in the world we live in, with "wheat and the tares" growing together, along with disease, and with our own imperfect human nature and human fallibility, which all cause enough trauma and adversity in our lives without Satan directly controlling and affecting the physical elements that surround us.

We can also many times consider death a very bad thing, and even "unnatural", though it is very natural and we will all pass into the next phase of our existence at some point in time.

Yes, in this passing there is deep loss, hearts are broken and there is deep mourning because of the transition of the one loved.

But along with this, do we ever _really_ consider eternity, and the thought of how amazing heaven must be, and that it may really not be a bad thing to go there?

I've seen a part of it, and it is way beyond amazing, far beyond anything we can even imagine. Each one of us individually is drawn into and reunited with the God of the Universe in perfect fulfillment of who we are in Him. Heaven is complete perfection, and perfect completion, in, and with our Creator. Forever.

I sometimes think of this next scripture when someone passes on to heaven, especially unexpectedly.

> *"The righteous perish, and no man lays it to heart: and merciful men are taken away, none considering that the righteous are taken away from the evil to come."(9)*

Do we ever consider that some "are taken away from the evil to come?"

Though we may feel a great and significant loss, this might certainly be considered the mercy and love of God.

> *"For now we see through a glass, darkly; but in the time to come, It will be face to face: now I know in part; but then I will know even as I am known."(10)*

One of the truths about our human condition is that we see through this observation glass darkly.

Ever try doing that? Ever try to look through an opaque, or clouded glass object? You can focus and squint all you'd like but it won't ever be truly clear, and all you can do for the most part is offer conjecture and hypothesize as to what is behind. Can we be correct in all of our observations if we can't quite see it all?

There are times we can see, and times when we can't.

That's why we have to go to, and to trust our Creator, especially in the times we can't see, because He can see. And He knows perfectly the answers and the fullness of all in all.

At the end of the Book of Job, just before God reveals everything to Job, He intervenes and asks Job,

> *"Will he that contends with the Almighty instruct Him? He that reproves God, let him answer."(11)*

> *"Will you also disannul my judgment? Will you condemn me, that you might be righteous?"(12)*

"Are you contending with Me and instructing Me, Job? Are you trying to void My judgment and are blaming Me because you consider yourself to be in the right?"

God is chastening Job here. Job still hasn't sinned by cursing God, but his accusations of God, and trying to justify his accusations of God by his words may still be in need of correction at this point.

God afterwards also chastens and corrects Job's friends, for not saying what was right about Job, and for not correctly saying what was right about Him or Who He was at all.

Do we sometimes do this? Do we say those things that may not be right about God?

It wasn't as important for the Lord to let Job know that Satan had been the cause of all his afflictions as it was to let Job know some very important things about Who his God was, and is, and to show Job a much better way to handle all of his earthly afflictions and adversity.

In our human condition, we should probably be careful about laying blame, especially on God, as Job and his friends did, as we only see through a glass darkly, and we may not really know or be able to see the source or the fullness of the events and circumstances before us.

And no matter what happens, we should always go immediately and directly to God.

As we'll see, the Lord shows Job and his friends a better way in the end.

And through Job, the Father is showing us a better way, too.

The Lord God has set the universe in motion...

Let us be very careful about blaming the One Who saves us.

God's Grace

"For by grace are you saved through faith; and it is not of yourselves:
it is the gift of God:"(1)

Before we go any further into what God might have as expectations for us, I think it is appropriate for us to understand a little bit about God's grace toward us all.

The grace of God is very similar and very much related to, and in synergy with, God's great Love for us. It is bigger than we can ever imagine, and it is in our lives for us to receive.

> *"Even when we were dead in sins, God has brought us to life with Christ, (by grace you are saved;) and has raised us up together, and made us sit together in heavenly places in Christ Jesus:*
> *That in the ages (time) to come He might show us the exceeding riches of His grace in his kindness toward us through Christ Jesus.*
> *For by grace are you saved through faith; and that not of yourselves: it is the gift of God:*
> *Not of (a person's) works, lest anyone should boast."(2)*

Nothing we have done, or not done, or what we can do, or can't do, has any bearing on, or relation to, God's grace toward us. It is His unmerited favor toward us. It is not earned, and indeed never can be. It is those things graciously provided to us by the Father.

And it's for everyone.

As the above verse points out, it can be given to us even when we are "dead in sins". There are no conditions to it or on it, and it is not a reward for something we've done. His grace is purely out of His unconditional love toward us.

His grace is a gift for us and to us, no matter where we are or what we have done.

God's grace is an undeserved gift, which only has to be realized, and received.

The middle verse from the above verse says,

"That in the ages to come" He might show us the exceeding riches of His grace..."

When is that? When are the "ages to come"? Is it off in heaven or in eternity at some point? Is it in some other lifetime?

No. We're in the ages to come right now.

"That He might show us the exceeding riches of His grace in his kindness toward us through Christ Jesus."

How does God show us these things, these exceeding riches of His Grace?

He gives us and shows us these things through Jesus, the Christ, and His Spirit, and through all He has given to us to be, and to use, and to share with others. These exceeding riches are all around us, and even within us.

> *"And now, my friends, I commend you to God,*
> *and to the Word of his grace, which is able to build you up,*
> *and to give you an inheritance..."(3)*

The Word is also by, or from, His grace. The Word is able to build us up.

This says that the Word also gives us an inheritance.

What might this inheritance be? Remember Jesus is the Word made flesh, and is the "Word of His grace."

All that Jesus did and all He gives to us, and all that we are able to do in Him including all we can accomplish with the authority in His Name, is the embodiment of that gift. And this is indeed a great inheritance.

What does this "Word of His grace" say?

That we can actually be and do all of the things the Lord said we could be and do.

That we can receive in its entirety all that He has given us, by His Word and through His Holy Spirit.

We already have these things; they have been given to us as gifts by God by His grace. Now, here, in this life.

We only need to realize and receive the fullness of them.

Once again let me reiterate that God's Grace is not earned. It is not anything you or I or anyone else can do, and it is no respecter of particular persons. It isn't given to anyone because of their works or merit, of how "Christian" or "Un-Christian" they are.

But just as God's love is given to anyone, so is His Grace given to us and anyone through His amazing Love. It is not deserved or to be expected or required. It is the unconditional Goodness of God, given to all.

And given to You.

Jesus came to show us, and to give us, God's grace.

The more we know of Him, the more we will understand His grace and His goodness, His forgiveness and His guidance, and His power and His strength. All given by and through His Love for us.

It is by God's grace, and by His Son Jesus, and through the Holy Spirit, that each one of us is offered all of the amazing things that the Lord has for us, much of which we have yet to realize.

This is His grace and His kindness toward us through Christ Jesus.

Mercy and Grace

"Let us therefore come boldly unto the throne of grace, that we may obtain mercy, and find grace to help in time of need."(1)

There are two elements of God's love for us which are often found together, and many times because they are similar, we take them as meaning the same thing. Both are tied together by God's love toward us, yet they are in fact very different with different intents and purposes.

These two "gifts" are God's mercy; and as we looked at in the last chapter, God's grace. So many times we see these two as one entity, which can cause some confusion, yet though they may be a connected whole, they are uniquely different in their character and characteristics.

Let's take a moment to look at each one.

Having **"mercy"** or being **merciful** means to refrain from harming a person or persons who have offended, and to not respond with repercussions that may be due. It is generally considered to be a release from punishment or reprimand.

God's Mercy = Not being punished for something done wrong; as in a sin or sins.

Some people say that God's mercy is "Not getting what we otherwise would deserve."

The Word shows that God's mercy is abundant toward us.

"But You, O Lord, are full of compassion, and gracious, longsuffering, and are plentiful in <u>mercy</u> and truth."(2)

"The Lord is gracious, and full of compassion; slow to anger, and of great <u>mercy</u>.
The Lord is good to all: and his tender <u>mercy</u> is over all his works."(3)

*"O give thanks to the Lord; for He is good: for His <u>**mercy**</u> endures forever."(4)*

91

God's mercy goes on forever. That means... yes, forever.

God has infinite mercy. Not just sometimes, but every day and all the time.

> "It is because of the LORD's mercies that we are not consumed, because his compassion never runs out. His mercies are new every morning; His faithfulness is great."(5)

God's mercy is renewed for each of us in our lives every day.

Let's go a little further and ask an earnest question regarding mercy. If mercy is not punishing us for what we've done wrong, and if it's true that God is plenteous in mercy, doesn't that mean that God does not punish us for what we've done, and that He has mercy on us always?

The first part of this question may contradict what we've always been taught or believed in the past. In talking about this with people, many admit that they think that our Almighty God is always standing over us with a big hammer and some instantaneous reprimand or rebuke, ready at any second to whack us over the head and/or to levy some form of punishment on us if we mess up at all. It's what we've been taught.

But is this really true?

Could the thoughts that we have, that God punishes us, be further evidence that our own misconceptions, via our own human nature, might also be misinterpreting the true character and nature of our God?

Could it be that the real truth is that God is indeed always merciful and doesn't punish us, and actually always forgives us for what we've done wrong, no matter what?

Jesus showed us this, as we'll look at later on.

Can you name something God has actually punished you, or any one, for?

I'm not at all saying that there won't ever be any form of punishment, as the Word talks about a Judgment Day. It is indeed written,

"Vengeance is mine; I will repay, says the Lord."(6)

But after all that we've seen in Jesus, the Christ, do we really think that God's vengeance will be similar to what our own vengeance might be or even look like?

Doesn't our very human nature tend to superimpose our own desires for retribution and retaliation upon or in place of God's desires? Do we feel that He would punish as we would have Him punish?

The Word says that we will be held accountable for our words and our actions while we were here on earth. But will this be in the way that we suppose?

God's ways are so much higher than our ways, which might suggest that the vengeance of God will be perfectly accomplished, yet will most probably be very, very different than what we would assume or can even imagine.

As to those 'not good' things that happen to us here, I would suggest that many times we receive the repercussions and the direct effects of things done wrong as a naturally occurring cause and effect, as a reaction to our own or someone else's actions, and we then receive the direct results of those actions. These consequences in many instances may be compound and severe, and we may have to live with the side effects of these actions for a long time.

But is this "God punishing us" for doing wrong? Or has He told us in any number of ways, in His Word and elsewhere, that by doing certain things, resultant consequences will occur? Is this a form of punishment, or are these the results and effects of ourselves, or others not heeding His really, really, really good advice, advice which has been given to us in His Word based on His knowing the complete truth about our nature and the natural consequences of our own humanity?

Don't we so many times ignore good advice and do things that might harm us or others anyway, regardless of what the consequences might be?

We can start with Adam and Eve…

Is His vengeance accomplished during our time here on earth?

Again, I am quite sure that God's judgment will be perfect in both the measure of its severity and its justice, and with His grace, in His much higher way. I would suggest that His vengeance is not for this time and place, but for after all is said and done in our lives, and again, nothing like what we might think it will be!

Let's look at this from Jesus' perspective, again considering that God's character was always being shown to us through His Son Jesus, the Messiah.

Did Jesus ever punish anyone? We asked this earlier. Did He ever put punishment or cause retribution to come on anyone while he was alive on earth?

Let's look further into at an example we looked at earlier. Jesus' disciples, after they realized the power they had in Jesus' name, asked the Lord if they could punish a village of Samaritans by calling down fire from heaven for wrongs they considered were done against Him.

> *"And when the time was come that Jesus should be received up, He steadfastly set Himself to go to Jerusalem, And He sent messengers before Him into a village of the Samaritans, to make ready for Him. But they did not receive Him…*
> *And when His disciples James and John saw this, they said, Lord, do You want us to command fire to come down from heaven, and consume them, even as Elijah did?*
>
> *But the Lord turned, and rebuked them, and said, you don't know what manner of spirit you are of. For the Son of man is not come to destroy men's lives, but to save them."(7)*

Jesus was telling His disciples that from now on, you are of the Spirit of God, and you are to have mercy and grace, just like your Father in heaven has mercy and grace, to forgive and to save.

This is also for us in this day as well.

> *"But I say unto you, Love your enemies, bless them that curse you, do good to them that hate you, and pray for them which despitefully use you, and persecute you;*
>
> *That you may be the children of your Father..."*(8)

What Jesus said here truly reflects God's character and nature toward all of us. The Father has mercy on all of us all the time, and asks us to do so to others as well. This is a good example that it's God's nature **not** to punish us for what we may deserve punishment for, and that we are to act as He actually does, with mercy toward others.

Can we even wrap our minds around the possibility that God does not punish us here on earth, but instead has mercy with us, and forgives us all the time?

Again, could this be something else that we have been very wrong about, and have been very wrong about Him, for a long, long time?

Let's begin to really know Who God is, and His mercy in our lives.

Okay, now let's take a little deeper look into God's *grace* toward us.

We've seen that God's *mercy* does not punish us when we deserve to be punished.

God could have stopped right there. This could have been all that we received (or didn't receive) which would have been great and amazing in and of itself. It could have ended solely with no punishment or retribution for us. Just His mercy, and then we would go on.

But God doesn't do that. He goes way beyond that, by and with His grace.

God's Grace = a greater undeserved good which is given to us by God.

Some say that grace is then "Receiving what we don't deserve."

Our Father, by His goodness, gives us gifts far greater than we can understand and/or even begin to realize.

One thing that God does by His grace is that He forgives us. All the time. He forgives us *completely*, so that our mistakes and sins are no longer remembered. He forgives us by, and through, His Son, Jesus.

Jesus died for us that by Him, and through His blood, our sins, or the things we've done wrong, are remembered by God no longer.

Jesus was the great and final sacrifice for this and for us.

It is also by Gods nature, and by His grace, that He forgives us over and over and over, all the time..

> *"Then came Peter to him, and said, Lord, how often shall my brother sin against me, and I forgive him? Up to seven times? Jesus then said to him, not just up to seven times: but up to <u>seventy times seven.</u>"(9)*

Jesus is showing Peter here that we should forgive others in the very same way that God forgives.

Jesus also lived this way always, having the character of His, and our, Father.

Another gift that the Lord gives to us by His grace is that if we're listening, and ready to receive, He shows us a better way.

Think about any time you've had to make a decision between something which is good and something which might seem good or enjoyable at the time but possibly has a degree of temptation or shade of gray to it, or even a time when it may have been full blown temptation.

Just before making that decision, isn't there an instant of consideration, a moment of opportunity, a certain point at which you realize that if you will intentionally act or react differently, the outcome will be different and probably much better?

Isn't there even just a moment in time, just before you decide to act, when you have the chance to go in a different direction, to get out of it, to avoid the desire and temptation and don't make that wrong move?

Unfortunately, we then many times go ahead and make the ill-conceived, ill-advised decision and action anyway.

> *"There is no temptation that can tempt you more than is common to man: but God is faithful Who will not allow you to be tempted beyond what you are able to handle; but will with the temptation also make a way to escape, that you may be able to handle it and escape it successfully."(10)*

When I was growing up, many of the cartoons of the day would personify the elements of good vs. evil. They would have an angelic character and an evil character each sitting on a person's shoulders and whispering opposing thoughts and reasoning's into a person's ears.

The good side was always the person's conscience, and the other side was temptation. Be guided by your conscience was the prevailing theme, inferring that the good choices were always the ones to be listened to and taken.

We've heard about our conscience, but what is our "conscience"? Is it something that comes to us from good traits we've learned? Are we born with a certain amount somehow of inherent knowledge of good? Is it somehow omnipresent throughout our lives?

We obviously have the capacity to hear it, and it is certainly something that can be instrumental and even dynamic in our lives.

Is it possible that these thoughts, or our "conscience", could be a gift given by the Lord and His Spirit speaking to us?

97

I won't delve into this further here, but if this "conscience" is indeed affiliated with the Spirit of God, then it is certainly marvelous and given to us as an opportunity by God's grace.

The Lords Spirit, and His grace show us a better way, whether we take heed of it or not.

I believe that Job had moments of opportunity in the beginning of his ordeal, during his time of contemplation and silence where he could have made different decisions on how he would react to all of his afflictions. Going to God was surely one of his options, but one he didn't choose.

God is the God of second chances, and in the end, when Job was ready to realize and receive it, God's grace showed Job how he could have handled his adversity in a better way, and could have gained so much by going to Him.

After realizing this, and asking, Job was then delivered and healed and blessed.

And not only this, but he also gained a much greater realization and understanding of Who his God was.

Again, all by God's grace.

So, God's goodness and greatness and love brings us mercy, and then He gives us grace in forgiving and correcting and blessing us. In the process He shows us a better way, and gives us a far greater understanding of Who He is.

Another vivid example in the Word of Jesus showing us the character, and mercy and grace of God, was with the woman who was caught in the act of adultery, caught in the very act.

As we observe today, there are two involved, and equally "guilty", but in Jesus' day Hebrew law said she was the one to be punished and stoned.

"And the scribes and Pharisees brought to him a woman taken in adultery;
And... they said to Him, Master (Jesus), this woman was taken in adultery, in the very act. Now Moses in the law commanded that we stone her: but what do you say?
They said this, tempting Him,
that they might have something to accuse Him with.
But Jesus stooped down, and with his finger wrote on the ground, as though he didn't hear them.
So when they continued asking him, he lifted himself up, and said to them, "He that is without sin among you, let him be the first to cast a stone at her."
And again he stooped down, and wrote on the ground.
When they heard it, they were convicted by their own consciences,
And they went out one by one, beginning at the eldest, even unto the last: and Jesus was left alone, along with the woman.
When Jesus got up again, and saw no one else but the woman, and he said to her, Woman, where are your accusers? Has no one condemned you?
She said, no one, Lord.
And Jesus said unto her, neither do I condemn you:
go, and sin no more."(11)

"Neither do I condemn you..."

Neither am I going to hold this over your head. I'm not going to punish you. I and My Father forgive you.

Then "Go, and sin no more." Go, and don't do it anymore. It hurts others and it hurts yourself.

"Neither do I condemn you" = God's mercy.

"Go, and sin no more" = God's grace.

Jesus was showing us of the Fathers nature and desire to forgive and then to give. This example is in very stark contrast to man's inclination to condemn, and the tendency of our human nature toward the condemnation of others.

"There is therefore now __no__ condemnation to them which are in Christ Jesus, who don't walk toward worldly things, but walk toward the Spirit."(12)

Jesus is also showing us that New Testament grace is much, much greater, and much more all-encompassing than the Old Testament was, though the two are very much connected.

It's all really very simple. The Lord has mercy on us and doesn't condemn us. Not only that but He has grace toward us and forgives us.

And not only does God forgive us, and gives us grace to go and sin no more, but He also shows us a better way.

And even greater than that, if we are looking, He also prepares us and gives us all of the tools with which to go and be a light to others in this life, to His glory.

With our desire and by His Spirit He thoroughly trains us in the use of all that He has given us, in all of His ways and in the things we can do through Him, so that we can go do all of the amazing works He says we can do.

In and through Him, we, and others, can have life, and have life more abundantly, and we can have great success in all these things, in Him, and all to His glory!

May we all learn to come boldly unto the throne of grace that we may obtain mercy, and find grace to help in time of need.

And may we learn to use all the many gifts, and tools that He has given us,,,

With Him,

And to His glory.

Judge Not

"Judge not, that you not be judged.
For with what judgment you judge, you shall be judged:
And with what measure you mete, it shall be measured to you."(1)

Job's friends could have had mercy and grace toward Job. They instead chose to judge and condemn him for things they knew nothing about.

Jesus said in the above verse, "Don't judge, or you will be judged".

Whatever judgment you make about someone, you will also be judged by that same judgment you yourself made. And not only that, but whatever the amount of that judgment that you judged someone else, that same amount of judgment, it says, will be given to you.

In short, if we judge, we will also be judged by that same thing, and to the same degree.

As we saw in the last chapter, Christ asks us not to condemn others, but to use mercy and grace to forgive others just as much as He forgives us.

Many times, in our own human nature, we try to judge and correct in others things we may actually know very little about.

And also, as a side note, if we look even closer at our human nature, we see that many times what we accuse others of, we are the ones that are guilty of it ourselves, and maybe even more so.

Have you ever noticed this? Have you ever noticed this in others? Have you ever heard someone accusing and passing judgment on someone else, and have absolutely known that it doesn't apply to the accused at all, but that it applies perfectly to the one doing the accusing?

Job's friends and their words, and then God's rebuke, suggest that judging others may not be a very wise course of action in our lives.

Again, Job's friends had the opportunity to have mercy and grace toward Job. They went to commiserate with him, and while they were there, they began to feel a certain obligation to judge and correct Job as well. They then began to condemn Job, and continued to do so until God stepped in and showed them that they themselves were wrong about it all. God at that point rebukes and corrects them, and then shows them all a better way.

It is the same with us. It is in our human nature to discover things, even about other people, but we should always do so, not by judging and being quick to condemn, but by the greater strength of God's wisdom, a certain knowing, and of mercy and grace.

We are certainly called to use discernment in our lives, and may discern certain things, but many times there are circumstances well beyond our knowledge which do not allow us to accurately assess a person or person's situations enough to judge and accuse and correct.

But God knows.

This is not saying that we should remain blind to events and attitudes and behaviors that surround us. We should not, but we can, by and through the Holy Spirit, discern the truth about those things and can respond accordingly without judgment.

Having discernment, and passing judgment on things and people are two very different considerations, and are indeed very different in direction, attitudes and in actions taken.

Discernment is the ability to be able to clearly perceive the truth about a person, persons or situation.

It is a knowing that you have. It is clearly and absolutely known to you in your heart and spirit. Nothing needs to be done about it. Nothing needs to be pronounced, spoken or judged, and no measures are needed.

Judgment or being judgmental is an action. It performs or metes out a punishment according to the punishers desires, either verbally or physically.

There is some sort of action associated with it.

So often in these instances the person judging is doing so by thinking they know all that's going on, and levying a judgment by their own perceived standards. What we find is that the judgment is many times only one sided, and truly not judicious, and does not know or recognize all that is taking place.

Our nature likes to find solutions, and many times we try to solve the puzzle presented before us while only having a few of the pieces, and then we pride ourselves on the completion, only to find that the assumption is completely wrong and the resolution badly flawed, and that there were important pieces missing. Though the assumption may have been a heartfelt feeling and it may have seemed at the time to be creative and imaginative, it also may very well have been, in actuality, harmful guessing.

I am talking strictly of personal judgment here, though sometimes it can become a certain type of social judgment.

We, as governed and governing entities, have been given the authority to pass judgment on the behavior of others via laws in our various social and communal systems. This pertains primarily to criminal actions and behaviors, so that pain and suffering might be prevented according to certain social standards, and that human chaos may be avoided. This has been necessary throughout time in order that we may attempt to live quiet and peaceful lives.

But what we are making reference to here is personally judging others personal lives. In this God is the only one Who can judge, and He will do so perfectly. It is only up to us to have mercy and grace with others and to forgive, as He does. 70 x 7.

Many times our perceptions of God can also be badly skewed by the words and actions of others, and even of other Christians, who, because of their/our human nature, may have a tendency to condemn others instead of having mercy and grace toward them.

People may even think of these others as "Godly" and then assume themselves to be inferior in the Lord by this condemnation, when it indeed is not the truth at all.

How many times have people been hurt by others judgment and condemnation, and then turned away from the Lord due to something someone has said to them or about them, out of their own, very human nature, and not from God or His nature?

How many times do people feel they have to be as "perfect" as the appearances of those they see as examples, in order to approach the Father?

The Word says, *"All have sinned and come short of the Glory of God."(2)*

All of us humans, anyway. It's in our nature to mess up at times in our lives, though we try not to.

Does God know this?

Yes. He created us.

Does He forgive us?

Yes. That's why He sent His Son, to give us a way back to Him, so that anyone and everyone can come to know the Father, and His mercy and grace, despite our very "human" nature.

And that's also why the Lord asks us to overcome our own human tendencies of judgment and condemnation, and instead to take on His nature, which is to *always* have mercy and grace toward others.

"Neither do I condemn you. Go, and sin no more."(3)

God's Expectation of Us

"Let us come boldly to His throne of grace..."(1)

We've looked at certain expectations that God may have had of Job.

What might be God's expectations of us?

First and foremost, the Lord wants us to have a relationship with Him.

He wants us to have this relationship with Him based on His Love, based on the 'yare' type worship which comes from knowing Him.

Jesus came to bring us and show us is that we can have this relationship and have access to both Him and the Father.

Have we been there, as the above verse says, to Gods throne room of Grace?

Do we ever go there? Do we go there often? Do we spend time in His presence? It's nice to already know where His throne room is, and how to get there, so when bad times or when things happen, we know exactly where to go.

Let's look at something.

> *"But this man (Jesus), after he had offered one sacrifice for sins forever, sat down at the right hand of God; from now on <u>expecting,</u> until his enemies are made his footstool."(2)*

This verse says that the Lord is expecting something. What is He expecting?

Jesus accomplished what He came here to do. He lived His life as a man, showed us of the Father through the Spirit via teaching, healing and wisdom, He gave us His Word, and He took all of our sins upon Him on the cross that we might be justified before God. It was there He said "It is finished".

Jesus also at that time and by His sacrifice brought us a New Covenant and all that we are now able to do in Him and through His name.

He did this, not only so that we could have the opportunity to have life everlasting, but also that we could know joy and peace and Life and His Power in us and with Him in _this_ life. He gave us authority and sent us the Holy Spirit to show us these things and to be with us in these things.

So what is He expecting?

Jesus is expecting for us to come to Him and to learn to use and exercise all that He has given us, that we would discover and realize, by this use, the height and length and depth and breadth of all that He has for us, and all that we can have, in and through Him.

One of those things is;

> "Having boldness to enter into the holiest (into the deep things of God) by the blood of Jesus. By a new and living way, which He has consecrated (cleansed and prepared) for us."(3)

In other words, Jesus wants us to go farther and deeper, and to know more and more about the Father, and about His Holy Spirit, who He sent, in His place, to be with us. He wants us to have and to know and to receive and to share more about who He is, and about the depth of the life He has already prepared for us.

He wants us to know all that He has given us by the Holy Spirit, and that we would use the power of His name in ours and others lives, to His glory, by and through His Spirit that lives within us.

One of the things ingrained in us and perpetuated by past misconceptions and misinterpretations of the Book of Job is the thought that we cannot know God. This may very well be partially based on the erroneous speeches and false concepts spoken by Job's friends to Job about God in the Book of Job.

Zophar - *"Can you by searching find out God?"*(4)

Eliphaz - *"Have you heard the secrets of God?"*(5)

Elihu - *"Behold, God is great, and we know Him not,,,"*(6)

In the end God Himself told them that they were very, very wrong.

The truth is that we **can** know Him, and not only that, but He **wants** us to know Him, even the deep things of Him!!!

We have so much to change in our thinking about Who the Father is, and what our part and place in Him is.

> *"...For this is good and acceptable in the sight of God our Savior; Who will have all men to be saved, **and** to come in to the knowledge of the truth."*(7)

Many teachings look at this verse and suggest that Paul is talking solely about the wonderful event of salvation.

Let's take a moment and look at this verse chronologically. If this were only about being saved, wouldn't it say that God will have all men to come in to the knowledge of the truth and then be saved? But it does not. It says that God will have all men to be saved, _and_ to come in to the knowledge of the truth, and _then_ _also_ to come into the knowledge and the fullness of _all_ He has given to us!

There is so much more that Jesus wants us to know. The Lord wants us to be saved, and also to *then* to come into the knowledge of **all** of the Truth. And He sent His Spirit to us that we could know and have these things!

We'll look at this again, but it is important to know that there is so much more for us to know and understand and realize about the Lord and His power within us than what little we know now. I don't believe we've even scratched the surface of what is available to us through God's Spirit, no matter how long we've been Christians.

Jesus said that when He departed, He would send the Comforter, the Holy Spirit, to be with us in His place so that the Holy Spirit would be able guide us into all the truth.

> *"But when He, the Spirit of truth is come, He will guide you into*
> ***all*** *truth: for He will not speak of Himself; but whatever He hears,*
> *that will He speak: and He will show you things to come.*
> *He will glorify Me: for He will receive from Me, and He will show it*
> *to you."(8)*

The Spirit of God will guide us into **all** truth.

Another question for us to answer individually is do we desire to have all truth? Do we desire to know these things, and to know more?

Jesus says to us over and over to ask, seek, and knock, and to find out more about Him, about Who He is, and about His righteousness, in other words about His <u>right</u>-ness. Paul says;

> *"God has revealed these things to us by His Spirit; for the Spirit*
> *searches **all** things, even the deep things of God."(9)*

The Lord has given us His Spirit specifically so that all these truths could be revealed to us. He's given us His Spirit so that we can discover even the "deep things of God"!!!

Paul goes on to explain that man's own human nature in and of itself doesn't know, and can't know the things of God, but the Spirit of God does know, and if this same Spirit of God is with us and dwells within us, then we too can know all of these things.

Keep in mind it doesn't say that we have to be perfect to know these things. All that's required is that we have received His Son, and His Spirit, and that we have a desire to know more and more about Him.

Paul at this point poses this next great question to those who were already Christians:

"Know ye not that you are the temple of God, and that the Spirit of God lives within you?"(10)

Paul is saying, "Don't you know?

Don't you know that not only are you the temple of God, but also that His Spirit, this same Spirit of God who knows all of the deep things of God, dwells and lives *within you*?"

Don't you know?

Have you gone as far as possible to find out Who the Lord is? Have we heard all there is to hear and know from the Holy Spirit?

As a side note, let me say something to those who may somehow be feeling inferior in all of this. We all have messed up. God isn't looking for a perfect temple. It would be impossible to find one.

What He is saying is that if you've received Him, He and His Spirit are in you and with you. He wants *you* to have *all* of these amazing things that go along with Him and who He is. He wants you to have them personally.

It's a part of the Lords expectation for us that we learn more about Him.

Let's switch gears for a moment and think about how we receive knowledge about anything. How do we really receive and learn?

Can our parents teach us? Yes, to a degree. Can others teach us? Yes, also to a degree. But how do we truly learn something?

We truly learn, receive, realize and understand something by actually involving ourselves in whatever it is, by doing it ourselves. We learn by discovering and experiencing the thing, first hand.

In the world, we have tools to learn such as books and information and teaching and training so that we might conceptualize what we desire to know.

But at some point, in order to truly understand the whole of it, we have to actually act upon it, or exercise that which we've learned.

It is the same with the things of God. We have the Word and His powerful Holy Spirit, and we have others who have gone before and those who have gone further who we can learn from. But in order to really know and experience the whole of all that we can have and be in the Father, Son and Holy Ghost, we have to _act_ upon His Word and experience these things for ourselves!

Then and only then can we truly go further. Both individually, and as the Body of Christ.

Paul writes about human nature and our lack of desire to actually experience the things of God. He talks about many of us;

> "...seeing you have become dull of hearing. And when you should now be teachers you desire that someone teach you the same things over and over again... and you have become like those that need of milk, and not strong meat.
> For every one that uses milk is not skilled in the word... for he is a babe."(11)

So many times we live our Christian lives just going through the motions of going to church, hearing about the things of God and Christ, receiving some insight, giving an offering, and then going home to live another way.

Is this the life Jesus expects or has in mind for us?

We indeed love the milk, and/or sometimes the milk shakes, but then we also tend to regularly avoid the broccoli and meat, which is actually experiencing the things of God or ourselves, by which we are made strong.

Think about this. If all you ever drank as adults was milk, what kind of physical shape would you be in? Would you be strong and healthy and have endurance? Or would you be weak and fatty and out of shape? Milk alone is great for babies to grow on, but in adults, not so much.

What about eating veggies and meat? Doesn't eating these proteins and vitamins give you strength, power and endurance?

Yes. Sometimes you have to chew on them a bit, but you grow stronger by doing so.

Figuratively speaking, I think many of us are more than happy to just drink milkshakes, when God is expecting us to be walking fully in His covenant, and receiving all the meat and vegetables we can possibly receive, so that we would have the strength to be able to do and share and experience with others the greater power and the love and the wisdom, and the communication of the authority in Jesus' name that we have, so that we and others might be greatly blessed.

God has not created us to simply acknowledge Him every so often as we go along in life. The Lord is not expecting us to go to church once in a while, or once or twice a week, or month, to listen to others talk about Him, while we occasionally and maybe only accidentally or incidentally actually receive something from Him.

God has created us to **_experience_** Him, in small, and great, and amazing ways in and throughout our entire life.

Do we really know what God can do in our lives??? Do you know Who the Lord is and what He can do with and through you?

Here's an example of someone realizing this very thing a long time ago.

How many people do we know that have walked on water? Would you say one?

Or maybe two...

> "And in the fourth watch of the night Jesus went to them, walking on the sea...
> And Jesus spoke to them, saying, Be of good cheer; it is I; don't be afraid.
> And Peter answered Him saying, Lord, if it is You, then ask me to come to You on the water.
> And Jesus said, Come.

And when Peter stepped down out of the ship, he walked on the water,
to go to Jesus."(12)

Peter walked on water too.

He couldn't have done that if he didn't have an idea of who Jesus was, and the power in His words, and what he might be able to do through Him.

Did Peter walk on water by magic, or in a dream?

No, he walked on water by the Spirit of the Lord.

But he also realized something else. He realized that much could be done through the power of the Word of the Lord, and by His Spirit.

After Jesus' death on the cross Peter went on to teach and heal and do many works in Jesus' name.

This same Holy Spirit is here, on earth, in Jesus' place and within us, to show each of us the truth of all the things we can have, and be, and all that we can do in the Father, and in the Son through and by the Spirit of God.

This is not based on one event of someone walking on water, this is just an example. It is based on the Lord's power and grace and love, and on the fullness of the times He and His Spirit have shown up to heal and save and deliver and to move in our world and in our lives!

The amazing part is that this is for every one of us.

We just have to be listening, and learning more and more about Who He is, and acting on all He gives us.

There are great and cool and amazing rewards that go along with all that the Lord shows us, and along with these things comes absolute joy and fulfillment to and in your life, and to and in others' lives as well.

Are you experiencing these opportunities of God for yourself? Probably to some degree if you're reading this book. Are you desiring to continue to experience the things of the Lord and go deeper into all that He is?

Again, being in God is not just a one-time event, then only to join some sort of club or spectator sport where everyone drinks milkshakes and seeks or watches the entertainment.

The things of God are to be experienced, one after another after another, each one building on our faith, and through these things we will be truly blessed. We will be a gift and a blessing to others, for the rest of our lives, and beyond...

Here is the second part of the earlier verse about the milk and the meat and the analogy Paul wants us to understand.

> But strong meat belongs to those, who **by reason of use** have their senses **exercised** to discern both good (things that are of God) and evil (things that are not of God)."(13)

Paul is writing specifically here about **using, exercising** and **experiencing** these things of God for ourselves. He is showing us that by doing these things we will find out Who the Lord is and what He wants for us, and we will grow deeper and stronger and greater in Him.

Yes, we need to keep the first principals close, as our base, in order to help others along the way.

But at the same time are we ourselves continually and intentionally growing into a much deeper and greater life with Him through the Holy Spirit?

Or are we just continuing to ride on what we already know and just listen and/or speak about the first principles again and again?

Jesus desires that we go deeper into all that He has prepared for us, no matter where we are in our walk with Him.

There is so much more to the Father. When we are experiencing God, and walking in all He's given us, then not only are we and others truly blessed, but God is also truly glorified in all that we do.

Jobs friends said,

> *"Touching the Almighty, we cannot find him out..."(14)*

And then Almighty God told them they were very, very wrong.

God, through Jesus, came to be with us, not to be away and separated from us. The Holy Spirit was sent by Jesus to be with all of us, and within us, and to show us **all** things of the Father.

> *"And they shall call his name Emmanuel, which is interpreted, God with us."(15)*

The Lord is expecting us individually to find out more about Him, and receive and experience Him, in all that He has for us,,,

Here and now,

In this life.

For all our lives.

Initiate Yourself

"Ask, and it shall be given you; seek, and you shall find;
knock, and it shall be opened to you..."(1)

The three things mentioned in the above verse, asking, seeking and knocking, are all action words. They are all pro-active words and phrases, with no passive nature to them at all. They all require some sort of action on our part.

When coming to God with anything, we, for the most part, must make the first move. We may be prompted to do so, but we also must actually initiate the action ourselves. This is how the Lord of the Universe has set it all up. The Lord has set the order of things so that we have to do something first, or 'initiate ourselves', which means we need to take first step initiatives toward Him.

When we do, He hears us and honors our actions with answers. It's part of His covenant with us. He hears according to our trust and our faith (not necessarily our emotions, as we'll see), as we make the effort to see and hear and receive from Him.

Let's take a look at some folks initiating themselves in the New Testament. Remember also that Jesus is always showing us the nature of God.

As you look at this group, notice that as Jesus performed miracles, the persons involved, or those around them, had to do something first. They had to make a move toward the Lord despite their limitations. They had to have trust in Him, and when they acted upon that trust, the Lord gave them what they desired.

> The wedding feast ran out of wine. The wedding providers came to Mary, who pointed them to Jesus. Jesus tells them to "go fill the vats with water". They did and then drew out the best wine ever.

> The woman with the issue of blood for 12 years, who had spent all she had on physicians yet only grew worse, had to press through the

115

great crowd of people to get to Jesus, which was no easy feat in that condition. She did so, and was healed.

➢ How about the friends who lowered the lame man through the roof to get to Jesus; again no easy feat taking him up there and breaking apart a roof. Jesus healed the man, afterward saying that the faith of his *friends* had made the man whole.

➢ When a few loaves and fishes were gathered first from any who had them, and then thousands were fed, twice, with leftovers.

➢ The Centurion knew that Jesus could just speak the word for his daughters healing, and he asked for this. Jesus was amazed that he knew this truth, and the Romans daughter was immediately healed.

➢ To the man with the withered hand, "Stretch forth your hand". Embarrassing at best. But with faith He did so and was made whole.

➢ The blind man, Bartimaeus, who wouldn't stop calling out to Him, and continued calling out despite the rebuff of others around him. Jesus then commanded that he be brought to Him, and he was healed.

➢ How about the woman with the spirit of infirmity eighteen years, who was bowed over and couldn't even lift herself up. She could barely move.

> *"And when Jesus saw her, **He called her to Him,,,"**(2)*

He did what? Didn't Jesus know she could barely move, let alone come to Him? Well, of course He did. He also knew that as she acted on His words, she would be healed. She did so, and she was healed completely.

In these examples is Jesus just being lazy or maybe disinterested in actually physically going to these people to heal them? No. He knew that His Father had set it up this way, that this is how these things were to be done.

Jesus heard from the Father by and through the Spirit of God, and He spoke the Word.

When it was mixed with faith/trust by the receiving person or persons, and when His words were acted upon, that which they desired was accomplished, and the Father was revealed to each one of them in an amazing way.

All were actions based on faith and trust, and on His Word.

➤ How about the man who sat by the pool of Bethesda for 38 years and couldn't move. 38 years. Jesus said, "Rise, take up your bed and walk." The man did it, and as he did he was healed.

➤ Jesus said to the fishermen, "Let down your nets". Even though they had caught nothing all night long, they did according to His words and received a massive overflowing catch.

These were all words of life given by Jesus for the benefit of those who would hear and act on what He said; on His Word. When people trusted and acted on faith, they received.

Note: Trusting and acting on Jesus' words is very important to the outcome.

At one point, there was a city in which Jesus could do no mighty works.

> *"And he did not many mighty works there, because of their unbelief."(3)*

Why couldn't He? Because there wasn't any faith, any trust to receive it. It was because of *their* unbelief.

Our trust, our faith, our belief, and acting upon that belief has a great deal to do with receiving the things of God.

Jesus tells us to seek, to ask, and to knock, and after that our joy would be full. Seeking, Asking and Knocking is part of initiating ourselves and acting on His Word.

Do we know this as a reality in our lives? Don't we know that by acting on His Word, great things can be and are done in our lives?

> *"And there are also many other things which Jesus did, which, if they should all be written, I suppose that even the world itself could not contain all the books."(4)*

And He is still doing these things today, through His Holy Spirit and through us.

This is how He has set it up. It is His nature to do these things. It's the nature of God.

He only asks that we believe and come to Him. He asks that we make the effort to come to Him, first. We must take the initial step, we must 'initiate ourselves', and direct ourselves toward God, and He honors that effort. That's just how it is. When we do, it allows God to show up and move on our behalf, and on the behalf of others. When we initiate ourselves, He hears us and His way is opened to us.

There are certainly those times when He overwhelms us with His goodness and love when we're not expecting it or looking for it. Those are incredible experiences which we completely receive, enjoy, may need, and/or are just a reminder to us that He's amazingly great and always there with us. Either way it is all out of His great Love for us.

But we can also reach these deep things of the Father even more so by spending time with Him and earnestly and diligently seeking Him.

There are also times when we may hear nothing, and see no immediate answer to a situation. We still must have trust and faith in Him. There are times where He may be waiting for us just to "be" in Him, and to rest in knowing that the Lord is still there, no matter what.

In these times we may not know how He moves, and/or what He is doing, but if we have trust in Him, and act on His Word, we will see the Lord and His Kingdom and His nature in operation in our lives.

Fear Not

*"For God hath not given us the spirit of fear;
but of power, and of Love, and of a sound mind."(1)*

God doesn't give us fear.

He didn't give Job fear. Job did that to himself.

The Lord gives us power, and His great love, and gives us a sound and functioning mind so that we can overcome any fear which might come our way. He has given us these things so that we will be able to receive and to discern what is real and what is not.

What happens when you come in contact with something that is new and much bigger than yourself, and when all you've heard about it is that it can possibly be bad? Your first tendency, your initial reaction, is to be wary of it and probably initially to have a certain amount of (pachad) fear about it. It's part of our nature.

What if you choose not to find out anything else about it? Does that concern go away? Or does it grow? The unknown always provides our minds with ample considerations and sometimes vivid imaginations of adverse scenarios, and many times even of worst-case ones.

On the other hand, if you find out more about the thing, spend more time with it, and as it becomes more and more familiar to you, you grow to know what you can and cannot do with it, then you find that the fear goes away, and is replaced by a certain knowledge and understanding and confidence in and of it.

As an example, what happens if someone has an odd unknown internal ailment that gives a measure of discomfort or pain and then persists? It many times is our nature to start to wonder if it is something more serious. The more a person wonders, the more they grow concerned. Could it be cancer? "I've heard that so many people die with cancer," they say. What if it is? "I will need to call everyone and I really need to make my will, and get my affairs all in order..." And it can grow all out of proportion.

Then after researching it or going to someone who has actual medical experience with the symptoms such as a physician, you find out it's just severe indigestion, probably because you've been worrying so much, and the remedy is easily available. You now have an answer, and a greater understanding, and the fear goes away.

Here's another example. You are starting a new job in which you don't have much experience. You wonder about it, a certain fear and anxiety grows, then pushing back the fear of the unknown, you get geared up for it, and set your mind to tackle and handle all that it encompasses. You dive in, go that first day, that first week, and as you learn more and more about the job, the worries start to go away and you become more and more a part of it. Eventually you grow to have a more complete and competent understanding of your place in it all. The fear disappears and you wonder what you were ever worried about in the first place. Not only that, but you have become proficient in it, have developed a certain confidence about it, and by this you begin producing results which leads to efficiently completing all which you are there to do.

It's the same thing with the things of God.

When you don't know about the Lord, and you've heard all kinds of good and bad stories about Him, and you haven't desired to find out more about Him, you may have a certain fear of Him. That fear or concern can grow until you don't want to hear anything about Him.

The only way to know for sure who He is, is to learn and seek and find out for yourself more about Him. As you do this, as you become more familiar with Him, you realize that He's not bad, but actually good, and even great after all. The fear goes away, and you forget why you ever were worried in the first place.

And as you continue to find out more, you find that you are very much a part of His Big picture, and that you are growing into a more profound understanding and appreciation for Who He is, His greatness, and His greatness in your life, and in you, and His greatness in all that surrounds you.

You receive from Him, and then as you become more proficient in all of the things He has given to you, you find that you are able to use and employ these gifts, these tools, for the benefit of others, and you then begin to produce results. And as the results come, you then start realizing and receiving the great rewards of all that is accomplished, which brings you great joy and appreciation and desire to do more of it!

> *"I sought the LORD, and He heard me, and delivered me*
> *from all my fears."(2)*

This is what happened in the end with Job too. God showed Job how he could have realized all of this in his life, and then he did!

The Word says, "*...for God is Love.*"(3).

The Word also says that *"Perfect Love casts out fear."(4)*

The more you know about the Lord and His Love, and the more you learn about Who He is, the more you will realize His greatness and the length and breadth and height of His perfect Love with you and within you.

By knowing these things, along with His power, you will also realize that fear, all 'pachad' fear, can be overcome and cast away from your life.

Completely.

Don't let fear of the unknown, or of what anyone else says or does, hinder you from going to God and finding out all there is to know, and all there is for you to have, in Him.

I Have Yet Many Things to Say to You

"I have yet many things to say to you, but you cannot bear them now.
But when the Spirit of Truth is come, He will guide you into all Truth..."(1)

Jesus did not tell the first disciples everything during His short time here on earth and indeed could not tell them everything. It can take lifetimes to know all about the Father, Son and Holy Spirit. His disciples had to get what Jesus needed them to know in just 3 years. That's why He said they couldn't bear it all now. They wouldn't be able to handle it all at once, all at one time.

So when were they going to get the rest of it?

Jesus said that when He went away, God would send the Spirit of Truth to us, that we would be able to know _all_ truth.

The Spirit of Truth Jesus is talking about is the Spirit of God, Who is the Comforter, who Jesus availed to be sent to us, in His place.

> *"The Comforter, which is the Holy Ghost,*
> *Whom the Father will send in My name,*
> *He shall teach you all things, and bring all things into your*
> *remembrance, of all I have said to you."(2)*

Jesus said that He would pray the Father, and He would send the Holy Spirit to us.

> *"And I will pray of the Father, and He will give you _another_ Comforter,*
> *that He may abide with you forever; even the Spirit of Truth;*
> *Who the world cannot receive, because in their worldly state they*
> *cannot see Him or know Him;*
> *But you know Him; for He dwells with you and will be in you."(3)*
>
> *"For He (the Spirit of God) shall not speak of Himself; but whatever*
> *He hears, that He will speak: and He will show you things to come.*
> *He will glorify me: for He will receive the things that are of Me,*
> *and will show them to you.*

All things that the Father has are mine: so I can say that <u>He will</u> <u>take of mine, and will show these things to you</u>."(4)

The Holy Spirit is here, in Jesus' place, to show us all things.

For anyone born after 33 AD, Jesus said that this was how He was going to work with us. He would come to us and be in us through and by the Spirit of God, sent from the Father, in His name.

So this is one of the primary functions of the Holy Spirit. This is what He's here to do. He has been sent here to show us all things, even the deep things of God, that we might know all that the Lord has for us.

King David also knew of all of the Lord's thoughts toward us, and His desire to be with us, and of all He wants to show us.

> *"How precious also are Your thoughts unto me, O God!*
> *How great is the sum of them!*
> *...they are more in number than the sand..." (5)*

The Lord has many things to tell us, and to tell you...

If the Father didn't want us to know about Him, He wouldn't have sent Jesus, and wouldn't have sent the Holy Spirit to be here with us in Jesus' place.

That's what both have come to do, to reveal to us the Father.

Do we know this? Are we ready for this?

Are we listening?

God Gives Great Gifts

"Or what man is there of you, if his son asks for bread, will he give him a stone?
Or if he asks for a fish, will he give him a serpent?
If you then, being evil, know how to give good gifts to your children,
how <u>much more</u> shall your Father which is in heaven
*give <u>good things</u> <u>to them that</u> <u>**ask**</u> <u>Him</u>?"(1)*

Gifts are things given by ourselves or others for the benefit and/or enjoyment of the receiver. Those from whom they come also receive pleasure in the giving.

In this case, the gifts we are talking about are given to us from the Father for our benefit and/or enjoyment..

This might be a great place to use a Christmas analogy.

During that marvelous time of Christmas, when you receive Christmas gifts, do you leave them all perfectly wrapped up in decorative paper and a bow under the tree, never opening them and never looking to see what's inside? Do you then put the beautiful boxes away in a closet with the intention of possibly taking them out to look at or open one day?

Or do you look at them with wonder and with anticipation about what could be inside, and then at the first moment you can, you open them with curiosity and excitement to find out what marvelous thing is there for you to have and to enjoy?

God has given us many gifts, and many we've never opened. Will we ever open them and realize all there is for us, or are we going to leave these amazing glorious gifts in the closet, unopened and unused?

Here are just a few of His gifts to us.

God's first and foremost gift to us is His son, Jesus.

Jesus came to bring the way for us to be reunited with God.

124

It is through Him and the Spirit of God that this life and spirit-changing event happens.

Jesus came that, *"we might have life, and have it more abundantly."(2)*

May we all receive the gift of Jesus and share it with others.

But this isn't just a one-time event. Jesus shows us in His Word that God has given great gifts to us in order for us to have a great, fulfilling and joy filled life in our time here. We'll talk more about this later.

The gift of God's Son, the Christ, also brought us the gift of good, and goodwill, from the Father. When Jesus was born, the angels proclaimed this to all of the shepherds nearby.

> *"And suddenly there was with the angel a multitude of the heavenly host praising God, and saying, Glory to God in the highest, and on earth peace, good will toward men."(3)*

May we always know that God's will toward us is always good.

Jesus is also, as shown to us by John, *"the Word made flesh"(4)*.

"The Word" is an amazing and great gift to us.

One of the things the Lord wants us to know is His Word, because in it is all of Him. He knows the great value and benefit of His Word to us, in and throughout our lives, and desires for us to have them within us.

The 'Word' I'm talking about is not only the written Word of God, but it is also His Words that we "receive" from Him in our hearts. These Words can also be described as a "knowing" we receive from the Lord.

This is from the Holy Spirit, showing us and revealing something to us. They may be the actual Word of God, or an extension of the Word in a situation, or it may be a discerning, or a certain understanding about a thing, and many times the very answers we are looking for!

The Lords Words are living and flowing and moving all around us in our lives. They may move through others as well, but know that the true Words of the Lord are certainly given to us by and from His Holy Spirit.

An example of what His Word is, and what it can do, is written in the book of Hebrews,

> "For the word of God is quick, and powerful, and sharper than any two-edged sword, piercing even to the dividing asunder (separating) of soul and spirit, and of the joints and marrow, and is a discerner of the thoughts and intents of the heart."(5)

Let's look more closely at this verse and about what this Word can do in our lives.

First of all, the Word is quick. This word "quick" in Hebrew means not only fast or speedily, but also that it revives or "quickens". His Word revives and/or enlivens; it is alive in our lives.

The Word is also powerful. It reveals things. Sometimes it reveals things in a strong or deep way, and other times in a more subtle or quiet way.

And it is also razor sharp. The Word doesn't whack at things with blunt blows or half-attempts. His Word is like a surgeon's scalpel which accurately and effectively separates truths, those things we need to know, and it reveals truth.

Let's look at the phrase "dividing asunder" here. What does "dividing asunder" mean?

To divide asunder means to divide accurately or to separate completely. It distinguishes between entities and/or ideas and/or situations. It clearly reveals the differences and the truths within or concerning each.

The Word is strong and can differentiate between some very important facets and circumstances that present themselves in our lives. It can separate what might otherwise be confusing, and can give us answers we need in situations we may find ourselves in, things in which we may need to deliberate and/or make decisions about.

As the verse says, the Word can separate between *"soul and spirit,"* *"bone and marrow,"* and the *"thoughts and intents"* of the heart. The Word can give direction and/or solutions we or others may need.

Let's go a little further in this.

Of these three aspects of the Word, the first is that it separates between "*soul and spirit*".

The *soul* of a person can be considered to be a person's emotions, as well as the reactions and effects of those emotions in or on a person. Our lives can many times be swayed by emotions.

Conversely, the *spirit* of a person is considered to be the essence or core nature of that person. The spirit of a person is many times called the "heart" of a person, and is that part of us which can, and does, connect with the Spirit of God.

The Word can separate or reveal what is coming from the soul, or emotions of a person, from what comes from the heart, or spirit of a person, the essence of that person.

The spirit of a person guides the true actions of that person in any given situation. The Word reveals these truths and reveals these valuable differentiations to us.

The next is "*bone and marrow*."

The marrow in our bones gives life to our whole body. It not only creates about 500 billion blood cells each day, it is also a key to our body's immune system which helps protects us. This all happens inside our bones.

The bone is what we may see and feel, but it is the marrow inside the bone which gives life to our bodies.

The Word and the Spirit can separate between what we see and feel, and what is really bringing life to or within a person, or to or within a given situation.

And lastly, but certainly not least, are the "*thoughts and the intents*" of the heart.

We all have many thoughts and they can vary greatly, from potential considerations to irrelevant imaginations. They can be all over the place and not necessarily in any particular order.

The intents of the heart are what a person is truly intending or planning (sometimes even subconsciously) to do. The Word is a "discerner of the thoughts and intents of the heart" and can reveal to us what might be the varied thoughts of a person, versus their actual intentions or plans.

Listening closely to a person's words can add to this discernment and reveal much.

> "Out of the abundance of the heart the mouth speaks."(6)

If we are listening, and listening to the Spirit of God, we can hear the truth about a person's intentions, and can many times *discern* or separate out what are just thoughts and what are the true intents of a person or situation.

There are times in our lives when we let our emotions overrule this discernment. We are not really listening to what someone's words may be because we are overcome or blinded by emotion. After these emotions wear off, we many times distinctly remember the things a person said which revealed their true intentions, and we wish we had listened much more closely.

All of this is to say that if the Word of God, Jesus, is within you, you can, by the Holy Spirit, observe the truth about many things, giving you real wisdom in being able to deal and discern, with much more clarity, the truth in life situations, and to discover wise solutions which we may otherwise not see or be oblivious to.

Part of King Solomon's great wisdom came in being able to realize and discern these truths by dividing or separating what was truth and what was not.

Solomon was able to bring incredible solutions to real life situations from that discernment.

> *"All Israel heard of the judgment which Solomon the king had judged; and they feared (yare-reverence) the king: for they saw that the wisdom of God was in him..."(7)*

What if we were able to do this all the time in our own lives?

The Word says we can, and that we can have this by learning and hearing God's Word and listening for the Lord's word and wisdom in our heart and spirit.

The Word is a very real guidebook to life and to all that we can have in Him. Just as a natural father gives and teaches his children many things so that they might be strong and courageous and able to use well all of the gifts that are given, so does our heavenly Father also desire that we know Him and learn from Him, and that we are able to have and use all of His gifts, that we might be strong, secure and wise, that we may show others of Him, and also that our joy would be full along the way.

Let us ask for wisdom, and practice with the Word. Let us be skillful with the Word. Let us seek to know the Word made flesh – Jesus, and all He has and says to us through the Spirit of God.

> *"For there are three that bear record in heaven, the Father, the Word, and the Holy Ghost: and these three are one."(8)*

There is so much that the Word can do in our lives, especially as the Father, the Word and the Holy Spirit of God are one, and agree as one, and are with us always.

Another great gift given to us is in the same verse at the beginning of this chapter, except in Luke it is written differently.

> *"How much more shall your heavenly Father give the Holy Spirit to them who ask Him."(9)*

As we've talked about, the Holy Spirit is a truly amazing and magnificent gift, and Jesus said it was very important that we receive and get to know the Comforter, the Spirit of God, after He went back to heaven.

One of the things our Lord and Savior desires of us is that we would have a true relationship, not only with Him, but also with His Spirit, the Comforter He sent to be with us.

> "The grace of the Lord Jesus Christ, and the Love of God, and the communion of the Holy Ghost, be with you all. Amen."(10)

Paul writes here that he would that we would have not only the grace of the Lord Jesus, and the love of God, but that we would also have communion, have relationship, with His Holy Spirit,,, the same Spirit who raised Jesus from the dead and who is with us always.

Merriam-Webster defines "commune" as "to communicate with someone,,, in a very personal or spiritual way."

Another familiar expression for commune might be "to hang out with", or "to chill with" another. When you commune with someone, you desire to be with them, you enjoy doing so, and you share and receive all that you can have together. In the end the result is a greater gain and understanding about the other than you had before.

It's the same with the Spirit of God. When you 'hang out' with the Holy Spirit and commune with Him, you will gain and understand more than you ever thought possible about the things of God, much more than you ever had before!

Think about this.

How often do you commune or "hang out" or "chill", or spend time with the Spirit of God?

As we are seeking the Lord more and more, and seeking all that He is, the Holy Spirit comes to us and shows us more and more about all that we seek, and all that He is.

In the process, we grow and overflow with all that He gives us, and we naturally "water" or share what we've received with all those around us.

As our cup overflows, it nourishes others, and we too are replenished. And just as anything that happens in the Father, the Son (the Word) and the Holy Ghost, everyone involved is uniquely and marvelously blessed.

And as the chapter verse says, all we have to do is ask.

There are so many other gifts the Lord gives us.

The Father has given us spiritual gifts. Many of them are written in the New Testament for us to receive and to share in our lives.

He not only gives us spiritual gifts, but He gives us His power in and over our lives, and even over the adversary we talked about earlier.

The Spirit of God is here to show us all things.

He is here to comfort us and guide us, to teach us and grow us and to show us the deep things of God. We have only barely scratched the surface of who this third Person of the Trinity, the Holy Spirit, is. There is so much more for us to discover and know and understand in Him.

> *"Do not err, my beloved brethren. Every good gift and every perfect gift is from above, and comes from the Father of lights with Whom is no variableness, nor even the shadow of changing..."*(11)

James is saying, "Don't get this wrong. Every good thing, every good gift, comes from God." God can't, and won't change.

Make the concerted effort to spend time with the Lord, His Word, and His Holy Spirit. They are all amazing gifts for us to receive, and to open, for our benefit, and to have an abundance of joy in.

And when you do, you will get to know your/our God, more and more, and greater and greater, and you'll begin to see and open all the marvelous gifts He has for you.

In These Things I Delight

"This says the Lord, Let not the wise man glory in his wisdom,
Neither let the mighty man glory in his might;
Let not the rich man glory in his riches:
But let him that glories, glory in this,
that he understands and knows Me,
and knows that I am the Lord Who exercises loving
kindness, judgment, and righteousness in the earth:
For in these things I delight, says the Lord."(1)

Job's friends said that no one can know God. God said very strongly in the end of the Book of Job that they were very wrong.

God wants us to know about Him. Not only does He want us to know Him, but He *delights* in us knowing Him!

Part of this begins with us understanding that God has good intentions toward us. Do we really know that God wants the best for us? Have we been taught otherwise or are we hindered by feelings that we don't deserve His best and how could we ever even consider such a thing?

Do we look at the Ten Commandments as behavior demanded of and forced on us to keep us in line, with the threat of punishment?

Or do we see them as basic guidelines given by God, out of His love for us, so that we will not bring injury and hurt to others and/or to ourselves?

Do we look at God as the perfect Father we always desired, or do we look at Him as a domineering boss who forgives nothing and punishes much?

Which one of these is God to you?

The Word says God is Love. God is strong, compassionate and powerful Love. His Son Jesus came to show us this love and of Who He is, to show us of the Father in all that He did, and all that He does through His Holy Spirit.

132

"If you had known Me, you should have known My Father also:
from now on you know Him, and have seen Him.
*Philip then said to Him, Lord, **show** us the Father, and it will be enough.*
Jesus said to him, Have I been with you all this time, Philip, and yet
you do not know Me? How can you ask this?
Whoever has seen Me has seen the Father.
Don't you know that I am in the Father, and the Father in Me?
The words that I speak to you I speak not of Myself: but the Father
Who dwells in Me, they are His words, and He does the works."(2)

Jesus was showing Philip, and us, Who God is.

As we asked before, was Jesus ever angry? Did He ever punish or put anything bad on anyone?

No.

What Jesus showed us was the true nature of His Father, and our Father, the Lord God Almighty.

Jesus felt this was so very important that He says it again.

"If you would know Me, you would know My Father also."(3)

Do we know God, and that He is good? Jesus shows us God's character throughout His Word.

Can we exercise our faith and know these things are true?

Yes.

There is so much more that the Lord has for us, for us to understand and to know about Him.

Let's consider the basic dynamics of any human relationship. There is a certain progression in getting to know someone.

First there is an introduction, and initial observations.

Then, with time spent together there comes a gleaning of knowledge and more observations.

As more time is spent together, there comes more levels of realization, and a gaining of trust and respect. Understanding and wisdom grow. There is a desire to know that person more, and to spend more time together as the understanding, rewards and enjoyment of the relationship continue to grow, until, with more experiences together, a true and strong friendship is established.

The same thing happens with knowing God, but in an even greater way all around.

One hindrance we have in establishing a relationship with the Lord is that many times we stop after our introduction, initial observations, and reception of the Lord,,, or after "Hello", and then we don't go any further into the relationship.

So many times, after "Hello", we stand at the door, and remain there, continuing in conversations about Who the Lord is before us, and then then we come back and reintroduce ourselves over and over, with our initial observations, to "Hello", without ever getting to really know Him.

If we do this, then we will never get to know Who He is, all that He is, and His power and His Spirit that is within us. We'll never find out Who He is more deeply, and more intimately, and more powerfully, and we end up not fulfilling, or not being fulfilled, in all that He has for us.

This "Hello" is truly a marvelous and amazing and life-changing event and we all should do our very best to allow everyone to have the opportunity for "Hello" in and with the Lord. This is a very important and integral part of the Great Commission.

By not stepping through the door and searching further, and by not *"coming into the knowledge of the truth"(4)* for ourselves, and by not continuing to develop and grow into the great depth of this amazing relationship, we will never fully realize the incredible life that has been prepared for us, <u>and which is readily available to us.</u>

134

When we step through the doorway and continue to move toward the great and true relationship and great fulfillment which is right there waiting for us, we will then find the depth and intimate understanding of our Greatest Friend.

The Lord wants us to take our salvation, take our "Hello", and go somewhere with it. He desires that we would go on to really know Him, and Who He is, and realize all that He has made available to us. His expectation and desire for us is that we would have a deep and real understanding and rest in and with Him.

> *"Come unto me, all who labor and have heavy burdens,*
> *and I will give you rest.*
> *Take my yoke (Spirit) upon you, **and learn of me**; for I am patient and*
> *kind, and humble in heart: **and you will find rest** unto your souls.*
> *My yoke is easy, and my burden is light."(5)*

Jesus said "Get to know me, and you will find the Father."

"Learn more and more about Me and you will also find the rest that you are seeking..."

And your **joy** will become full.

May God delight in each one of us as we more fully come to understand,

And to really know,

Him.

Know God

"Be strong and courageous; and be not afraid, or dismayed:
for the LORD your God is with you, wherever you go."(1)

Know the Lord. Know that He is with us. Know that He is with You, and within You, wherever you are and wherever you go.

Always.

One of the greatest things that Jesus came to bring to us was an amazing and beautiful access to God.

"For through him (Jesus) we have access by one Spirit to the Father." (2)

Knowing the Lord begins with realizing that we indeed have access to the Father through Jesus by the Holy Spirit, and we can go there anytime we want. This verse and the Word in general do not say anything about our access being limited in any way, if we are seeking Him.

Jesus is the door to knowing more about God through the Spirit of God.

The more time you spend seeking the Father and spending time with Him and the more you seek to understand Him, the more you will learn of and know Him.

"And we have known and believed the love that God has toward us.
God is love; and he that dwells in love dwells in God, and God in him.
In this is our love made perfect, that we may have boldness in the day
of judgment: because as He is, so are we in this world.

There is no fear in love; but perfect love casts out fear: because fear
has torment. He that fears is not made perfect in love."(3)

The Lord wants us to come to Him, and to know Him and His love well enough so as not to fear, and then move on to receive the strength and fulfillment of the great rewards and of the things of God that He has for us, in this life.

Let us go on to learn and receive and know the profound fullness and fulfillment of His Love for each one of us.

King David said,

> *"Blessed be the LORD, because He has heard the voice of my requests.*
> *The LORD is my strength and my shield; my heart trusts in Him,*
> *and I am helped:*
> *Therefore my heart greatly rejoices; and with my song will I praise*
> *Him."(4)*

Read this last verse again. Does this sound anything like the words and attitude and outlook expressed by Job, especially during his afflictions?

In the next chapter we will look at David's attitude toward God, in contrast to Job's.

I would like to suggest here that if Job had put his trust and desire for God first, and had not let his 'pachad' fear of God take over all of his senses, then he would have been able to immediately and boldly go to the Lord and ask for, and receive, the help of the Father.

Zophar said,

> *"Can you by searching find out God?*
> *"Can you find out the Almighty unto perfection?"(5)*

Maybe not to absolute perfection, but the greater answer is Yes, we can find out so very much more about God, and in fact, as much as we desire to receive. And we have only scratched the surface of Who He really is.

Jesus said,

> *"It is written in the Word, "And they shall be all taught of God."*
> *Every man who has heard, and has learned of the Father,*
> *comes to Me."(6)*

When we know the Fathers nature, which Jesus came and showed us, and when we start to know Him more, we will find that we can, with ease, and with anything, come to Him for comfort, for help, and for answers.

> *"Behold, I give unto you power to tread on serpents and scorpions, and over all the power of the enemy: and nothing shall by any means harm you.*
> *Because of this don't rejoice that the spirits are subject unto you;*
> *But rather rejoice because your names are written in heaven."*(7)

The Lord has given us great power and authority in His name. He knows that if we rejoice in our lives, rejoice in Him, and know Him as our refuge and our strength, that not only can nothing by any means harm us, but that we can also exercise this power and authority for good. And by doing this, by using what He's given us, we will accomplish much, and our joy will be full to overflowing.

Jesus, and all that He went through, died so that we might know, and delight, and live in God.

He died that we might receive and realize the things He's freely given to us, including the authority and power of His name.

He died that we might have access to all that God has given to us, so that the Father would be glorified, and in turn that our joy, and our lives, would be full. Jesus came to this earth that we might know the Father, and that we might receive the fullness of all that He has for us.

Let us search and seek to know Him more and more.

Job and David

"Death and life are in the power of the tongue:
and they that love it shall eat the fruit of it."(1)

The above verse in Proverbs gives a profound life principle. It says that both those who speak life and those who speak death will eat the 'fruit', or receive the results, of whichever things they speak.

In other words, if you love and speak evil and discouragement, and are saying negative things all the time, you will receive the 'fruit' of those things, or whatever the byproduct of negative and discouraging things in your life.

On the other hand, if you speak life and encouragement and that which is good, you will likewise receive the 'fruit' of those words of life and good and positive encouraging things as a byproduct.

Either way, you will have the "fruit", the end results of the things that you say.

Have you ever been around someone who was always telling you and others about all of their ailments? Have you ever noticed that they are always sick? How about people who always have bad things happen to them or people who are always negative? How about those who always have drama or gossip going on? What are the fruit of their words?

It manifests in their lives.

How about those who are positive all the time?

Do we use our words for good? The Lord wants us not only to be aware of what we say, but He is looking for us to powerfully use the words we have been given to communicate, from our heart to Him and into the lives of others, that which is good and life giving.

This is part of what this book is all about, and what His Word is all about. It is what the Lord wants for each one of us.

What words did Job speak as a reaction to all of his afflictions? Job talks much about God with his friends, extolling God's virtues, while at the same time speaking miserably and negatively about the rest of his life, inferring blame on God for all that had happened, and speaking extensively about all of the bad things he thought God was doing to him.

The very next Book in the Bible, after Job, is the Book of Psalms. In it is David, who we're told was a man after God's own heart. David was continually going to God, and the Word shows him knowing God as his fortress, his deliverer, his help, his comforter and his joy, even in extremely difficult life-threatening situations.

One of the questions I always wondered about the Book of Job was, "Why is the Book of Job right in the middle of the Word of God?"

"Why is it right there in the middle of Your Book, Lord?"

In the process of writing The Secret of Job and realizing all that the Lord has for us through Job, what became amazingly clear and extremely profound was that the Book of Job has indeed been purposely and perfectly placed, right in the middle of His Word.

It was perfectly situated right next to the Book of Psalms, and put there for a reason, with a marvelous purpose.

One of the great things the Lord showed Job in the end, and I believe is one of the great 'lessons' of the Book of Job, involves how we handle adversity in our lives.

These two books paired together show us a truly magnificent contrast between Job and David, and between the attitudes and reactions of each of these men when dealing with adversity.

It is an amazing comparison and example to all of us of how we can deal with any or all of the things that oppose us in our lives.

Even though Job and David both had gone through very difficult and extreme situations and events in their lives, they each handle the adversity in distinctly different ways, and in very stark contrast to one another.

Jesus said in the New Testament, *"Out of the abundance of the heart, the mouth speaks."(2)*

You can tell a lot about a person by listening to what they say.

Let's take a look at the words of David and the words of Job and see how each approached God in their adversity.

Job: *"Know that God has overthrown me, and has compassed me with His net. Behold, I cry out of wrong, but I am not heard: I cry aloud, but there is no judgment.*
He has fenced in my way that I cannot pass, and He has set darkness in my paths.
He has stripped me of my glory, and taken the crown from my head. He has destroyed me on every side, and I am gone: and my hope He has removed like a tree.
He has also lit His wrath against me, and He counts me as one of His enemies."(3)

David: *"Hear, O LORD, when I cry with my voice: have mercy also upon me and answer me.*
When You said, Seek my face; my heart said unto You, Your face, LORD, I will seek."(4)

Was God doing all of these things to Job as he says? No. Did God count Job as one of His enemies? No. Was Job revealing anything about his perspective toward God? Yes.

David is saying "I will seek Your Face, Lord."

No matter what.

How does each approach the subject of going to God?

Job: *"Even today is my complaint bitter: my stroke is heavier than my groaning.*

Oh that I knew where I might find Him, that I might come even to His seat!

I would make my case before Him, and fill my mouth with arguments. I would know the words which He would answer me, and understand what He would say unto me...(5)

David: *"Hear the voice of my cry, my King and my God: for to You I will pray. My voice You will hear in the morning, O LORD; and in the morning I will direct my prayer to You, and will look up."*(6)

Job, in his mourning, argues about asking God anything.

David prays.

How much faith, how much trust does each have in God?

Job: *"I cry to You, and You do not hear me: I stand up, and You don't regard me.*
You have become cruel to me: with Your strong hand You oppose Yourself against me."(7)

David: *"Be merciful unto me, O God, be merciful unto me: for my soul trusts in You:*
In the shadow of Your wings will I make my refuge, until these calamities be over.
I will cry unto God most high; unto God that performs all things for me."(8)

David has faith in God as a power and a refuge in his life.

Job responds without faith to what he thinks God is doing to him. He has made the decision that God Himself is against him, which is not the truth, and doesn't come to God with anything.

Was Job trusting and looking to the Lord for answers, or for help, or comfort? No.

Was David?

Yes.

There are many, many more examples of this contrast throughout Job and Psalms.

These last two verses I have included summarize very well the attitudes and perspectives of each man:

David: *"Hear my cry, O God; attend unto my prayer. From the ends of the earth I will cry unto You, when my heart is overwhelmed: lead me to the Rock that is higher than I.*

For You have been a shelter for me, and a strong tower from the enemy. I will abide in Your tabernacle forever: I will trust in the cover of Your wings. Selah."(9)

Job: *"Oh that my grief were thoroughly weighed, and my calamity laid in the balances together! For now it would be heavier than the sand of the sea: therefore my words are swallowed up. For the arrows of the Almighty are within me, the poison whereof drinks up my spirit: the terrors of God do set themselves in array against me."(10)*

David: *"My help comes from the LORD, Who made heaven and earth..."(11)*

Both books are filled with many words and attitudes toward the Father.

David spoke life, and the Life of God into his situations. Job spoke only of loss and suffering and of death. And there were never any arrows or poison or terrors given to him from God. That is only how Job perceived it himself.

The juxtaposition of these two Books again is perfect. All this time the Book of Job has been right next to the Book of Psalms and we've never really known why.

Through Job, in the Book of Job, God is also showing us how to, and how **not** to, deal with adversity.

In Psalms, the Lord gives a wonderful example through David's attitude and words showing us a much greater way, of how to live and to deal with trials and adversity in our lives.

We will all have some degree of adversity in our lives at some point. It is part of this life. It is a given. Our Father is showing us the best way to handle and to deal with it when it comes our way.

Jesus reminds us in John that in the world we will have tribulation, and then He said for us to be of good cheer, as He, our Lord and our Savior, has overcome the world, for us.

Let us learn by the examples of Job and David how we can best deal with adversity in our lives. Let us seek and come before God as David did. It may not be easy to do at first, but once you start, with trust and in faith knowing Who God is, knowing that He is good, and cannot do bad or evil, and that He is always with you, you will find that His Spirit will bring you comfort, and you can receive life and peace, and the good things of God, no matter what you are going through.

He desires for us to come to Him in Spirit and in truth, to know Who He is in our lives, and to know all the good that He has for us.

He desires that we would know these things in good times,,,

and even more so, in the not so good times.

> *"I have set before you life and death, blessing and cursing;*
>
> *Therefore choose life,,,"(12)*

Our Refuge

"GOD is our refuge and our strength, a very present help in trouble.
Therefore we will not fear, though the earth be moved, and though
the mountains be carried into the midst of the sea..."(1)

Did Job know the Lord as his refuge?

Do you know the Lord as your refuge?

Do you know Him as your refuge from all earthly cares, fears, worries and troubles? Do you know that He is a fortress, and that His refuge is available to you 24/7?

Let's look at the above chapter verse and the David/Job comparison a little more.

The verse starts with David saying that God is his refuge and strength. And because of that, he will not fear, no matter what adverse things happened to him.

As we saw in the last chapter, how did Job handle the adverse things that happened to him?

> *"Even today is my complaint bitter: my stroke is heavier than*
> *my groaning."(2)*

He puts his own misery and fear first and paramount in his life, and doesn't put his God, the One who provides a refuge and a fortress for him, first.

David had the attitude and understanding of God's goodness and great strength when he had to handle adversity.

> *"The LORD is my rock, and my fortress, and my deliverer...*
> *in Him will I trust:*
> *He is my shield, and the horn of my salvation, my high tower,*
> *and my refuge, my Saviour; He saves me from violence.*

I will call on the LORD, Who is worthy to be praised:
so shall I be saved from mine enemies."(3)

"When the waves of death compassed me...when the sorrows
of hell were all around me; the snares of death prevented me;
In my distress I called upon the LORD, I called to my God:
And he heard my voice...then the earth shook and trembled..."(4)

David didn't just think this. He knew this to be true. He had experienced God, knew Who He was in his life, and trusted Him.

The Lord desires us to know Him as our strength and our refuge and Who He is in our lives as well.

Can we know the Lord in this way? Yes. If we personally get to know Him, and His greatness in our lives, then we can go to Him for protection and strength and rest, regardless of what is happening around us.

Jesus' original disciples, after they had been imprisoned, beaten and threatened, went to God and began to ask for boldness. They started their prayer like this.

"Lord, You are God, Who has made heaven, and earth, and the sea,
and everything that is in them..."(5)

When you begin a prayer, or going to God, by speaking of Who God is, His Creation and what He's done, you are putting everything else into its real and proper perspective.

So many times our difficulties overwhelm us emotionally and become all we can see, and we are unable to realize the bigger picture, the real truth of the matter. And then when we try to handle it all by ourselves it can get bigger and bigger.

What happens when we put the Lord first in our lives and then go to Him, we become able to realize how good and how much greater He is, and how much bigger He is than any of our problems and situations and circumstances.

When we start to realize this, it puts our emotions in their proper place and also puts us in the right frame of mind to receive Him, and to have all that we need with which to go on.

When you begin to realize how great and how good the Lord is, and how much greater He is than anything you're going through, you'll see that the seemingly huge emotional giant in the problem begins to shrink and diminish, and what you're dealing with becomes less overwhelming, and then becomes more realistic, and you begin to see a much truer perspective of it all. The difficulties then become more manageable and you are then able to deal with them.

Sometimes realizing God is with you and in you in it is by itself an answer for us. We gain a sense of security in it. He gives us rest and peace and we receive clarity when we need it most.

At other times it is within Him, as a Fortress and strong Tower, that we can find a badly needed break, or rest. It is after this rest, even if momentarily, that we are able to plan and re-engage in all that is going on, from a rested and clearer and stronger frame of mind and heart.

All with His peace and power with us and within us.

King David said,

> "Be merciful unto me, O God, be merciful unto me: for my soul trusts in You: In the shadow of Your wings will I make my refuge, until these calamities be past."(6)
> "He alone is my Rock and my salvation: He is my defense; I shall not be moved.
> In God is my salvation and my glory: In God is the rock of my strength, and my refuge. Trust in Him at all times; pour out your heart before Him: God is a refuge for us."(7)
>
> "He that dwells in the secret place of the most High shall abide under the shadow of the Almighty.
>
> I will say of the LORD, He is my refuge and my fortress: my God; in Him I will trust."(8)

David knew who the Lord was, and the Bible says he was a man after Gods own heart.

But he isn't the only one.

So can we be.

Trust God

"Without faith it is impossible to please God..."(1)

Even though I have used this verse over and over and taught on it at length, I have always endeavored to make 'faith' easier to understand, and to relay to others the depth and fullness of what "faith" really is.

Faith has a somewhat elusive "real" meaning for many, and I have always searched for another expression of it in order to present a clearer understanding of what 'faith' truly is.

Then one day I asked the Lord about it.

This next verse then immediately came to me. Though I had heard it and spoken about it thousands of times, I knew I needed to read it again and to look at it even more closely.

> *"Faith is the substance of things hoped for,*
> *and the evidence of things not seen."(2)*

You've probably heard it a thousand times too, but let's look at it again.

Okay, so according to this verse, "faith" is substance, and it is also evidence.

If it indeed has actual substance and is evidence, then you can have it, and believe it, and you can even see it.

We'll talk about this in a later chapter, but the absolute end result of believing in something, after experiencing it, is "knowing" it.

If you absolutely know something to be true, you have no doubt at all and you firmly trust it.

So if faith is substance and evidence, then you can believe it. And if you can truly believe it, you can trust it.

From this progression came the realization that the word 'faith' can actually be, in fact, easily interchanged with the word 'trust'.

Trust equals Faith. Faith equals Trust.

- ➢ *"The just shall live by "trust."(3)* Yes.
- ➢ *"Without "trust" it is impossible to please God."(4)* Yes.
- ➢ *"Trust" is the substance of things hoped for, and the evidence of things not seen."(5)* Yes it is.
- ➢ *"I have not found such great "trust"...(6)* And his servant was healed.
- ➢ *"Abraham was strong in "trust"...(7)* Yes he certainly was.
- ➢ *"According to your "trust" be it unto you."(8)* Yes.
- ➢ *"Your "trust" has made you whole"(9)* Could it be?
- ➢ *"Have "trust" in God."(10)* Yes!!!

I then began to use the word 'trust' wherever faith was talked about.

It has since given a much clearer and more marvelous understanding of what faith is. I now use both words interchangeably.

Try using 'trust' wherever you find the word 'faith' in the Word of God and see if it doesn't add depth to your understanding of what faith is.

As a matter of fact, Trusting God is what the whole Word of God, and what our life in Him is all about!

Faith all the way, or faith "all-in", is *Trust*.

Here is an example whereby the substance and evidence, and trust, is there, without it even happening yet.

"I have faith that the sun will come up today."

Well, yes there is a highly remote chance that it won't, but my faith that the sun will come up is a true belief, which by experience is a 'knowing', with the end result being a very high level of trust. I can't see it yet, but the believing and the trust is solidly there.

Do we discount the whole day and doubt every day for the rest of our lives just because of the remote possibility that the sun might not come up? No. We have seen it enough times to know that it will.

Have we seen God's hand (and attributed those things correctly to God) enough to know how much He works in our lives? Have we used our faith, our trust, enough to understand that the Lord God is right there with us, and He is always available for us to come to?

Have we endeavored to understand and to know Who He is and how we should go about communicating with Him personally, so that we might grow our faith, our trust, in Him more, in order to receive all the things which He gives?

Did Job trust God? Did he have faith in his Lord?

It is so easy to trust or to have faith in God when everything is going great, when you are physically, emotionally and financially at ease, and it's smooth sailing. Job was that very way. Job was a guy who had it made. He was very wealthy, he had family and friends, lands and livestock, and he made it a point to help others and to worship God along the way.

It is in these times when faith is wonderful, believing and trust is easy, and God is marvelously and comfortably Great.

But when do we need trust, when do we need faith in Him the most?

Exactly. When things are horrible, upside down, when the situation is dire, when it's awful, and when there are a million more questions than answers.

The hardest time to have trust is in the middle of the storm.

And that's when we need to have it the most.

God knows this about us. He created us. And He also has created the solution to be able to find our answers. It's all in Trust.

What about Job? Did he have trust in God as his Victory, as his Fortress during these afflictions? Did he press into faith and trust that his God was going to help him and even save him?

What happens to *your* faith and trust when you find yourself in adverse situations?

To have faith and to have trust during these hard times is a real and pure faith. It is trust "tried in the fire" through adversity.

It is faith and trust exercised and worked, over and over. Everything in your being wants to call it quits, wants to give up, and maybe even to give up God and live in the misery of it all. It is faith and trust truly fought for, and at times to its very lengths.

What are our natural reactions in these times of adversity? Do we regress into a passive, helpless and hopeless state, as Job did? Or do we ramp up our worshipping and praise of God to meet the need, as David did?

Do we become more determined to be strong in the Lord and in the power of His might? Or do we resign ourselves to "fate" and say "It must be God doing this to me, so it must be God's will, and He does whatever He wants"?

Do we believe, and act on our beliefs? Or do our beliefs change with the circumstances, and we end up questioning everything in life, losing sight of our trust, and gaining nothing?

These times are really a test of what we truly believe, whether we like the test or not. I know it's hard, I've been there.

Jesus says, *"Have faith in God."(11)*

The actual Greek translation of this is, *"Have the faith __of__ God."*

What is the greatest underlying theme throughout the Bible?

Trust God.

What should the very core of our own belief system tell us, despite what our situation is or what it looks like?

Trust God.

Seek the Father, the Son and the Holy Spirit. Learn about Him. Have Big Faith, and Big Trust.

This can not only save you but it can also produce amazing results and can indeed work real and true miracles in your life.

> *"I have come that they might have life,*
> *and that they might have it more abundantly."(12)*

Trust God in the good times,

And <u>even more so</u>, in the not so good times.

The Power of God

*"That your trust should not be in the wisdom of men,
but in the power of God."*(1)

So you/we believe in God.

The Word of God says that so also do devils, with trembling.

Why do they tremble?

Because they **know** the reality of the Power of God.

Do we truly know and believe in the reality of His Power? Or do we just
believe in who we think He is and what we've heard He's done in the
past?

Do we live our lives comfortably enough simply acknowledging that He
must be powerful because He is God, and then just go on?

As I said earlier, we are not meant to live solely acknowledging God, but
we are to realize that He has created us also to know and experience
Him.

Part of knowing and experiencing Him is realizing His power in our
lives.

So what are some of these things of God we can experience?

Many of us have experienced His Son. There is so much more for us to
know there. We can experience His Word. There is so much more for us
to know there. We can experience His Spirit. There is _far_ more for us to
know there.

And we can experience His Power. We have much to learn and realize
about His good, and His great, Power.

The word "power" we're talking about in the verse above in the Greek is
the word "Dunamis", which means to have miraculous ability,

miraculous acts and amazing works. It means having the ability, the greatness, the abundance of might, and the exceptional strength to make things happen above and beyond what is considered natural.

"Kratos" is another Greek word for "power" which is also used in the Word and means great dominion, and might, and strength.

All of these describe the greatness, and the awesome power that God is, and has, and accomplishes for good in our lives.

We are not only to believe that He is, or that He exists, but we are also to believe and to know His power, and that it is both with us and within us.

The Lord desires that we would know what He can do, in a moment, in a life, and in a lifetime. He desires that we would have faith and trust in His amazing "Almighty" Might.

Do we really know and believe in His Power? Do we know that His Power is all around us and within us? Have we experienced His power in our lives? Do we see it and realize it on a regular basis?

Do we believe He is good, and uses His power for good in ours and others lives?

> "For God has not given us the spirit of fear;
> but of power, and of love, and of a sound mind."(2)

Job said over and over that God had put great fear on him. What we see in the above verse is that this is something God doesn't do. He doesn't put fear on anyone or cause any form of "frightened/scared" fear.

He does though, as Hid Word says, give us power, and love and a sound mind.

He gives us His power, to overcome fear. He gives us His Love, which casts out fear. And he's given us a sound mind which can put fear in its proper perspective and place. All of these are able to put fear far from us and even remove it as we trust in Him.

Job's own reasoning considered the power of God to be something it wasn't. He had turned what he knew about God into something that was not of God.

Do we also do this at times?

Do we sometimes attribute to the Lord and His power things that are not of Him? Do we feel He uses His power to do harm or to punish?

We see the results of this kind of reasoning vividly in Job. By his actions, it is apparent that Job didn't truly know Who his God was; and didn't know the nature and character of God and His power.

Do _we_ know the nature of God's power? That it is great, and it is for us, and for good in all things?

This is one of the things we can know by the Spirit of God, Who has come to show us all things. God's power is in and with His Spirit.

The Lord expects us to believe not only in Him being good, and great, but also to know that His power is also very much good, and great, and that His powerful Spirit, which created everything by the word of God, is with and within us.

Jesus, throughout the New Testament, was continually demonstrating the true power of God.

> *"The Spirit of the Lord is upon Me, because He has anointed Me to preach the gospel to the poor; He has sent Me to heal the brokenhearted, to preach deliverance to the captives, and the recovering of sight to the blind, to set at liberty them that are bruised, and to preach the acceptable year of the Lord."(3)*

And He did just that, and more.

Paul, concerning his experiences with and in the Lord, said,

> *"For the kingdom of God is not in word, but in power."(4)*

The things of God are shown to us by and with the power of God, and they become real and alive to us via His power.

So many times in our lives we try so very hard to do things _for_ God. We try to do it all ourselves, even the miracles.

What we need to know is that it is the Lord Who does these things, and what He desires of us is that we would ask for, and then allow, His Spirit and His power to move through us in great ways.

It is for us only to ask and to truly believe, and then watch and receive as He accomplishes the works by His Spirit.

This may be quite a relief to some of us. And a great hope for others.

There is also an amazing rest in it all when we know how the Father, His Son (His Word) and His Spirit work, and when we **_know_** His power to affect change, many times in small, personal but meaningful things, and at times in amazing and miraculous and completely out of the ordinary things.

The Lord desires for us to know His power so well that we can find rest in it, and rest in it easily, and know that He is the One Who is doing and accomplishing it all via His Son and His Spirit. Then not only can we have a part in all that is accomplished, through our trust, but we can also take part in His power being demonstrated, and watch as the works of God come to pass!

In the words of the Apostle Paul,

> _"My speech and my preaching was <u>not</u> done with enticing words of man's wisdom, but (it was) in demonstration of the Spirit and of power:_
> _That your faith should not stand in the wisdom of men, but in the <u>Power</u> of God. ..."(5)_

Paul is saying that it wasn't his words that had any creative or powerful or enticing ability, but that it was the _works_ of the Holy Spirit and the

Power of God that were evident and alive and real and demonstrated through his words and works in people's lives.

It is the power of God which accomplishes much, and bears much fruit, and brings good things to life.

Again, it is not our 'words of wisdom' that accomplish anything.

We may speak something along the way, but our main job is to speak and to ask and to believe, and to trust, in Jesus' name, and allow the Spirit of God to work through us. It is then He who powerfully and wonderfully finishes it all, to God's glory.

Jesus not only knew this very thing, He embodied it. All the works that He accomplished as He spoke were done by the Father, and by God's power within Him, through the Holy Spirit.

> *"Don't you believe that I am in the Father, and the Father is in Me?*
> *The words that I speak to you I don't speak of (from) Myself:*
> *but it is the Father who dwells within Me, He does the works."(6)*

And Jesus said that <u>we should also walk in this</u>...

> *"And Jesus said unto them, Go into all of the world, and preach*
> *the gospel to every creature. He who believes and is baptized*
> *will be saved; but he that doesn't believe shall not be.*
> *And these signs shall follow those who believe;* **In My name** *they*
> *will cast out devils; they will speak with new tongues; They will take*
> *up serpents; and if they drink anything deadly, it will not hurt them;*
> *They shall lay their hands on the sick, and they shall recover."(7)*

This isn't just some poetic thought, only for a few chosen people. This is the power of God, alive in Jesus' name, given to all of us, in our lives.

Many works are being done, even today all over the world, by those who believe and in the power of Jesus name, to the glory of God.

> *"Then Peter said, Silver and gold have I none; but what I have I will*
> *give to you:*

158

In the name of Jesus Christ of Nazareth rise up and walk.
And he took him by the right hand, and lifted him up: and immediately
the man's feet and ankle bones received strength.
And the man leapt up and stood, and walked with them into the temple,
walking and leaping, and praising God."(8)

The Fathers power and Spirit are in Jesus' name.

We need to know that Jesus has given us the authority to use His name, just as He did Peter, that we would know His power, and that it is for us to have and use for good in ours and others lives.

Paul talks about the Lord demonstrating and confirming these things to us and through us and in us, with power, to His glory.

"That the God of our Lord Jesus Christ, the Father of glory, may give
you the spirit of wisdom and of revelation in the knowledge of Him:
That the eyes of your understanding would be enlightened;
That you might know the hope of His calling, and that you would
know the riches of the glory of His inheritance in us, that you would
know what is the exceeding greatness of His power to us (you) who
believe, according to His mighty power,,,"(9)

The *"exceeding greatness"* of His power is to all of us who believe...

"Which He created in Christ, when He raised Him from the dead,
and set Him at His own right hand in the heavenly places,
Far above (and greater than) all other principality, and power, and
might, and dominion, and every name that is named, not only in this
world, but also in that which is to come:
And has put all things under His feet, and made Him to be the head
over all things to the church, which is His body, the fullness of Him
that fills all in all."(10)

We are His church and His body, and the fullness of Him. He is the Head. If this is truly the case, then we, through Him, and as part of His body, can be and are, very useable instruments of His Great and Good power.

"Now unto Him that is able to do exceeding abundantly above all that
we ask or think, according to the (His) power that works in us..."(11)

It's His power that works in us. His power is _to_ us and _for_ us, and works _in_ us and _through_ us.

> "For this cause we... do not cease to pray for you, and to desire that you might be filled with the knowledge of His will in all wisdom and spiritual understanding;
>
> That you might walk worthy of the Lord to all pleasing, being fruitful in every good work, and increasing in the knowledge of God; being _strengthened with all might, according to His glorious_ **power**_..."(12)_

The Lord desires that we would be strengthened - _with all might_ - by His amazing and glorious power working within us.

He also desires that we would be fruitful, or that we would bear much fruit; meaning that we would accomplish results in every good work, by and through and in and with His power.

As we talked before, God is only good and His power is also only good.

> "We also pray for you, that our God would count you worthy of this calling, and fulfill all the _good_ pleasure of His _goodness_, and the work of faith, **with power,** that the name of our Lord Jesus Christ may be glorified in you, and you in Him, according to the grace of our God and the Lord Jesus Christ."(13)

Not only are we to fulfill His goodness, but that we would do it through works of trust with His power. Not only believing in Him, but believing also in His power also has a great deal to do with us being fruitful in every "good work".

In his letter to Timothy, the apostle Paul talks about how people in the last days will have a form of godliness, but unfortunately will deny the power of God that is so important to and in their lives.

> "This also know, that in the last days perilous times will come. Men will be lovers of their own selves, covetous, boasters, proud, blasphemers, disobedient to parents, unthankful, unholy, without natural affection, trucebreakers, accusing others falsely, without self-constraint, fierce, despisers of those that are good, traitors, heady, high-minded, lovers of pleasures more than lovers of God;

160

Having a form of godliness, but denying <u>the power of God</u>."(14)

The Lord wants us to realize Who He is, and to have faith and trust in Him, and in His power, and to know that His Spirit and His power are there, available, and able to work in us and through us.

Another aspect of the great power of God is in His Holiness.

Learn of His Holiness. In it is more power than we can ever know. I've seen it, and yet I only glimpsed a fraction of the unspeakable depth and greatness of it.

In Jesus' name there is might and power and truth and healing and release and relief and miracles and all that which is good through God.

➤ There is power in His Name
➤ There is power in His Word.
➤ There is power in His Spirit.
➤ There is power in His Truth.
➤ There is power in His Holiness.
➤ There is power in His Grace.
➤ There is power in His Salvation.
➤ There is power in His Mercy.
➤ There is power in His Wisdom.
➤ There is power in His Love.

God is the most powerful force in all of Creation. He *is* the Creator, and the might of Creation. It is all His Creation.

His power is nothing we can create ourselves. Remember how God told Job "if you could do these things..."

The Lords power is greater than anything we can imagine. It is all mighty and it's all of and from the Father, via the Son, and Spirit of God.

As His children, He wants us to personally experience Him and His good and great power in our lives. He wants us to ask for it and use it in our lives, to His glory.

God's soliloquy at the end of the Book of Job remains a great and tangible description of God's physical creation in our world, but His power is so much more than that. His power is personal, tangible, deeply meaningful and intimately involved in every aspect of our lives.

His desire is that we would know His power, and that we would know that He, His Son, and His mighty Spirit will be with us and in us and through us in all things of Him.

Always.

May we learn and know and trust in His power, and in all that He has for us.

> "Finally, my brethren, be strong in the Lord,
>
> And in the Power of His might."(15)

Patience

"Let patience have her perfect work..."(1)

Patience and hope are tied together and many times are paralleled with afflictions and tribulation in the New Testament.

> *"But we glory in tribulations also, knowing that tribulation works (or creates) patience; and patience, experience; and experience, hope:*
> *And hope doesn't cause shame; because the love of God is full and filled in our hearts by the Holy Spirit Who is given to us."(2)*

Why didn't Job just "curse God and die" as his wife suggested? I believe it is because throughout it all, deep down, he still had hope in his God.

This also may be what James is referring to when he says,

> *"Take the prophets for an example of suffering affliction, and of patience. Behold, we count them happy which endure.*
> *You have heard of the patience of Job, and have seen the end of the Lord; that the Lord is very compassionate, and of tender mercy."(3)*

Job is greatly blessed by God in the end.

As we look at the Book of Job in depth, it seems that the patience of Job may only have been that he didn't curse God during all of his afflictions.

Job may even have had a certain amount of patience in dealing with his friends and their strong accusations against him, but even that was wearing very thin in the end.

In the past much has been said about the 'patience of Job'. This view is many times inferred in teachings as one of the most important aspects and considerations of the Book of Job.

Let's look at something else.

Since the second round of Satan's afflictions Job had been dwelling in his misery and is continuously blaming God for everything.

God had been listening to Job and his friends, and to all the things they argued and discussed, in all their error, for some time.

In fact, The Lord had been listening and waiting for 35 chapters, and He continued to listen, for whatever actual time frame it was, until it was very clear that Job was not going to stop mourning and blaming Him, that Job was not going to come to his God for anything, and Job's friends were not going to stop their accusations, and speaking what was "not right" about Job and what was also "not right" about God Himself. The same debate and discussion between the characters continued on and on with nothing being resolved.

So after all of this, God finally steps in and sets the record straight, sets Jobs friends straight, and delivers Job.

As we look at the story of Job more closely, it would appear, that, other than the very beginning in his initial reactions and his silence and in his "not cursing" God, Job seems to have exercised very little patience at all.

Are we like this as well? Do we exercise little patience with God in our lives? Does our patience wane even if/when we know that He greatly cares for us?

How long, and what does it take for us to "get things straight" in our own lives? How long does God have to wait for us to realize He is with us, and in us, and Who He really is?

As we look into the Book of Job, and as we begin to see the 'lessons' and the bigger and clearer picture of Who the Father is, I believe we will find that the "patience of Job" may not be one of the more important aspects of Jobs story as we've always been taught.

We might even start to see, as we look deeper into it, that one of the more relevant aspects of the Book of Job might in actuality be...

The Patience of God.

Praise

I will praise You, O LORD, with my whole heart...(1)
While I live I will praise the LORD:
I will sing praises to my God while I have any being...(2)

One of the truest expressions of a person's trust is Praise.

The Merriam-Webster Dictionary defines praise as to "commend the worth of, or to glorify..."

When you praise something or someone, you are, first of all, from the inside, verbalizing and revealing your gratitude and giving outward honor to that person or thing.

They have done something great in your life, and they have been someone worthy of recognition and worthy of your commendation. They have made a profound difference to you and in your life.

As we mentioned earlier, in the beginning of the book Job worshipped continuously and would even offer up special offerings to God when he thought his children may have sinned in their feasting days. Even when Satan afflicted Job the first time, it says he worshipped;

> *"Then Job arose, and rent his mantle, and shaved his head,*
> *and fell down on the ground, and worshipped..."(3)*

This scripture is the last time we see any reference to Job worshipping or praising God - until the end of the book when God reveals to him the truth, and Job realizes the fullness of it.

David knew the power of praising God regardless of what was happening in his life.

He also made it his *will* and desire to praise God, and made it a point to praise and worship God all the time regardless of what was going on around him.

He was going to praise the Lord, no matter what.

> "I **will** bless the LORD at all times: His praise shall continually
> be in my mouth.
>
> My soul will make her boast in the LORD: the humble will hear of it,
> and be glad.
> O magnify the LORD with me, and let us exalt His Name together.
> I sought the LORD, and He heard me,
> and delivered me from all my fears..."(4)

Do we really trust God? If we do, then we can also praise Him no matter what is going on. As we know the Lord better and better, we will be able to do so automatically and naturally regardless of what is happening, and we will receive blessing from it.

Did Job do this?

Not until the end when God showed up, held a mirror up to him, and revealed to him his heart and actions.

And I believe this is one of the biggest reasons Job repented so strongly and deeply at the end. He realized that he had stopped praising and worshipping the God he revered and loved.

Praise is not only the expressed thankfulness for what the Lord has done in our lives, but it is also an expression of the anticipation of what God is going to do in our lives. It is looking forward to all that He has for us.

Praise is endeavoring to be in God's presence and rejoicing in Who He is, and what He is doing.

I've heard it said that if you are low on fuel, you re-fuel, and if you are low on joy, you rejoice!

When we praise and worship God, the purpose is not to somehow appeal to or to appease God's ego, as might again be suggested by past teachings of Job.

Quite the contrary, praising and worshipping the Lord renews and revives you and _your very own_ connection with the Father, by the Son and through the Holy Spirit.

It opens the doors and clears the channels to Him, so He can hear you and so that you can hear Him. It brings you into His refuge, into His strength and into His love for you.

It brings you into His Presence, into that perfect place, into the throne room of grace.

In Him and with Him.

Let us always remember to praise and worship the Lord.

And let us remember to do so, maybe even more boldly, when our situation is at its most trying and dire.

For it is in those times when we need it, and need Him, the most.

The
Great Irony

The Great Irony

*"Then the LORD answered Job out of the whirlwind, and said,
Who is this that darkens counsel with words without knowledge?"(1)*

Let us look at a brief, somewhat literary overview of the Book of Job.

The story of Job begins with the introduction of the main characters, and then moves into a marvelous portrayal of the inner workings of the realm of heaven. It then evolves into God's praise of the primary character and protagonist, Job, which ushers in a challenge by the antagonist, Satan. The challenge is considered and accepted by God. Satan then causes an onslaught of afflictions to come upon Job, to prove that Job will indeed not go to God for help and will instead curse God to His face. As Job's afflictions from Satan take place, God possibly anticipates that because of Job's perfection before Him, Job will come directly to Him as his fortress and refuge, to be comforted and healed.

The story then takes an unexpected turn when the protagonist, Job, reacts to these events in an entirely different way than anticipated and fails to go to God at all. This unexpected reaction in turn completely and dramatically changes the outcome of the story. Subsequent and lengthy discussions ensue between Job and his friends about Job and about God. These elaborate pontifications continue in a wayward direction away from the truth for a considerable period of time.

Job continues to wholly commiserate in his misery, and even though he doesn't curse God, he infers blame on God for everything, and even as his 'friends' blatantly blame Job himself.

In his heart Job questions God, his friends question Job, and all of them continue to try to explain it all with well-crafted words, words which though may contain partial truths, but as a whole turn out to be "words without knowledge" about God.

The Father listens, and waits for the debate and discussion to change (for 38 chapters out of 42). Then when it is apparent that none of them are going to get it right, He steps in and sets the record straight.

It is at this point where God is more concerned that Job understand the bigger picture of the need to come to Him with everything (as Jesus teaches), than to let him know exactly what has happened by Satan's hand.

He proceeds to show Job, as only the Lord can, the understanding of the error of his reactions, and creates the environment for Job to realize what he should have done in the first place and all along.

As Job begins to comprehend all that God is showing him, he acts on this revealed understanding first with reverence, then deep repentance, and then with prayer.

He then finds himself in the place he should have been from the very beginning; he worships God, asks of Him, and receives from the Lord. He ends up with far more in his life than he ever had before. And he also gains a much deeper and greater wisdom and understanding of Who God really is.

It's profoundly simple really. A man of God starts out well, but because of a flaw in his nature, chooses and goes in the wrong direction. The Father steps in and shows him his error and brings him back to the truth. The man is forgiven and ends up being greatly blessed.

For generations we have read so many adverse things into all that transpired with Job. As part of our nature, we've commiserated with Job and have tried to justify his actions, just as he himself tried to do. We then pontificate and speak earnest generalizations about who God is, and make great proclamations and create teachings about things we don't really understand, and then end up with the same "non-answers", just as those in Job did.

We have made the same presumptions and conclusions, that somehow God was undeservedly punishing Job, in the very same way Job and his friends did in all of their various discourses.

170

And even though we have much more information about the scenario than Job did, we end up the same way in not realizing any sound answers, and we (just as they) have surmised and guessed at the understanding of it all.

In the end, we, again just as they, have found ourselves speaking "words without knowledge."

By doing all of this, we have made the Book of Job heavy and profound, in an uneasy sort of way, which has allowed and perpetuated a certain gravitas of the unknown, basing all of our hypotheses almost wholly on the dialog and "words without knowledge" spoken by Job and his friends.

The irony in the Book of Job is that we, by our own extrapolating, pontificating, expounding and commiserating, have acted and reacted in the exact same way as Job and his friends.

We have endeavored with all our best efforts to explain it all, and in doing so have made it far more involved, complicated, difficult and burdensome than it was ever intended to be.

And by this we have also completely missed the point of Job.

Human Nature

"Gird up your loins now like a man:
I will ask you, and you will give Me the answer..."(1)

The Great Irony of the Book of Job is that this great and marvelous story is actually entirely about **Us**. It is an amazing study in, and a reflection of, our very own, very human, nature. And it is presented to us by our very own God and Father and Creator.

The story of Job involves our tendency to consume ourselves with our selves and our own limited vision, and as a result not seeing the bigger picture of it all. It is also about our inability, for any number of reasons, to go to our Creator for help in time of need. It is about the human condition, and about who or what we put before God in our lives.

Let's again take a closer look.

What do we do when something bad or something we consider bad happens in our lives? What are our natural tendencies and reactions?

After initial shock, do we not find ourselves in an abstract and wholly redirected state of mind? Don't we begin, out of our emotions, to question everything, and to look for answers and explanations? In our commiserating we realize a variety of emotional reactions, and when the conditions are severe enough we certainly can find ourselves in misery, which sometimes can last for a long time.

As a side note, I have always personally felt that there is a part of our human condition which can, at times, find some sort of abandoned resignation and even comfort of a sort in this particular state of being. Some can tend to remain and/or dwell there, and some find themselves in these places for long periods of time and some even for lifetimes.

What else happens around us? Friends arrive and attend to us, and in their earnest desire and compassion, make great efforts to empathize with us.

172

This is a beautiful emotional element of our nature. It lends itself to wanting to comfort and to be comforted. We commiserate, mourn, and have a need to show our compassion to those in need, and to receive this comfort when in need ourselves.

Then in our desire to put it all in a big logical box, we consider a variety of in-depth thoughts and discussions and dialog with the hope and intent of somehow having it all explained to our satisfaction, that there might indeed be relief and answers in it all. We find ourselves searching for understanding and comprehension, trying to glean as much wisdom as we can from others and/or from anyone who might be able to tell us more about our present state, in order that we might find the answers and immediately solve and resolve the whole of it.

During these difficult times and subsequent searching, all kinds of conjecture is made and scenarios hypothesized. We talk about God, and our particular states of being, and of how we wish it could all be different somehow. Though the questions are never really answered, the elements of empathy are comforting, and we go on. Along the way we might offer up a "I hope you're here" thought to God, or we may even have the understanding that He is with us, yet we may never actually make the effort to go directly and diligently to Him for comfort. Or if we do, it is many times out of our present emotional state, and not out of knowing who He is and how He works in our lives, that He indeed is a strong 'tower' and great and perfect 'refuge' for us.

Then at some point there is a realization and a resignation that our friends may not be able to truly understand what we are going through. We are thankful for their friendship, concern and compassion, but we also realize that when it comes right down to it, they can't actually help with the situation, and it's once again left to us. This can be a lonely place to find ourselves in.

It is in these times that if we really think about it, and if we know the Father, we will realize that the only one who can truly understand and help us with all that is going on is our Lord.

The One Who created us.

Gods Ways

"For as the heavens are higher than the earth,
so are My ways higher than your ways,
and My thoughts than your thoughts..."(1)

Okay, now let's look at this above chapter verse. Maybe read it again.

I can hear some of you now... "Okay, here he goes. We knew he'd have to come back to this at some point, as after all, this is what we've been taught and have heard all along about Jobs trials; that God is God, and we can never understand Him, and He does whatever He wants, whenever He wants, good or evil, and we can never really know Him."

Ah,,, No.

God's ways are way higher than that.

First of all, as we've discussed, God cannot be and/or do both good and evil. He does only good, and also brings good out of bad.

That's His nature. It's Who He is and what He does.

Secondly, as part of what we've done so many times in our lives and throughout generations, we, by our very own nature, consistently and wrongfully attribute many of our own human traits and faults to God.

We attribute to God, as Job's friends did, the human trait of being a punishing God.

In our human element and our own nature we punish, and we have also inferred this trait and accusation on God, that He is a 'punisher' for all that happens.

As we talked about in the Mercy and Grace chapter, God does not punish, or do bad things to us. He's not schizophrenic, but He does bring good out of the bad we find ourselves in.

At the end of the Book of Job God strongly points out that the words spoken by Job and his friends were very wrong about Him, including the perception that God is a punisher, and that He does bad things to us.

We have also attributed to the Lord God the human traits of pride and boasting in His soliloquy at the end of Job. We suggest that God is just reiterating and/or soundly emphasizing His Majesty to Job as if Job and his friends don't already know how great He is.

Or maybe we think that God may just be grandly boasting, or extremely egotistical and making very sure that they, and we, fully understand how great He is and that He is far greater than they or we are.

So by these conclusions we've made, and because there appear to be no other viable explanations of the events of Job, we've created and perpetuated a belief that there really *aren't* any other reasons for it all, and our answers default to "because God is God, that's that, and we can never know Him."

That's our nature.

The thing about this is - look at this - God <u>knew</u> that we would respond in this manner.

Let me say this again. The Father knows and **knew** that we would react and respond to Job in the way we have for all these years!

God created us. He knows exactly how we react to events and adversity, and He knew that we would react, in our very own human nature, in very specific ways to Job's events and his adversity.

The Lord had the story of Job put into the middle of the Word of God, knowing that we would look at this whole incredible scenario of Job solely from and through the eyes of Job.

By our very own nature He knew that we would commiserate completely with the man and his trials.

Our focus was entirely on Job's misery, and through our own inclinations and nature and perceptions, we could see nothing else.

He knew that we would view the afflictions of Job from a personal misery perspective, and that we would react in the same way as Job and his friends by blaming God and then pontificating about Him in trying to explain it all to ourselves.

We have hypothesized and inferred the fault of God, just as Job did, and have continued to make all sorts of conjecture, as Job's friends did.

What is truly amazing, and how the "Higher ways" verse beautifully applies here, is how God has woven into the events of Job a depth and a perfect visual and visceral portrayal of our very own human nature, and how we ourselves react to events and to adversity in our own lives!

God has wonderfully disguised and marvelously revealed our own human nature to us through the characters and events of the Book of Job. He is showing us our own nature, and then is also showing us our very own perceptions and misconceptions about Who He is.

And we have behaved in the exact same way as Job and his friends did, through our own actions and reactions to Job and his afflictions.

All of the expansive thoughts and explanations spoken by Job and his friends about God and about Job's trials are *identical* to the expansive explanations and pontifications about the Book of Job that we've perpetuated for all of these years!

In the end we've gone on with our great and grand presumptions and assumptions of our own making, without benefitting from, or asking for, any answers from the One Who created it all, and the One Who created us in the first place!

Not only is the Father revealing to us a clear and perfect reflection of our own human nature in and through the characters of Job and his friends and their actions and reactions, but He has done it in such a way that He has profoundly demonstrated it to us in real time, in and through our very own actions and reactions! We have become the very participants in it all...

And we've played our parts perfectly!

The dialog of Job and his friends is an amazing mirror image of what we actually do, our thoughts and reactions, especially in time of need, toward God.

Through the events of Job, God has shown us, just as He showed Job, that our perceptions and presumptions of Him may not be Who He really is, or even close to His true nature at all.

It turns out that what we have not looked for, or may never have even considered, is the view from **God's** perspective in and by and of the events of Job.

We have not looked at it from the perspective that God might be trying to show us great and amazing things about ourselves through Job, and about handling adversity, and about Who He really is, in order to help us in our lives!

We have only looked at it through our own commiserating emotions and through our very own, very human, nature.

And He hid this mystery right where He knew we wouldn't see it, right before our very own eyes.

He knew we wouldn't see it that is, until we stepped beyond ourselves; and by searching for more of Him, began to see a very different and much larger picture, from His perspective and vista.

The thing Job's friends got right was God's greatness, and strength, and wisdom.

What they got wrong was Who He really is and His great desire for us to know Him, and by this to have a great true friendship and relationship with Him.

He was also showing them, and us, more about His nature than we've ever seen before.

He was showing them, and us, that His nature may be very different than what we have been told, or what we've learned in the past, or how we've presumed Him to be.

He's showing us how to step out of our own nature and perspective and to look at how we perceive our Father, and at Who we are discovering Him to be.

God is always with us; He is *always* waiting for us to come to Him; He is in reality a great refuge and strength for us.

We **can** find out answers and find out about Him; We **can** have an amazing and full and 'real' relationship with Him, and His Son and His Spirit; and we **can** always come to Him and receive from Him.

The great irony of the book of Job is that we have always thought the writings of Job were about Job.

In reality, the writings of Job are all about us.

As we take a closer look, we begin to see many amazing and profound perspectives and truths in the Book of Job,

And we find that God's thoughts and ways are indeed higher than our thoughts and ways.

Way higher.

God Knew

*"Jesus answered and said to them, it is given to **you**
to know the mysteries of the kingdom of heaven,,,"(1)*

As we have just discussed, God's ways are truly marvelous and much higher than ours.

Let's take this even one step even higher. Look at this…

God allowed Satan to have excessive powers over Job to prove a point.

The original challenge was, at face value, apparently won by God, but seemingly barely, as Job, to his credit, never actually curses God to His face, but also has not come to God.

So if we believe that God knows all things, then the Lord would also have known from the very beginning what Job's real time response would be, to and during all of his afflictions. God would have known *exactly* how Job was going to react to it all the whole time - even when He was talking with Satan.

So then if God already knew what Job's actual, real time responses would be, that Job wouldn't come to Him and would even blame Him, doesn't it follow that God might not have agreed to Satan's challenge in the first place?

Unless there was far more to the story than the challenge itself.

Was this challenge with Satan, of Job 'not cursing God', done so that we would know that "God is God, and we're not"? Could this have been God's only intention by the Book of Job?

Or what if, from the very beginning, it was not the challenge from Satan that God was concerned with, but all along it was His purpose and desire to use these events, to allow these one-time happenings to transpire in Jobs life to reveal to all who followed, including us,

179

something more, something larger, a far greater view and perspective about Job and his friends concerning their reactions and responses?

What if from the very beginning it was His purpose and His desire to show us about our own selves and our own naturally human responses, and to show us things that would benefit us as well, as we too would deal with adversity and difficult times in our lives?

What if from the very beginning it was His purpose and His desire to also show us more about Himself, and Who He really is, not just Who we think He is or Who we've been told He is?

By this very observation, that God knew all of this beforehand, and that the whole purpose of Job was to show us more about ourselves, and more about Himself, then Satans challenge was not just barely won by God, but was in fact **perfectly** *completed,* **fully** *accomplished,* **completely** *successful and* **wholly fulfilled** *in* **everything God intended by and through it!!!**

Could it be that Job went through all of this so that we might know a better and more successful way in which to react in the face of adversity in our lives?

Could it be that Job went through all of this so that we might see our very own nature, and by that to realize that we can indeed know God and His nature, and have a greater trust and faith, and have an in depth relationship with and in Him?

Could it be that the very next Book of the Bible, Psalms, was put there in direct contrast and comparison to Job in order to show us a better way to live through adversity, and how to better be able to handle ourselves during difficult times and events in our lives?

Could it be that Job went through all that he did with his friends so that we might be more careful about condemning others?

Could it be that Job went through all that he did so that we might be more careful about blaming God for things we don't understand?

Could it be that Job went through all of this so that we might be able to discover a greater and far deeper understanding of Who our God is and the truth about how good our Father really is?

Could it be that God was showing Job, and us, that we can come to Him always and with anything, anytime, and that He is a very real refuge for us?

The answers are Yes, Yes, Yes, Yes, Yes, Yes, and Yes!!!

There appears to be much, much more to the lessons and examples of Job than what we have heard or have been taught before.

And we just haven't seen it,,,

Until now.

The Question

"If you continue in my word, then you are my disciples indeed; and you shall know the truth, and the truth shall make you free..."(1)

Another part of this Great Irony refers to the question that has been perpetually asked and taught as the old school main theme question posed by the Book of Job.

This question is "Why do the righteous suffer?" or, "Why does God allow the righteous to suffer?"

Let's take a look at this.

As we know, all of creation has been set in motion by God, and as a result of previous Garden events, part of our human element is the fact that everyone faces suffering at some point or points in their lives.

Why does anyone suffer?

Because it's part of our human experience and existence here.

So do we have an answer for, or have ever found an answer to, "Why do the righteous suffer", or "why does anyone suffer" question?

We could go into very long, in-depth existential conversations as to why we would even be able to ask this question in the first place, let alone answer it, and I think it would work our noodles for a very long time, and in fact has.

Can we actually solve it?

Probably not. Not in this life.

The theoretical progression of this particular question then becomes, "How do we deal with, or handle, or assimilate a question we are not able to answer, seeing we have not been able to answer it for all of our existence?"

We have tried to generate and extrapolate answers, but for the most part have only been able to come up with partial, hypothetical ponderings and explanations, and then when more deeply considered, all we end up with is once again defaulting to "because God is God and He created it that way..."

This particular infinite and indefinite question posed about suffering and the righteous suffering has been attributed to the Book of Job for centuries, and yet has never been answered.

Here's the reason why it's never been resolved, never been explained, and it is really quite simple.

It's not the question.

"Why do the righteous suffer" is never answered in Job because it is not the question, nor the purpose, nor even the consideration ever posed by the Book of Job.

I can hear many of you breathing a collective sigh of relief.

The Lords yoke is easy and His burden is light. What we have been doing for years with all the non-explanations of Job is heaping upon ourselves our own heavy burden of non-answers and confusion.

The real question that is presented to us in the Book of Job is not "Why do the righteous suffer," or "Why does God allow the righteous to suffer."

It is in fact the question, "How do we handle suffering when it comes?"

"What are our reactions and responses to trials and tribulation when adversity happens in our lives?" "How do we best deal with the suffering and adversity when it comes?"

What do we do when suffering comes? What should we do that will give us the best or optimum outcome?

More specifically how are we as Christians, to deal with the afflictions and suffering that is inherent at times in our human condition?

How are we to deal with adversity in our lives? What will bring us peace, and bring to us those things that we truly need during it all?

The Lord God knows that we will have adverse situations in our lives.

It's part of life, it's part of the deal.

He also loves us, and cares for and about us, and He desires to help us through these challenging times of adversity. As part of that, He gives us examples in His Word to help us.

He has also given us keys to the answers to this very question in the Book of Job.

Through Job's responses and actions, and then through the contrasting of David's responses and actions in Psalms, The Lord is guiding us, and showing us a light and a path through adversity to success and victory in our lives.

The Lord desires for us to know to how to respond to, and how to best handle adversity, so that by His great help and refuge, we can have great personal success in time of need and anytime.

Through Job He has given us the answers to dealing with adversity successfully, so that we might live life more abundantly, in Him.

Do we know the Lord well enough to know this?

Do we go directly to God as David did?

Or do we hide from God and blame Him as Job did?

Do we remain far from God and live continually in fear, and even in misery, hiding from Him and blaming Him, as Job did?

Or do we go immediately and directly to the Lord as David did in faith and trust, knowing God as our refuge and our strength, our Rock, and knowing that He alone has the answers for us?

Do we go to the Lord for help?

Or do we go somewhere else?

Do we really have faith and trust enough to know that He can help us and indeed wants to help us?

What do we do?

What do <u>you</u> do?

> *"Many are the afflictions of the righteous:*
>
> *But the LORD delivers him out of them all."*(2)

Revelation

Revelation Rock

"...for flesh and blood has not revealed this to you,
but my Father in heaven (has revealed it to you)."(1)

Our God wants us to know more about Him.

So how is this accomplished in us, and how is this information given to us? How does the Lord reveal these things to us?

The Father shows us things in many different ways. He reveals things to our hearts as we seek Him. He reveals things to our spirit as we learn more about Him. Our spirit and the Holy Spirit connect and we receive understanding.

He reveals when we seek for and hear His Word. He reveals things through others, especially when we desire to know more. He enlightens and enlivens moments and words spoken and we realize the importance of them in and to ours and others lives.

The things God shows us through His Word and His Spirit may at times come to our understanding all at once. These instant realizations are called "revelations".

A revelation is a complete understanding of a thing, revealed in a given moment of time.

To put it in our modern vernacular, this type of information and understanding transfer can be considered a "download" or an "instant download" of "God" information. This understanding which is downloaded is profound to us, and what is even more amazing is that it is given, directly and personally to us, from the Lord by the Holy Spirit.

Let's look at these downloads and instant downloads in a couple of different ways.

Throughout our education in life, both formal and experiential, as part of learning about a subject, we first receive, or "download" information and data about a subject into our knowledge "bank" or cognitive brain. As our learning progresses, we at some point gain a working understanding of the thing. We start to "get" it.

We first receive the knowledge, and then there is a particular point in time when the knowledge is put into motion or acted upon, and it is at this point when we realize the connection and the understanding of how it truly works. We use, or exercise the knowledge we have gained when it is converted into understanding. At this point you know it, you now have it, it's yours, and you own it.

It is the same thing with understanding the things of God.

Revelation from God is "revealed understanding" about God and the things of God, and all the things He desires to show us.

These revelations are so much more profound than our earthly learning as they involve and connect completely with our Creator, and if you will, with all Creation itself.

I often see, as a perspective, that the learning of things of the world are one, or at most two-dimensional, while these downloads of God and the instant downloads received from the Holy Spirit are multi-dimensional, multi-layered, and truly amazing in depth and meaning.

They are personal, inherently profound, and they apply directly to our lives, our growth and our understanding of situations and people. And of God.

Jesus explained the character or nature of these downloads when speaking with Peter:

> "When Jesus came into the coasts of Caesarea Philippi, He asked His disciples,
> "Who do men say that I am?"

And they said, some say that You are John the Baptist, some say Elijah, others say You are Jeremiah, or one of the prophets.

He then said to them, "But who do you say that I am?"
And Simon Peter answered, "You are the Christ, the Son of the living God."
And Jesus said to him, "You are blessed Simon, for flesh and blood has not revealed this to you, but My Father in heaven (has revealed it to you). And I say also to you, that you are Peter, and upon this rock I will build My church, and the gates of hell shall not prevail against it. And... I will give to you the keys of the kingdom of heaven..."(2)

As Jesus and His disciples discussed the things being said about Him, comparing Him to prophets and other great men who had gone before, Jesus asked Peter, "Who do you say that I am?" Peter then spoke from what had been revealed to him from his time with Jesus, and from all that he had seen and heard, and from the understanding he had been given by God, that Jesus was indeed the Christ, the Messiah, the Son of God.

This wasn't just a good guess. This wasn't Peter just trying to say the right thing to appease Jesus. This was what he now personally knew to be true and had been revealed to him by the Father. He didn't know this from what others had told him, or what he had heard somewhere else, he knew this by experiencing first hand all that the Lord had for him.

Peter didn't receive this understanding by physical means either, by "flesh and blood", or by physical observations of others. Jesus was saying that Peter had received this understanding as a result of a direct and personal download from God.

The verse goes on to say "that you are Peter, and upon this rock I will build my church..."

Was Jesus saying that He would build His church on Peter?

No.

He wasn't talking about Peter.

189

Jesus was pointing out or referring to the "revealed understanding" that Peter had received, and was using the metaphor of Peters name (originally Simon Bar-Jonah in Hebrew, Jesus gave him the Greek name Petros meaning Rock) to show the great strength that this "revealed understanding" and these downloads from the Lord would have in Peters life, in our lives, and in the life of His church.

The Lord is continually revealing things to us.

Are we listening? Are we continually receiving and experiencing these downloads and all that the Lord has for us?

Look at the last line of the last verse, directly after he talks about these revealed truths from God. Jesus says that by this revealed understanding He will give us the keys of the Kingdom of heaven.

Keys are tools or instruments which allow for entry into something.

What are these keys Jesus is talking about?

They are these very revelations from the Lord, which we can have, and which unlock all that is in God's Kingdom...

As we truly seek the Father, He gives this revealed understanding to us individually and personally, and it comes from the Lord via His Holy Spirit.

Jesus asked Peter, "Who do you say that I am?"

Who do _you_ say He is?

That is a really big and important question for us to ask ourselves, in order to begin to gain true insight and in order to find out more about Him.

When we start spending time in and with the Lord, and begin to understand more of Who He is, more and more is revealed to us.

This becomes the solid 'Rock' that the gates of hell can't stand against.

God revealing Himself to us grows us, makes us stronger, and brings us into all that He would have us to know and to be.

And He desires that we go further, as far as we can desire into all the amazing truths of Who He is and all He is doing, and the things He desires to do in us, with us, and through us.

When you are seeking and receiving the revealed things of God, and when you are realizing and experiencing the things of the Lord, the adversary can't stop it. As it grows and grows within you, and as you then share it with others, it continues to multiply, exponentially, inwardly and outwardly, growing and abounding in your life and in others' lives, and then from us and each of them it goes into others' lives and so on until it is everywhere. This 'receiving' bears fruit, and this fruit, or the results of these things grow in others outwardly and exponentially, "abounding to your account", and abounding to the glory of God!

"Flesh and blood has not revealed this to you, but My Father in heaven has revealed it to you."

Again, this isn't something someone has told us. This isn't some second-hand information. These are things specifically and personally shown us by the Lord and experienced through His Spirit.

And it is available to all of us.

Let's look at this next scripture, which we used in an earlier chapter, in a little different light. Paul is writing about <u>experiencing</u> God in our walk in the Lord.

> *"...and have become like those that have need of milk, and not of strong meat.*
> *For everyone that uses milk is unskillful in the Word of righteousness, but strong meat belongs to them that are of full age, even those, who, **by reason of use**, have their senses exercised to discern both good (those things that are of God) and evil (those things that are not of God)."(3)*

A new perspective in this verse came to me, that those who are only receiving the milk of the Word, and nothing else, are persons who only hear or receive someone else's revelations, somebody else's revealed understanding and have only lived in Him through second hand experiences.

They either don't know that they can receive these things for themselves from God, or don't desire to make an effort to see the things of God first hand in their lives.

I think many of us live only desiring the milk of the Word. It's all we desire to know. We'd rather hear a good story or two about someone else's revelation, week after week, than to experience these things for ourselves. It is easy and "sweet" to do this, and can help us continue in the Lord, but it doesn't help us grow any stronger, or grow in Him ourselves, and it also limits us in how far we can go in Him.

Paul is admonishing/strongly inferring here, that we should seek to and experience the things of God for ourselves.

This actual experiencing of God, and the personal downloads from Him as we seek Him, is the 'strong meat' Paul is talking about. He is intensely and intentionally urging us to seek these things, so that we would have these interactions with the Lord and His Spirit often in our lives.

One of the results if we do this is that the gates of hell will not be able to stand against us.

Paul is also saying that if we do not **_exercise_** our own spirit, if we don't 'exercise our senses to discern', if we don't search out the Holy Spirit and revelations of God for our own, then we will not be as strong in the Lord as we can and should be, and as we need to be, to have great and amazing fulfillment of and in our Christian walk.

Another way the Lord reveals these downloads to us is by God's Word.

God uses His Word to build our faith. Many, if not all of the things we need to know and understand can be found in His Word. In it can be found all the fullness of God. It is **the** Guidebook. It has lifetimes full of revelation from Him that the Holy Spirit can show us. Most of the time the answers we are looking for are already right there in His Word.

> *"All scripture is given by inspiration of God, and is profitable for doctrine, for reproof, for correction, for instruction in righteousness: That the man of God may be perfect, throughly furnished to (and for) every good work."(4)*

The whole of the Bible has been inspired by God and given to men. How was it given? It was given by the Holy Spirit of God to each writer as they wrote. By this we know that the whole Word of God can be considered divine revelation or revealed understanding, given to us by the Holy Spirit from the Lord Himself.

As a side note, I really like the word *"throughly"* here. It has a deeper connotation than the word "thoroughly" which otherwise might have been used, and portrays His Word becoming fully a part of us and inside us, through and throughout us.

I am always amazed when I randomly open up the Bible to a particular page which is perfectly relevant to what I am going through. Or when I'm seeking the fullness of a theme, I find even more truths, as well as the revealed understanding that comes with it.

It is also amazing when the Lord reveals something to our hearts, and then we see it in the Word of God, or vice versa. We may have read a particular verse many times before, but have never really known it until it is revealed or shown to us by His Spirit. It then jumps off the page. It is at this point the understanding comes and we realize it, we take possession of it, the truths are revealed and we now have it. It becomes completely relevant and becomes a marvelous confirmation of things that have already been revealed to and within us.

There are so many layers of truths to be found in the Word of God. Each one of these truths is multi-faceted. I've heard it described as peeling back unlimited layers; that there are more and more "revelations" the farther and deeper you go.

Gods' answers for us are right there in His Word, and His revelations await us. They are revealed to us through the Fathers deep and gracious, amazing and holy, Spirit.

As we seek and ask, we can receive this revealed understanding by His Spirit and/or through His Word.

When we diligently search for the things of God, and they are then revealed to us personally, and it becomes not only incredibly profound, but it also becomes truly relevant to us and within us for the rest of our lives.

All it takes is for us to seek, and ask.

This same thing happened with Job. In the end, God directly revealed the truth, the understanding, and the revelation of his situation to him.

He showed Job a better way to handle his adversity, and showed Job more about Who He was, and then all that Job had realized became completely relevant and purposeful and life giving, in and for the rest of his life.

As we search for and receive these things from the Lord and the Spirit of God, we will find what we are looking for.

And we will much more clearly see God.

> *"I have heard of you (said Job),,,*
>
> *But now I see you for myself..."*(5)

Your Thoughts Unto Me

"How precious also are Your thoughts to me, O God!
How great is the sum of them!
If I should count them, they are more in number than the sand..."(1)

Okay, more in number than the sand? How much is that? Let's see,,, deserts, beaches, oceans,,,

How many "thoughts" does God have toward us?

The Lord's thoughts to us are coming to us all the time.

As we talked about in the last chapter,

> ➤ He reveals Himself to us through His Word.
> ➤ He reveals Himself by and through His Spirit
> ➤ He reveals Himself to us via downloads to and into our hearts and minds.
> ➤ He reveals Himself to us through others.
> ➤ He reveals Himself to others through us.

The Lord desires to show us and to communicate to us life, and the things and understanding of all life, of His Creation, and of Him.

> *...The words that I speak unto you, they are spirit,*
> *and they are life."*(2)

The Lord wants us to know all of the truth, and all of the things that He has for us. Jesus sent the Comforter, the Holy Spirit, to be here in His place, to show us of the Father, and to help us see Him.

The Apostle Paul wrote,

> *"I don't stop giving thanks for you, making mention of you in my prayers,*
> *That the God of our Lord Jesus Christ, the Father of glory, may give to*
> *you the spirit of wisdom and revelation in the knowledge of Him:*

195

That the eyes of your understanding would be enlightened; that you may know what is the hope of His calling, and what are the riches of the glory of His inheritance in the saints (in You), and what is the exceeding greatness of His power toward us who believe, according to the working of His mighty power...”(3)

This is a huge and powerful statement. Paul is talking to Christians in Ephesus, but is also talking to all of us. He prayed that the Lord would give them, (and us) *the spirit of wisdom and revelation in the knowledge of Him.*

Paul goes on... That each of us would know and understand the hope of God's calling, and the riches of all that He has given us, and that we also would **know** the greatness of his power both to us and for us and in us!

The Lord wants us to know Him, and He wants us to learn of and receive all that He has for us, and for all of our lives. I will say this again. We have only barely scratched the surface of this understanding! There is so much more for us to know, so much more than we ever have known before.

One of the primary purposes of the Holy Spirit, what He has been sent here to do, is to reveal to us all of the truth of God.

The Lord desires for us to hear and receive all of these things from Him and His Spirit, that we might know Him more and more, better and better.

Jesus said, *"My sheep hear my voice..."(4)*

Many are His thoughts toward us...

Are we listening?

Tuning In

*"The grace of the Lord Jesus Christ, and the love of God,
and the communion of the Holy Ghost be with you all..."(1)*

Are we continually looking for the Lord and His Spirit to reveal things to us? Have we put ourselves in a position to hear these things and to hear Him, or is He going to just have to bonk us on the heads on the fly to get anything across to us?

Bonking would be great, but that is not how God, in His infinite wisdom, has set it up. We probably wouldn't want it, or even receive it that way, much less realize the fullness of it, and we certainly wouldn't have the reward that comes from the searching and the finding of it.

So how can we hear more clearly from the Lord?

As we said earlier concerning anything in or of God, we have to 'initiate ourselves'. One of the ways we can initiate ourselves is by endeavoring to tune ourselves in to the Spirit of God.

Keep in mind we don't have to be perfect to hear and to listen (and we actually can't be, as we're all sinners and mess up at times), but we *do* have to desire to, and make the effort to listen, and to hear.

Hearing from the Lord through the Holy Spirit happens as we tune ourselves to Him. These things are not heard physically with your ears. They are heard with your heart, with and within your very own spirit.

Hearing from the Spirit of God is started by an internal asking, and then can be described as a 'knowing' or receiving of an understanding. It is a word or words that are understood by and with the heart, or 'heard' in the spirit of a man.

*"The Spirit itself bears witness with our spirit,
that we are the children of God."(2)*

The Spirit of God "hooks up" with our own spirit.

This is the connection.

Each of us has our own spirit, which is who we in essence are. The Spirit of God "bears witness" or "connects" with our spirit within us. In this particular case Paul is saying that the Spirit of God tells our spirit that we are the children of God, and then we know it.

The Holy Spirit connects with our spirit about many things, and, if we're listening, tells us even of the deep things of God.

For those who need a more tangible or visual description of this connection, think of your spirit/heart as a live wire or conduit connection to the Spirit of God. Or better yet think of it as a "wireless" connection where the Holy Spirit of God transfers 'files' of information concerning the things of God to our heart and spirit. This is where we receive it, and then our heart and spirit send it to our minds for the application.

This "God information" is given to you, and you then perceive and receive it, you understand it, and know it to be true on the inside of you.

> "The wisdom that is from above is first pure, then peaceable, gentle, easy to be asked for, full of mercy and good fruits, without partiality, and without hypocrisy..."(3)

It is pure and peaceful and easy to ask for and easy to receive. And because it is from the Lord and His Spirit, it is always good.

This wisdom, this "God" information and understanding, comes easily when we're listening, and asking, and it is always good.

Our part in it all is to initiate the dialog, to start the conversation, and to ask, which opens the channel. Again, every once in a while, He'll amaze us with something, or bowl us over with some great and profound truth when we're not looking, but most of the time, in order to have more, we have to be intentionally listening and moving in His direction.

I like to think of the Spirit of God connection to our spirit as tuning in a radio dial (think of the old AM/FM radios). You have to concentrate on listening to hear the desired frequency and then turn the dial back and forth and then ever so slightly until it becomes absolutely clear.

It can take some time to do at first, but then, as you continue to adjust the dial and to listen, and as you do it more and more, you will find that finding the frequency becomes natural to you and you get to the point of being able to quickly tune in or adjust whenever wanted, and you can clearly hear all that's coming across to you!

Also, like a radio station, what you hear from the Father, Son, and the Holy Spirit, the content, is not something you can direct or control, but is there to be received. The amazing thing about your Holy Spirit station is that the Lord has just the right content, just the right information, on just the right frequency for you!

All you need to do is be tuned in to it, and as you do, much will be revealed.

What is also wonderful and amazing is that the Holy Spirit bandwidth is infinitely long, and everyone can be tuned to different channels from and within the same Spirit.

The effort, and the reward, is in finding your station, what channel you are to be on, and staying tuned in.

From my own experience, I prayed for years to be able to hear from the Holy Spirit. Others said they could hear, but I wasn't sure what that meant and I wondered if I ever would be able to. One of the things I always wanted to know was which way I should go, and what was next for me; but I felt like I wasn't hearing any of that sort of thing.

As I think back on it, I'm not sure what I was expecting.

It was a little further down my "walk" when I started turning the dial and paying more attention to it when I realized that the Holy Spirit was already there, in my heart, moving in me and through me strongly in many different ways.

199

If I had been more open to all that was possible with God I would have seen that He was continually giving me purposeful insight into Who He was, and all of the thoughts and revealed understanding I was writing down was what the Spirit was really communicating to me personally, on the Holy Spirit channel.

I realized that even though I didn't think I could hear anything, the Lord was all along sending information my way. As I began to see this, I realized that I had been moving closer to Him the whole time, without ever even knowing it.

As you continue toward Him, know that He will honor your efforts and will reveal Himself to you in a very personal and profound way. Know that He sees and knows the desire that is in your heart. Take comfort in this, and keep tuning in!

To help with your listening, know that the Holy Spirit speaks in an inside voice, not an outside one. It's a heart thing, not a head thing. As you listen and seek Him more, you will find your channel. You may not recognize it at first, but as you continue to make the effort to tune in, you will understand it more and more and you will find that it's been there the whole time. It is your very own station and channel and frequency from the Lord, not like anyone else's!

I would like to make the disclaimer here that God is Love, and the only thing you will ever hear on the Holy Spirit channel will be related to the love of God and the God of Love. There will never ever be anything from hate or anger or evil, and you will never hear anything that has to do with injury or harm to anyone. The Holy Spirit channel is of God and conveys only good and only the good things of God.

So find your channel with the Father, Son and Holy Spirit. Chances are you are already listening to it, but endeavor to keep adjusting the dial and tuning in a little more so that you may always hear all you can,,,

,,,and receive all that the Lord has for you!

"Ask,,, and it shall be given you;
Seek,,, and ye shall find;
Knock,,, and it shall be opened unto you:

For everyone who asks, receives;
and he that seeks, finds;
and to him that knocks, it shall be opened.

Or who of you, if his son asks for bread, will give him a stone?
Or if he ask a fish, will he give him a serpent?

If you then, being evil, know how to give good gifts to your children,
How much more shall your Father which is in heaven
Give good things to them that ask Him?"

Mat 7:7-11

Seek

Knock

Ask

Seek, Knock, Ask

"For every one who <u>asks</u>, <u>receives</u>;
and he who <u>seeks</u>, <u>finds</u>;
and to him who <u>knocks</u>, <u>it shall be opened</u>..."(1)

One of the most profound secrets or truths found in the Book of Job is that Job never went directly to God.

In the end, God shows Job that he could have come to Him and could have received His help, and His answers the whole time.

Jesus tells us over and over that we can come to Him, anytime, and we can also receive from Him.

One of the Secrets of Job is that we can know Him and we can come to Him and receive from Him the things we are looking for.

Keep in mind that many of our answers and the wisdom of God in situations are already found in His Word. Job didn't have this resource in his day, but we have it and more.

Another resource Job didn't have was the Spirit of God, Who is here to show us all things, and we also hear and receive of the Lord by and through His Spirit.

Let's rearrange the above chapter verse a little bit. We'll keep the same phrases, but we'll put them in a different order.

For he who seeks, *finds*;
To him who knocks, *it shall be opened*;
And every one who asks, *receives*.

I very much like this progression. It is more in line with the steps we can take to find and receive from the Lord.

Seek, Knock, Ask.

And as you do this, as the chapter verse says, the Spirit of God will begin to show you personally and profoundly all that the Father has for you.

As we, as you, seek, knock and ask...

...You will find; it will be opened to you; and you will receive...

All of the things of our Father, Lord, and Creator.

Seek

Seek First

"The LORD is good to them that wait for Him,
to the soul that <u>seeks</u> Him."(1)

Let's look deeper into this next similar verse, and at some of the ways we can initiate ourselves toward God.

"But <u>seek first</u> the kingdom of God, and his righteousness;
and all these things shall be added unto you."(2)

"<u>Seek first</u>..."

Seeking is an action. It is an initiated action with the purpose of obtaining a result. It is not just asking a random question; it is delving into the things of God for a particular reason. Of all the things we do, the first thing we should do is to seek.

"<u>The Kingdom of God</u>..."

What is the Kingdom of God? It is everything that pertains to God. By seeking this, and Him, first, we are going to the Maker of all Creation from the start in whatever we're doing. Seeking Him and the His Kingdom gives our hearts and minds the right perspective and puts us in position, and sets us up to find Him.

Everything good is within God's Kingdom.

I sometimes refer to the Kingdom of God as a great cornucopia. The traditional image of a cornucopia, or "horn of plenty", is a natural horn shaped basket, overflowing with fruit and produce of many different kinds, and is symbolic of unlimited abundance. It is all we could ever want or need, overflowing with a variety of all good things.

I then like to think of each individual type of fruit as anything we can desire in our lives. Each fruit has its own shape, texture and taste, as do those things we desire. Each contains the related rewards which each particular desire can provide.

Many times we find ourselves desiring individual items during our lives, and we may have them at various levels of importance to us including at times making them paramount in our desires.

Let's relate several of these desires to a certain thing that grows, and consider them for a moment.

If all we desire in our lives is a partner, who we initially may feel will give us everything we are looking for (we'll relate this to an 'apple'), what we will find is that we can receive in our lives only the things that an apple, or mate, can give. If we are seeking money (we'll call this an 'ear of corn'), we can only receive what corn, or money, can give us. If we seek social relationships (we'll call those 'grapes'), we'll have only the tastes and textures that grapes alone can give us.

It's the same along those lines with anything, including the basics of food and shelter and clothing and anything else we might desire. If we're only seeking each of these things individually, we'll only have what those things in and of themselves can provide.

But if we seek the Lord and His Kingdom, then we can have everything in the whole cornucopia, not only personal needs and desires in our lives, but everything else the Lord has for us. With God it's not just great relationships, or a mate, or provision, but it's also all of the much greater things He's prepared for us of and in and through Him, for ourselves and for others!

"*And His righteousness…*"

His righteousness means His "*right*-ness". This means that we are seeking all that is good and right and true, and all that He correctly Is. It is seeking and finding all that is in Him and in His Greatness.

Here's the result which comes from doing this.

"*And all these things shall be added to you.*"

As we seek Him, and His Kingdom and His "right-ness" or righteousness, all things not only might, but the Word says they **will** come to us.

We can have it all through Him. The whole Cornucopia.

This seeking isn't just passively or randomly looking for something. This isn't just an obscure hope something might happen or be revealed someday. This isn't trying to get it all by some form of osmosis. It is a conscious and conscientious decision to actively seek Him.

This also isn't just a one time, salvation type event. This is for us to do and desire and to be a part of, for all of our lives.

The verse that follows the above verse is:

> "Take no thought for tomorrow: for tomorrow shall have its own concerns. There is enough to think about in just today."(3)

This is saying that that we shouldn't be concerned with the things of tomorrow because there will be more than enough things to think about when that time comes. There are already plenty of thoughts and considerations to handle today without worrying about tomorrows "stuff".

I heard someone say once that our emotions and mind (our souls) were only designed to handle the concerns and activities and workings of a single day, not for multiple days.

I've also heard it said that 98-100% of everything you fear never comes to pass.

We have been given emotions and vivid imaginations, but they were not intended to be used for worrying. We need not be overly concerned about the things of tomorrow; there'll be plenty of time to deal with them at that time.

The above verse is telling us not to be worried or be afraid.

The words "Fear not" or "do not be afraid" appear over 84 times in the Word of God, so it must be important. The Lord doesn't want us to spend our time worrying about what might happen in the future.

There is nothing positive or helpful in this activity.

"Worry" can be defined as "prolonged fear". The natural progression of things that are worried about is to see them grow in size to the point of blocking or obscuring our true originally clear and positive view or outlook, our goals and possibilities, and things of greater importance in our lives, such as seeking and finding the things of the Lord.

So instead of spending all of our time worrying and in fear, which causes confusion and distraction and even at times torment, let us put our sights on His Kingdom and His *right*-ness. The worry will fade away and we will be able to see the great cornucopia and all that God has for us with much greater clarity.

Did Job seek, knock or ask anything of God?

No.

He spent his time in fear and worry.

Give it to God. Speak to the Lord. And leave it with Him.

> *"Casting all your cares (worries) upon him; for he cares for you..."(4)*

And you will find peace, and answers, in your seeking.

> *"Seek, and ye shall find;... For every one that seeks, <u>finds</u>."(5)*

Peace

"And the peace of God, which is beyond all understanding,
will keep (protect, comfort) your hearts and minds
through Christ Jesus."(1)

What are we really looking for when we are going through trials or adversity in our lives?

Certainly that the trials and/or adversity would end.

But if they go on longer, or if they have to play out, what do we really want, what do we really need from the Lord to get through them?

What is the purest and truest desire that we have?

Most assuredly it is to have Peace. To have Peace in the storm. There is nothing like it.

And peace is one of the primary things the Lord, the 'Prince of Peace', gives to us when we seek Him.

It is the nature of this peace that is so amazing. When it is from God, it passes or "goes far beyond" our human understanding. It is something we can know and feel, but nothing we can truly explain or "wrap our heads around." It far surpasses anything we can try to do ourselves, and there is no rational explanation for it. No reasonable person could possibly have this much calm, this amazing peace, in difficult situations.

Unless it is something that has come directly from our Creator, by His Spirit, to comfort us and to give us this relief in time of need.

He moves in our lives by and with His peace.

What do you think Job really wanted most of all while going through his trials? He was worried about everything and fear was constantly very heavy on him...

What Job really wanted, what he really needed to the depths of his being, was Peace.

This is also what we desire, and even need, in our daily life, and most definitely during times of trials.

A million dollars won't do it, though we think it will. I can tell you from experience, that doesn't work. To have a loved one back would seem to be the perfect solution for us, but may not be possible. We might believe that to have a situation resolved to our satisfaction quickly would certainly be the best outcome for us. Then again, it may not.

But the one thing that we can have, and experience from/in the Lord, anytime, no matter what is happening in our lives, is His peace. It is an amazing personal refuge, with an overflowing, overwhelming comfort, and it comes when you know and trust Him, and His love, in the midst of the storm.

Peace in the storm. There's nothing like it. And it is one of the great and amazing things the Lord has for us.

Fear and worry had blinded Job, and he allowed it to have complete control over him. When this happened, he could no longer see God. He didn't put God, and the peace that God brings, first in his life at all.

One key to hearing from the Lord and receiving this peace is to remind ourselves of how Great God is. This will start to remove fear and worry out of your mind. The mind is where fear originates, and when coupled with our imagination, can make fear far bigger than it should ever be.

Initiating ourselves to remember how great, and how much more powerful the Lord is than any of our troubles, and to realize Who our God truly is, and then to ask Him (because He is always with us), helps us receive His peace.

Jesus gave us an excellent example this, and of where to find His peace.

"Now it came to pass, as they went, that He (Jesus) entered into a certain village: and a certain woman named Martha received Him into her house.
And she had a sister called Mary, who sat at Jesus' feet, and heard His word.
But Martha was busy with much serving, and came to Him, and said, "Lord, don't you care that my sister has left me to serve by myself? Please ask her to help me".
And Jesus answered and said unto her, "Martha, Martha, you are careful (worried) and troubled about many things: But there is one good thing which you need: and Mary has chosen that better way, and it will always be with her."(2)

Mary had chosen to put aside her "busy"-ness for a time to be with the Lord. Jesus was telling Martha that this was a good thing and she too needed to do this and find His peace by being with Him.

We so many times fill our lives with being busy. What we will find is by finding rest and peace in Him, we will then gain what we need in order to go on and accomplish our goals and desires.

The Word says *"Seek peace and pursue it."(3)*

We must desire to have this peace, and seek it, and even pursue it.

Searching and seeking for God and His peace has much to do with finding it and obtaining it. This involves initiating ourselves, coupled with our faith and trust in Him (which we all have been given a measure of), and with an earnest desire to find it. This is where this peace is found.

"And let the peace of God rule in your hearts, <u>which is your calling</u>; and be thankful."(4)

We must not only **seek** peace (and pursue it), but we must **let** this peace of God **rule and reign** in our hearts.

This means that we need to initiate ourselves and allow this peace to have the highest place in our lives. We must purposefully and consciously not only make room for it, but make a high place for it, put it on the very top of all of our priorities, and to put things aside to attain and obtain it.

"Which is your calling..." We are even **called** to do this.

We must give Peace the highest place, allow it to have the utmost preeminence in our lives, and to let it rule in us, and reign over and in us, at all times and in all things, always. No matter the situation or conditions.

The second part of this verse, and knit very closely with peace, is the action and attitude of being thankful.

Let peace rule and reign in your hearts, which is your calling, "*and be thankful.*"

Being thankful helps to bring many good things into our lives, and one of those things is peace.

Being thankful, and finding Peace is so very important in our walk and in our seeking and asking. Without peace, our asking can be skewed by fears and emotions, and the way to God may not be as clear as when we are asking from our spirit and heart and from trust and peace.

This peace is available and applies as much to ordinary decisions in our lives as it does to crises. In both, fear and worry can blind us to the way and the truth in what we're looking for.

As an example, years ago a friend of mine was at a crossroad in her life, where she had to make an important decision on which way to go, which road to choose, and she had been genuinely and constantly worried about it for some time. She came to me with her concerns one day, and as we were talking, it came to me that she needed to find the peace and "rest" of God first, and if she would find His peace, and put the worry and fear aside, she would then find her answers.

The next time I saw her she ran up to me, and excitedly began to tell me how she had applied herself to finding the Lord and His Peace, and said that when she did this, the worry faded away, and when she realized that God would be there for her no matter which way she went, she found the rest and the trust, and the very peace of God she was looking for.

It was at this point that her answers came to her and it was perfectly obvious to her which way she should go. She was thrilled about it. She absolutely knew. She just had to get past the fear and the worry that was a blinding obstacle to her.

She had found her way through His peace.

"For God is not the author of confusion, He is the author of peace."(5)

I sometimes like to think of our requests being sent or going through a cylinder or pipe or a channel to the Lord. When we have peace and trust in Him in our asking, along with thanksgiving, the channel is clear and open. When we ask in fear and doubt and emotions (or blame, as Job had), we find obstacles in the way of that flow.

We always want to make sure that the channel is as clear as possible to the Lord whenever we go to Him.

Seek Him, and while doing so, find peace and let it rule and reign in your heart and life. Then, with trust and thanksgiving and you will find and receive all that you are looking for and much will be accomplished!

Another great benefit of being in that peace is that you know that you don't have to worry one bit.

Calm will come over you. It's all taken care of and you have this complete knowing that in the end, everything will be okay. It is complete trust. You may not know how or when the situation will be resolved, but you know it will be.

If you care to receive it, I believe the Holy Spirit showed me several years ago about the role of peace in our lives in the passage in His Word about the mark of the beast.

> *"Here is wisdom. Let him that has understanding count the number of the beast: For it is the number of man; and his number is six hundred threescore and six."(6)*

This verse has been the subject of considerable debate and conjecture for generations, and I can only relay what I feel had been revealed to me as a part of the understanding of it.

The number here in Revelations, is six hundred threescore and six, or 666, or the number 6, three times. The number 6 is the number of man, as this verse says, and also in Biblical numerology. The verse is talking about the beast, or the entity which will be adversarial, or the adversary of God and all that is good.

This number of the beast appears to be the number of man, three times.

What came to me was that the "beast", the number of man three times, will be prominent and preeminent in the world, and placed above the three Persons of the Trinity - the Father, Son and Holy Spirit. Instead of the Father and Son and Holy Ghost, the predominance will then be man, man, & man.

Can't we see this happening so vividly and rapidly in our society and world today? Man trying to replace God in all things and insisting that it is man alone who knows and controls it all. Consider also what is being done with AI now, and what might AI do?

I brought all this up to say that in the verse right after that one, John says that those who would be in and of the Lord would have the seal of God in their foreheads. It impressed me that one amazing aspect of this this "seal" would be Peace.

No matter what happens, no matter what awful or chaotic events may be, or may be transpiring, those who remain in and of God will have Peace and Trust in Him. They will not have a wrinkled brow, or worry on their forehead. Only peace.

The Lord, the Prince of Peace, our Prince of Peace, is there for us always.

> *"Grace to you and <u>peace,</u> from God our Father, and the Lord Jesus Christ..."(7)*

> *"Now the <u>God of peace</u> be with you all."(8)*

The original apostles knew what this was. These last two verses were written 26 times in the New Testament.

Find out about the peace of God which passes all understanding. The Father has this peace for you, and He wants you to receive it, because He knows it will help you.

You/we just need to ask.

> *"Peace I leave with you, My peace I give to you:*
> *It is not what the world tries to give.*
>
> *This is My peace.*
>
> *Let not your heart be troubled, neither let it be afraid."(9)*

His Peace.

It's in Him,,,

And it's for you.

God Rewards

"But without faith it is impossible to please God:
for he that comes to God must believe that He is,
and that He is a <u>rewarder</u> of those who diligently seek Him."(1)

There are three important parts in the verse above that directly apply to us.

The first is that we must have faith and trust in order to honor our God. It says that it's impossible to please Him otherwise.

We've talked fairly extensively about the importance of trust when coming to the Lord. The Word says in Romans 12 that we've all been given a certain measure of faith, or trust, and also that it doesn't take much of it to do great things.

I'd like to add something here to our understanding of faith. Faith is not something that is "out there" somewhere. It is not something to be acquired or to "go out and get", or to search for or get more of.

The truth is, we already have it.

We've all been given a certain amount of faith and it is already within us. It has been given to us from the Father, in just the right measure for each of us, and we have all we need to go out and use it.

He's already given it to us. All we have to do is realize it is within us, and then exercise it, grow it, and develop it into something He can use and that we and others can benefit from!

What it's saying in the first line of above verse is that faith is of limited value unless we activate it, and exercise that trust within us when we come to Him.

Which ties in with the second line in the verse above that says that if we want to come to the Lord, we must believe that He is.

*"Jesus answered and said, This is the work of God,
that you believe on Him who He has sent."(2)*

Sometimes it's real work to believe.

Jesus said that this work of God within us comes solely from believing in Him. It is a continual "work" and is an active thing, not a passive one. It is the action of believing.

We also need to keep in mind that the Father not only sent us Jesus, but also sent His Holy Spirit to us through Jesus.

The third line in the beginning chapter verse is very profound and seems to always have been hidden behind the other two. It says that he who comes to God must not only believe that He is, but he must also believe and know that God is a <u>rewarder</u> of those who diligently seek Him; that He **rewards** those who diligently seek Him.

It is saying that not only must we believe that He "is", but we must also <u>know</u> that He rewards us when we diligently seek Him. It's part of trusting Him and part of God's plan for us.

Have you developed your faith and trust to the point of knowing the Lord rewards you? Have you built your faith and trust to the point of expecting the good things of God to happen when you go to Him?

The Lord has given us plenty of faith, not only to believe, but also, as the verse says, to receive from Him. He desires this, and it's already within us!

Here is another opportunity to step it up in the Lord a little bit. Just as we clarified the word 'faith' with the word 'trust', we can also do the same thing with the words 'believe' and 'know'.

Webster's Dictionary defines 'believe' as "to take as true or real." When you've actually experienced something that you have believed, you find that you no longer just believe it, but that it changes into something else. You now know it. It is yours. You have no doubt of it. You own it.

218

In this we see that the word "believe" can be used interchangeably with the word "know".

Try using "know" in place of the word "believe" in your expressions and see what happens. I would suggest that doing this will add a greater understanding to your believing, and a greater understanding and 'knowing' to, and in, your Christian walk.

So we are to know that God rewards us. It is Who He is, and what He does. He is a Rewarder. He honors and rewards us when we seek Him.

These aren't little trinket rewards either. God is great and He rewards greatly. We find this out as part of our 'knowing' who the Lord is, and receive more as we grow to learn and understand more about Him.

The last part of our original verse says that He rewards us *when we diligently seek Him.*

We've seen this before. Let's look at "diligently seeking Him" and its meaning.

Diligently, or diligence, is defined as persevering, with careful effort, and with earnest desire, in order to attain something.

Combining these efforts with seeking, asking, and knocking directly on the Lords door, is diligently seeking Him.

Let's look at this diligence another way.

Jesus asks Peter,

> *"But who do you say that I am?"(3)*

As we talked about earlier, this is a fairly important question for us to ask ourselves.

What is our answer when the Lord asks us,

"Who do **_you_** say that I am?"

Are we, with earnest desire, spending even a little time finding out who the Lord is, who "the Word made flesh" really is? And as a result of this do we know Him well enough to know that one of the benefits of seeking and finding Him is that He rewards us when we do so? Do we endeavor to make the time to find out more about Him, despite all the things that distract us?

Doing this is diligently seeking Him.

This is where the true rewards are; when we personally seek out God and He answers us. It's amazing, and profound and most incredible when you receive knowledge of Who God is and/or what He does; and it is given directly to you in a very personal way by the Lord and the Spirit of God! And it becomes all yours. It's like the understanding of the universe has been personally handed to you, in a moment in time, and you realize that the understanding you've received is deep, powerful, profound and eternal.

There is nothing like receiving wisdom and understanding personally and directly from the Lord and from the Spirit of God. Not only is your faith (trust) built up, but the Lord shows up in you and all around you.

These rewards are great and they come when we diligently spend time listening for, and searching in and for the things and the kingdom of God.

I like to use an analogy of our "working" lives when talking about seeking God and the rewards of the Lord.

What happens when we get a new job, which will provide well for ourselves and our families and will give us a certain amount of satisfaction in life?

We look forward with anticipation to all that we will be able to do and to accomplish, and we also look forward to receiving all of the rewards and benefits that come along with it.

Don't we also at the same time make the effort to learn more about our jobs and what we are supposed to be doing in order to accomplish what we are there for? Don't we, in the process, endeavor to learn our role and how to produce results, learn how we can be more effective, how to perform better, and how to become more proficient in what we do?

This in turn has the added benefit of providing more rewards for our families and for those around us as we continue to grow in it.

What if we were to go to work and sit at our desk, or stand in our correct place or station, and do nothing all day long, all week long, all year long, and continue to do nothing for our entire time there? Then, at the end of our career we hope that by at least showing up regularly, that we will have somehow done or accomplished something? And hoping the whole time that the boss will forgive us for whatever we haven't done, and that we'll be granted a spectacularly rich retirement with great rewards...

Many times we act out our Christianity in this way. We get the job, assume the position, and then sit at our "Saved" desk for years and years, never learning what we are supposed to do, not finding out more about what we're supposed to be there for. We remain in that state, not learning or becoming experienced or proficient at all in the tools that are available to us, that have been given us to use which would produce deep and meaningful results in ours and others lives.

Because of this we miss out on many or even most of the great rewards and benefits we could have had in our lives. Yes, we go to company meetings and picnics regularly, but we still choose not to really search personally to learn more about God and our place in Him. And by doing so we are in reality deciding and choosing **_not_** to produce results in the Lord for ourselves and those who could benefit greatly by our efforts, abilities and understanding.

And in the end, despite all our non-efforts, we somehow hope that The Boss will forgive us and give us a great and rich golden "Retirement."

Well, because of His really great and amazing mercy and grace He will probably forgive us and give us a great heavenly eternal home...

...But what will we have fulfilled in our lives while we were here?

What will we have accomplished in this most important walk in the end? Will we, in this life, receive all of the true rewards that the Lord has made available for us and others here and now?

When you spend time in the Lord and in the Holy Spirit, seeking, knocking, and asking, God's Word says the answers will be found, opened, and given to you. The things of God shall be revealed to you, and you will realize amazing rewards.

Zophar, one of Job's friends said, *"Can you by searching find out God?"*(4)

Zophar's doubt was strongly corrected by God in the end, and the Lord Himself gave him, and us, the answer.

Yes, you can.

And we can have all the "finding out" we can possibly desire...

Did Job know this, and did he have faith in God during his trials?

No.

Did Job diligently seek God in it all?

No.

Job actually realizes all of this at the end of the Book of Job. He sees and comprehends all that God has shown him, he then repents, and receives all that God has for him.

He receives great and profound understanding, and his life is turned around completely; and he is then greatly and overwhelmingly rewarded and blessed.

God says in His Word that He rewards those who diligently seek Him.

We in some way believe this, but do we **know** that He is a great and true rewarder when, and as we seek Him?

Do we truly know this?

"Seek <u>and you shall find</u>..."*(5)*

Desire

"Through desire, a man, having separated himself,
seeketh and intermeddleth with all wisdom"(1)

I love this verse. The five parts of it reveal how to discover the deeper things of the Lord and how to get to the point of huge reward in Him.

"Through desire..."

Do we really want to know God? Do we really want to know wisdom? Do we really want to know the Lord who gives wisdom liberally and wants for us to have it in abundance? Do we want it badly enough to ask for it, and also believe that we will get it?

Just as in so many things in our lives, along with effort and heart, and with perseverance, comes reward.

You have to really want to. You have to have a desire that will work through anything to get what it's after. God honors that kind of desire, and especially when that focused desire is in Him. He sees it and is pleased when your desire is directed toward finding out more about Him.

"A man..."

No, it's not gender specific here, it can be anyone.

"Having separated him/herself..."

Sometimes one of the most difficult parts of all this is that you have to separate yourself. This means from all distractions, from those things that easily arise and take you away from your focus on the Lord. This is why many don't ever go into a deeper relationship with God. You must find, and you must make moments to set yourself apart. Apart from all the easy to come by distractions, whether it be work, or play, or family, or friends, or technology; anything and everything that can take you away from seeking God.

Jesus said go into a closet. It doesn't matter where, but it needs to be a place with as few distractions as possible. Even if it is just for 5 minutes, you need to want it enough to separate yourself, and God will honor that effort. There are times when you can hear from the Lord on the fly, but seeking God and communing with the Holy Spirit is far more powerful and enduring and takes separation time.

"But I don't have time..."

Go back and look at the *"Through desire"* section again.

You will find the time.

"Seeks..."

This is what this chapter, as well as the New Testament and the Book of Job in particularly, bring to light and enliven. We are admonished or shown to seek Him, His kingdom, and His righteousness. It is a state of mind, and especially a state of the heart. We are to seek, to knock, and to ask. It is the act of our heart, turned toward the Lord, and guided by the Holy Spirit.

You will find that the Spirit of God shows up when you start focusing on the Lord. The Holy Spirit of God wants to show you all about the Father.

Jesus said that it's about God <u>with</u> us, not just us with Him. His Spirit shows up when we dedicate ourselves to Him. This is a marvelous aspect and result of our seeking.

"And intermeddles with all wisdom..."

I love this part. This is the part of the experience which is amazingly deep, incredibly profound, and fully rewarding. Not only are you fully understanding the things of God which are revealed to you by the Holy Spirit, but you are going further, and even "intermeddling" with all wisdom, and with all understanding! You are in it, and handling it and applying it in and to all of Creation. You are able to involve yourself fully, or "throughly," and intimately and part of it all.

It is hard to describe the amazing greatness that this, treasure, truly is.

I also love this word "*intermeddleth*" in the original old English because it encompasses the whole of it so well. "*Intermeddleth*' just sounds the part. You are in it. Your heart and mind and soul are completely involved in the things of God, and in the things of His Creation. You are intermeddling with His great wisdom. Just as in a treasure hunt, you've searched diligently and have found what you were looking for, and more than what you were looking for! And as you find it, you gaze at it, you handle it, you joy in it and are amazed that you now can see it so clearly. You bask in the bounty of it, and in the heart thought that it has been given for you to see, and you rejoice greatly in the One Who has given it to you. This treasure of understanding and wisdom is as marvelous seemingly as your Creator Himself, and in fact is a part of our Creator Himself! It is so complete and perfectly profound.

And in it you realize you have received, and are receiving, *great* reward.

Solomon talks about this in Proverbs:

> "Happy is the man that finds wisdom, and the man that gets understanding.
> The merchandise of it is better than the merchandise of silver, and the gain of it is better than of fine gold.
> She is more precious than rubies: and all the things that you can desire cannot be compared to her.
> Length of days is in her right hand; and in her left hand riches, and honor.
> Her ways are ways of pleasantness, and all her paths are peace.
> She is a tree of life to them that lay hold upon her: and happy is everyone who retains her."(2)

God gives us wisdom through His Spirit. We all (even and especially You) can have this wisdom and everything that comes with it, and it is available for all of us to experience.

> "Listen for wisdom, and apply your heart to understanding;
> If you cry for knowledge, and lift up your voice for understanding;
> If you seek her as silver, and search for her as for hidden treasure;
> then you will understand the reverence (yirah) of the LORD

and you will find the knowledge of God."(3)

Is there anyone who doesn't want wisdom, and to be able to find the knowledge of God in their lives? It is better than anything else we can have here in this earth! As we seek God He gives us this amazing wisdom and understanding, and by seeking and finding Him, and His wisdom, we receive such great and amazing reward.

Seek for His wisdom, and the Lord will give it to you.

Another way you can move forward in your "desire" is when you give up something to seek the Father. God sees this and honors it. Our conscious acts can reveal to the Lord our desire to know more about Him.

Fasting is one of these ways we can live in that desire.

I can hear it now, "Oh no, not *that....!*"

I'm not talking about 40 days or years out in the desert wilderness or such as that. I'm talking about any time frame, and with anything you desire. Whether it be for minutes, hours or days, and whatever it is, whether it be a certain food or foods or TV or technology, or a hobby or past time, any effort, no matter how small, even if it is just one meal, or one item, or a morning or two with the Lord, seeking Him in your heart, God will honor it, and it clears the way for Him to come into your life in a much greater way.

The rewards of laying things aside for the Lord are truly great. And it is enhanced further as you replace the things fasted with spending time in His Word and Spirit.

God speaks about fasting in Isaiah,

> *"Is not this the fast that I have chosen?*
> *That you loose the bands of wickedness, that you relieve the heavy burdens, and let the oppressed go free, and that you break every chain of bondage?"*

"Is it not to give your bread to the hungry, and to bring the poor that are cast out to your house? Is it not to cover the naked, and to not hide your own errors from yourself?"

"Then your light will break forth as the morning, and your health will spring to you speedily: and your righteousness will go before you; and the glory of the LORD will be your reward. Then you will call, and the LORD will answer; you will cry to Him, and He will say, Here I am."

"If you take away from you the chains of bondage, and the condemnation of others, and speaking of vanity; and if you draw out your soul to the hungry, and satisfy the afflicted soul; then your light will rise in obscurity, and your darkness will be as the noonday: And the LORD will guide you continually, and satisfy your soul in drought, and make fat your bones: and you will be like a watered garden, like a spring of water, whose waters fail not..."(4)

Wow, what truly great reward!

I can tell you by experience that you will, by and through fasting, climb higher and deeper in the Lord more and more every time. And I've also found that when you do this, and truly give up something to seek the Lord, that you won't want to stop.

Jesus said:

"Up until now you have asked nothing in my name: Ask, and you will receive, that your joy may be full."(5)

Desire the things of God. Jesus says ask for this, and you will receive it, in a very fulfilling way.

The Lord wants us to have all of these treasures in our lives, including full and overflowing joy.

And it all starts with our desire to know Him.

Knock

Knock

"Knock, and it shall be opened to you...
for to him that knocks, it shall be opened."(1)

Knock is also an action word.

Knocking is an action which results in actively presenting one person to another. It is a conscious act which initiates the communication of one with another.

In this context, I would suggest that it is the action necessary to present ourselves to God.

There is a degree of boldness which goes along with knocking on a natural door. It is the same with knocking on God's door, but with God we can have a confidence and faith, and know that our God and Lord will gladly open His door to and for us.

> *"Let us come boldly unto the throne of grace*
> *that we may obtain mercy,*
> *and find grace to help in time of need."(2)*

Did Job knock, and go boldly to God, to the throne of His grace?

No.

Can we knock, and go boldly to God, to His throne of grace?

Yes!

I had a friend who in a particular time in life was being barraged continually by all manner of difficulties and challenges. She was a sweet, quiet, meek (teachable & kind) person, but was going through an awful time.

She eventually asked God for an answer, and in prayer she saw the story of Moses and the rock in the wilderness, and that the only way Moses was going to get life giving water out of that rock was to strike it with his staff, as God had told him.*(3)* She realized from this that she had to begin to be much more active and more assertive in her spiritual life, and began to strike back against that which was obstructing her. She had to do it, and did it, with determination, with God's Spirit, and with prayer.

She became proactive in her asking by the Spirit of God, and as she did this, the difficulties and obstructions began to diminish, and then became no longer a threat, and eventually they were gone!

She had also become stronger in the Holy Spirit in her life, and realized what it was to be actively knocking and going boldly to Gods throne of grace, by using and exercising the spiritual authority given to her by the Lord. She heard, acted, overcame and conquered. She was still meek and sweet, but had become much stronger in the things of the Spirit of God.

We all have the ability to do this. The Lord has created us to knock, and when we act on what He's given us, He says that the doors shall be opened wide to us. It doesn't say that it "might be" or "could be" opened, it says that they _shall_ be.

There is no mold or model or formula for any of this. We are all created by the Lord marvelously. He knows each of us, and He knows our characteristics and personalities individually. Part of our walk in the Lord is realizing who we are in Him and how we can come to Him, and come into our own in Him, in our own very individual way, the way He created in us in the first place.

The Lord looks forward to this and is blessed by it. He loves it when we come to Him in Spirit and Truth, and via who we are in Him. We can't pretend to be someone else, we must be ourselves. That's how He knows us and that's how He hears us.

Let me also say that going boldly to Gods throne does not necessarily mean going loudly. It means going with confidence in who you are, and who you are in Him. For this we need to know personally who we are in God. We need to know that the Father works through us, and all that he has given us, and through our own personality, that we might learn and know Who He is and who He created each one of us to be.

"If you, being evil, know how to give good gifts to your children, **how much more** *shall your Father which is in heaven give good things to them that ask him?"(4)*

I've found that a helpful way to look at God, as we knock, is to see Him as the Perfect Father, one who would be everything you always wanted in a natural father in your heart and life. Our human fathers cannot be everything to us by their/our own human limitations,,, but God can be everything to us.

Can you picture in your mind, soul and spirit (heart) how it would be going home to your perfect Father? How would you enter?

Wouldn't you knock and go right in with the confidence and trust and the love of a loved and loving child, knowing that He would receive you with joy and a desire to help in any way He could? Wouldn't you go right in, and right up to your great Father with joy, and boldly and marvelously right up to your Father with Whom nothing is impossible?

Wouldn't that be wonderful? You would be warmly and greatly welcomed and you would know that it was good and strong and life giving just to be there, to feed at the table, and to know that you will always be blessed and that you will always come out far better off than you went in!

His home would always be open for you to remain, for you to rest in His refuge, in His strong tower, for as long as you needed, until you were ready to go out and face the world again.

And you could ask for any good thing and He would give it to you.

Wouldn't that be amazing?

Your Father God has this very thing for each one us, and all we have to do is learn of Him,,, and knock.

"To him that knocks, it shall be opened..."(5)

Ask

You Have Not Because You Ask Not

"...You have not, because you ask not.
You ask, and receive not, because you ask amiss..."(1)

In the verse above, James says that we don't have or that we don't receive, because we don't ask.

If we don't ask, why don't we?

Let's go back to Job for a bit.

We see in the Book of Job a number of factors at work as to why Job never goes to God. He had made a decision, possibly both consciously and unconsciously based on uncertain conclusions by which he decided that he just wasn't going to go to God.

Let's take a closer look at some of the possible reasons why he didn't.

"Behold, I cry out of wrong, but I am not heard: I cry aloud,
but there is no judgment..."(2)

Job says, "...I cry out of wrong, but I am not heard...". God was in fact listening the whole time, hearing every word.

"God has cast me into the mire, and I am become like dust and ashes.
I cry to You, and You do not hear me: I stand up, and You regard me
not."(3)

As we said earlier, this was probably as close as Job came to asking anything of God. Job "cried out" from of his misery, out of his emotions, and "out of wrong".

He never actually directs this cry as a request to God nor does he ask anything of God. He again says that God doesn't hear him, but this is only a supposition, not the truth.

He isn't asking anything of God here either, and is certainly not asking anything by faith and trust in Him.

Later on we will look at and compare asking God out of our emotions, vs. asking out of faith and trust in the Father, which are two very different things.

What we'll see is that it's not fervent emotions that God hears, but a fervent and trusting heart.

> *"Let Him take His rod away from me, and let not His fear terrify me: Then would I speak, and not fear Him; but it is not so with me."*(4)

There are several important things to see in this verse. We talked previously about how Job's 'pachad' fear of God completely overruled his worshipful 'yare' understanding of who God is, and we can see this plainly here. It was Job's own fear that was terrifying him, and because of that he said he wouldn't speak to God.

Do we let our emotions and fears rule over us, especially when faced with the unknown? Do we lose sight of the truth at times because of this? Are we afraid to go to God? Does this type of fear cause us not to seek or approach Him, as it did with Job?

Let's look at something else very apparent in this verse. Job is saying. "If God will remove all this from me <u>first</u>, then I will ask and will not fear."

As we looked at earlier, we find that Job is not asking anything of the Lord. What we do see here is Job is actually putting conditions on God and his going to God before he will even consider asking. He is setting the terms and/or the priorities for God to fulfill, before he will ask God anything.

Do we put conditions on God? Do we suggest that God do something or some things first before we go to Him? Have we decided, as Job did, that we are not going to go to God until certain events happen, or until God does something?

If we do indeed put conditions on our going to God, that we would have Him do some thing or things first before we come to Him, then where does our trust come in? Where is our faith, which is required in all of our asking?

235

So Job actually has this backwards. It should be that we ask first in trust, and then be ready for God's answer, not to have God do something first and then have faith later. Job sees this at the end of the Book of Job when he finally goes to God, and God then answers and blesses him greatly.

We also saw this earlier in the 'Relationship' chapter as to why Job didn't go to God but it is worth looking at again here.

> "Only don't do two things to me: then will I not hide myself from You.
> Withdraw Your hand far from me: and let not Your dread make me afraid.
> Then You can call, and I will answer: or let me speak, and You'll answer me..."(5)

"If _You_ stop doing two things to me, I will stop hiding from You."

Again, the verse not only shows that Job hasn't come to the Lord and is intentionally hiding from and refusing to go to God, but it also again suggests that unless God makes the first move, he will not go to God at all.

Job is making any communication with God conditional upon God resolving his demands first.

Also keep in mind that the two things Job is asking God to do, or stop doing, God is not doing whatsoever, and they are due solely to Job's own perceptions. The Lord's hand has not been upon Job at any point in the story. Not once. Job has falsely assumed that God has put these afflictions on him, and has based all of his accusations and misery upon that assumption.

And neither has Job's great 'dread' and 'fear' been given to him by God, but has been brought on by his own reactions and emotions during all of this. Yes he was afflicted by Satan, but the dread that Job has, has not been given to him by God.

So Job has allowed his emotions to overwhelm him and then finds himself in this fearful state, being encompassed by the inevitable results of his own fears, thoughts and emotions.

This is all because Job has not gone to God and maybe has not even really known his God at all.

He has not used his faith and trust in his God as his Refuge and as his Deliverer. His overwhelming emotions are not tempered or redirected at all by the truth of knowing Who God really is in his life.

Can the Lord change Job's perceptions, even when Job is blaming Him for things He is not doing?

In the end the Lord indeed does do this, and gives Job the information and the opportunity to change his perspective completely by showing him the truth of his situation, which Job finally sees and then acts upon.

But throughout all this time and up until the point God intervenes, Job has continued to make everything much more difficult on himself, and has prolonged his misery, all by not going to God.

Do we also do this?

Do we not go to God, and then inevitably make it much harder on ourselves by not doing so?

Do we knowingly or even unknowingly make conditions on our going to God, and/or leave it all up to Him to make the first move?

Do we not come to Him because we don't really know Who He is? And because of this do we "hide ourselves" from Him, and not make our requests known to Him?

Job is asking for God to remove things that are already in his own control, and which are being perpetuated by his erroneous assumptions and decisions, and by his self-proclaimed pachad (scared) fear of God.

Wasn't that up to Job to remove? Even with his faith?

Isn't that up to us to do, by our faith?

Sometimes it all has more to do with our own faith and trust than any efforts that could be made by our Lord God.

Many times it's our own "stuff" that gets in our way, and it's this "stuff" that prevents us from clearly seeing or asking anything of the Lord.

We have been given a certain amount of faith by God. What have we been given this faith for? Why do we have it?

Think about this for a minute.

Couldn't it be that we have it so that we can come to Him and ask?

Selah... Let's continue.

Even though the Lord knows our thoughts entirely, we must exercise our faith and trust by asking.

If we don't ask, He may not have our complete faith or trust to work with. And with nothing to work with, and nothing to honor, we may find that we have nothing to receive.

Let's put it this way. The Father knows what we need before we ask,,, ***but we still need to ask!***

I believe this is where many times we fall short. How many times have you thought or wished something would happen?

When we don't actually ask anything of the Lord by trust, and then when we don't subsequently receive any answers for our 'non'-questions, we default to "I guess God doesn't love me/us, and doesn't want to answer my prayers", or "It must be God's will",,, when we haven't even asked anything of Him in the first place!!!

There also seems to be something in our nature that many times doesn't want to ask, or is hesitant to ask. Whether it is because of fear or pride or timidity, or even our own personality or nature, or anything else we've talked about, these are things we can and need to overcome.

If we can see clearly enough, we can initiate ourselves to overcome whatever holds us back, in order to open the door to the Lord and receive the things of God.

Jesus said in Revelations,

> "Behold, I stand at the door and knock: if _any_ man hear My voice, and opens the door, I will come in to him, and will sup with him, and he with Me.
> To him that overcomes will I grant to sit with Me in my throne, even as I also overcame, and am set down with my Father in His throne."(6)

We need to overcome anything that causes us not to go to Him, or not to ask Him, by intentionally initiating ourselves, opening the door, and asking. The Lord and His Spirit are there to help us do this. And They will help!

As we talked about before, the Lord has created this whole system in which we must come to Him first in order to receive. This applies to our asking as well. It's just how it is.

So if we don't make the effort to ask, if we don't take an active role in our requesting, and we take a passive "whatever will be, will be" position, according to Gods system we are not really making any requests at all. If we don't ask, can we then really expect to receive anything from Him?

Especially when He has repeatedly and specifically told us, over and over and over, to ask...

One of the reasons the Father wants us to know Him is so that we would know His Refuge and Strength. He knows we will need this in our lives and He wants us to know that these things are available to us.

> "Casting all your cares (worries and concerns) upon Him; for He cares for you."(7)

Asking and casting all of your cares on Him means giving the Lord all of your concerns, worries, thoughts,,, everything, so that in return you might have His peace.

Cast your cares upon Him....

The Apostle Paul also admonishes us to pray or ask without ceasing. We can do this by creating an environment in our lives where we naturally and automatically come to God with everything.

I have intentionally refrained from writing a chapter about asking amiss because the more important consideration I want to get across is that we need to ask. There are those who may be overly concerned as to how they ask, and by not wanting to ask amiss, they might subsequently never ask at all.

The important thing we need to know is that we need to ask, and know that the Father will also help us ask through His Son and His Spirit.

We also need to know that we don't have to be perfect with our asking, as the Lord and His Spirit know our hearts, and will help us with this.

The Book of Job shows us that we should not hide from God, that we should not let our emotions get the best of us, and that we should come to Him sooner rather than later. It shows us that we should initiate ourselves, trust Him, and ask.

These are the elements and conditions given to us. If we decide, consciously or unconsciously, not to go to God, it may very well be that our answers will remain far from us.

But if we find out more about God, learn that He wants us to come to Him, and always go to Him and ask, the Lord says that He will hear and that we will have those things which we desire.

"Don't forget to say your prayers...!"

This phrase has been said for generations to our children before bedtime. Not only is it a good thing to teach our children, but the greater action of this applies even more so to us.

Don't forget to say your prayers.

Don't forget to ask.

Don't children ask their parents for things all the time?

How much joy do we as parents get when we are able to deliver on their asking?

The Lord loves our asking.

And He loves to Give.

Our Heavenly Father, His Son, and His Spirit all say "Ask".

Just do it.

Just ask.

<u>Make</u> your requests,

And <u>*make them known*</u> to God.

> *"So far you have asked nothing in my name:*
>
> *Ask, and you shall receive, that your joy may be full."(8)*

Jonah

"Then Jonah prayed..."(1)

What Job did by not going to God and by saying that he was hiding from God reminds me very much of the events and reactions of another Old Testament person and example - Jonah.

You remember Jonah. God asked him to do something and he went the other way.

Here's a brief recap chronologically.

God asks Jonah to go to Nineveh and tell them of their impending doom unless they repent and get things right. Jonah's response is to hide from God (sound familiar?), so he gets onto a ship going in the opposite direction of Nineveh. Soon after the ship leaves port a great storm comes upon the ship and its crew. The wind and waves become so strong that it strikes fear into even the seasoned sailors who were on board. They had never seen such a storm and decided that it must be someone's god or gods who were causing it and that they'd better find out who it was and take care of it before they all died. So they cast lots, which pointed to Jonah who was sleeping in the hold of the ship. When awakened by the crew, Jonah admits that he is running away from the Lord God of Heaven.

> *"Then were the men exceedingly afraid... and said to him,*
> *"Why have you done this? What must we do to you that the sea*
> *may be calm for us?" for the sea was tempestuous.*
> *And he said unto them, Take me up, and cast me into the sea;*
> *and the sea will be calm for you..."(2)*

Though Jonah tells them to throw him overboard so that the storm will cease, the crew throws everything else overboard except Job and keeps trying to bring the ship to land. They soon realize their efforts are in vain and then, after apologizing to God, they cast Jonah into the sea.

The waters immediately become calm, and the Word says that after this happened the crew greatly feared God (yare, reverential fear is used here) even more.

> "Then the men greatly feared (yare) the LORD, and offered a sacrifice to the LORD..."(3)

So Jonah up to this point has been tossed about in a boat, persevered in a violent storm knowing that God has asked him to go to a certain city for a purpose and has gone the other way, and has now been thrown into the sea.

> "...cast into the deep, in the midst of the seas; and the floods were all around me: all Your billows and Your waves passed over me."(4)

God then has very big fish ready, a whale, which swallows Jonah, and he ends up inside its belly for three days and three nights. It was most certainly nasty inside there, with seaweed wrapped around him, dead fish everywhere, no place to stand, and it was pitch black and surely stank. While he is there Jonah goes on a wild and crazy ride, probably upside down half the time, with unbearable ocean pressures on him, to the depths of the sea, for hours and days on end.

> "The waters compassed me about, even to the soul: the depth closed in around and about me, the weeds were wrapped around my head. I went down to the bottoms of the mountains; the earth with her bars was around me forever..."(5)

Then... I just love this next verse. After all that had happened, after the floundering ship, then being thrown into the ocean, then after being swallowed by a whale and dragged to the depths of the sea and back, the Word says,

> "Then Jonah prayed..."(6)

Well I guess so. It's about time!

> "When my soul fainted within me I remembered the LORD: and my prayer came to the Lord, and into His holy temple."(7)

"And the LORD spoke unto the fish, and it vomited out Jonah upon the dry land."(8)

So only _after_ he has gone through all of these horrible things, Jonah finally prays to the Lord God, Who then delivers him from all of this.

Jonah then goes on to perform what God had asked him to do and the whole city of Nineveh is saved.

Does this story sound familiar? Doesn't it sound a lot like the story and events of Job?

God seems to have had a certain expectation of both Jonah and Job.

They both hid from the Lord while going through their individual and considerable events, trials and afflictions.

And neither of them prayed,,, until after they had gone through so very much.

Both Job and Jonah had the opportunity to go to God, and if they had done so, they would have ended up with good and productive outcomes, and gained much, without having to go through their extended trials.

So why did it take both Jonah and Job so long to pray?

Why does it take us so long to pray?

They both had the opportunity to go to God right away…

And so do we.

Ask

"Ask, and it shall be given you...
for every one that asks receives..."(1)

Okay, so if we are seeking the Lord, and we are knocking, and entering into His throne of grace, what do we do next?

Then we abide. And ask.

The above verse comes just before this next one.

> *"...how much more will your Father in heaven give good things*
> *to them that ask Him?"(2)*

Let's look once again at how we perceive God.

What good things do we want for our children?

Everything, of course.

How much greater does God, as our giving Father, want to give good things to us?

Do we know God as a giving Father who wants to give us greater gifts than even we do as mothers and fathers to our children? Do we know that the Lord wants to give us so much more?

Do we really know that God desires good for us?

> *"...for love is of God; and everyone that loves, is of God,*
> *and knows God... for God is love."(3)*

See this. If we know what love is,,, this very love is the love of God, and because we know love, we know God.

He does all that He does through Love because He *is* Love. The Father comforts and delivers and restores and heals and is a great strength for us, all by and through His Great Love.

He also desires that we would share these things, and His Love, with others, and He moves through us, for them, when we do.

We looked at this verse earlier.

> *"God has not given us the spirit of fear, but of love and of power, and of a sound mind."(4)*

This also applies to our coming to Him and being with Him and asking.

We should come, not in fear, but in love, knowing that He is powerful Love. We should come in strength in Him, knowing His power and His strength and His Spirit are all within us. And we should come boldly, knowing that He has given us a complete and sound mind to know Him.

We need not come to Him asking in emotions and worry, but we can come soundly in faith and trust, knowing Who He is and the power of those things which are of Him.

The Word tells us that the Father knows our thoughts and our words even before we speak them. We know this to be true and understand that the Lord knows all.

Let us again keep in mind that even though the Lord knows our thoughts even before we ask, *we still need to ask.* God has set it up this way. By asking, we exercise our trust, our faith, and He is able to honor and answer us in our lives.

> *"Again I say unto you, that if two of you shall agree on earth about anything that they shall ask, it shall be done for them by My Father which is in heaven."(5)*

One day we will know how much we could have accomplished just by asking...

> *"Ask, and it shall be given to you... for everyone who asks, receives."(6)*

Do we know this?

> *"And all things, whatever you will ask in prayer, believing, you will receive."(7)*

Do we know that when we ask and believe (know) we will receive?

And again Jesus says,

> *"And in that day you will ask Me nothing. Verily, verily, I say to you, whatever you will ask the Father in My name, He will give it to you.*
>
> *Up until now you have asked nothing in My name: Ask, and you will receive, that your joy may be full."(8)*

"In that day..." What day is Jesus talking about? Is it someday in some other era or generation, or maybe in heaven? Is it for some other world somewhere? Is it just for back then?

No.

It's right here, right now, and for us in our lives!

As we've seen, Jesus, the Word, talks at length about spending time with the Lord and His Spirit, and speaks often about asking and praying.

Are all of these verses where Jesus talks to us about asking just idle conversational expressions by our Lord, for no one in particular? Are they just random hypothetical thoughts and suggestions that maybe only He and God might understand, but which really didn't or don't apply to us, and don't have any meaning or bearing on our lives in this world? Were they just off-the-cuff remarks only to be said and not really considered or followed? Were these just words that apply to some make-believe people or place somewhere else, to people other than us?

Or are they absolutely true and the reality being that He desires us to be walking in this in our lives, for ours and others great benefit!

Our Lord knows we can have all these things, and desires that we would know and realize the greatness of asking and receiving all He has for us, here and now, in this time, in our lives. Now.

Another reason that Jesus wants us to know God, and the things of the Father, and to ask, is not only to build our faith/trust, to lead and help others along the way, which happens naturally as we dwell in Him, but it is also that **our joy**, our very own personal joy, would be _full_ and overflowing because of it!

He created us and knows exactly what will bring us true joy, and the Lord very much wants us to have that joy. He created us for it, and it for us!

So many times in life we don't really know what will bring us complete joy. But the Lord does, and He's showing us how to have it through His Word and His Spirit and through asking and receiving.

Jesus says that by learning and knowing more about the Father, more about Himself, and more about the Holy Spirit, and by exercising our faith, we will be able to have more and more **life** in our lives.

That by asking we will receive, others will be blessed, and our joy will be full and even overflowing.

The Lord wants us to spend time in Him, and to ask. The results will be wonderful and sometimes amazing, with accomplishments both in our lives and in others' lives in this world.

That it would be commonplace in our lives.

And that our joy would be full and complete.

Here and now!

Asking Effectively

"The effective fervent prayer of a righteous man avails much."(1)

So now that we know to ask, how <u>do</u> we ask?

We can certainly ask what we will very simply from our heart and with faith in the power of God. It doesn't have to be long, and it doesn't have to be perfect, and indeed cannot be as we are not perfect. Not even close.

And the Lord hears us.

Our Father knows our thoughts, even before we ask,,,

But we still have to ask.

We have to initiate ourselves, and ask.

I believe that as with anything we do in this life, we have a certain desire to try and be more effective in whatever we do.

It's the same thing with the things of, and going to, God.

Let's talk about how we can become more effective in our asking, as we come to know the Lord more and more.

> *"Be careful for nothing; but in everything by prayer and supplication, with thanksgiving, <u>let your requests be made known to God.</u>"*(2)

Remember back in the first chapter of Genesis God "spoke" everything into existence?

> *"And God <u>said</u>, Let there be light: and there was light."*(3)

In the beginning the Father created it all by speaking it.

"God said..."

God didn't "think" all this into existence. He didn't "hope" it all into existence. He didn't somehow "will" it into existence.

The Word says He **spoke** it into existence.

If our Almighty God spoke the things He desired which became this great physical and spiritual manifestation, it follows that we too need to speak those things which we desire, and we are not somehow exempt or exonerated from doing so.

Along these lines, in order to make our requests or petitions <u>known</u> to the Father and in order to receive, we too need to *verbalize* our requests and desires and/or questions.

I know that this may step on some preconceived ideas that we have about going to God, but I believe it's important that we realize this in order for us to be more effective in our asking.

I might also suggest that any other form of asking without expressing it in words from our hearts, remains only a thought, or an idea, and is not a deliberate and intentional request being "made known" to the Lord.

There is power in our words, especially as children of our God. Not only is there power generated by speaking these requests, but our words at the same time have the additional effect of confirming our belief and trust in Him which we need to have along with our asking, which gives the Lord the opportunity to act upon the things spoken.

This is how the Lord of All, the God of Heaven and Earth has set things up.

Speaking your requests gives them traction.

King David said,

"Hear my prayer, O God; listen to the words of my mouth."(4)

Thinking or hoping a request in our heads is easy. Speaking it from our hearts takes a much more concerted and involved and intentional effort and belief in what is actually being said or asked.

Try this. Take just a moment and think of a request, something to ask the Lord.

Now go ahead and speak that request. Actually speak it out loud.

Go ahead, try it. I'll wait...

If you've tried this then you've just realized that speaking it is a whole different form of expression than just thinking it. You have to initiate it (like knocking) and you really have to consider and formulate what you're asking in order for you to verbalize it, and then you have to make the effort to actually speak it.

At the same time, it takes a certain conviction and decision to believe in Who you are speaking it to in order to speak it out loud.

I believe that God honors this spoken effort of a request when it is accompanied by even a seed of faith and trust, and this effort not only gives the Lord something tangible to use and to answer, but at the same time you are also building your faith as part of the asking!

> *"For verily I say unto you, that whoever will <u>say</u> unto this mountain, Be removed, and be cast into the sea; and will not doubt in his heart, but will believe that those things which he <u>says</u> will come to pass; he will have whatever he <u>says</u>."(5)*

"Whoever will say..."

That's anyone who believes.

Also by doing this, we are exercising trust and faith in Him, and by speaking our requests to Him we initiate the process for amazing and powerful answers in and from our God.

Along those same lines, let's look at something else Jesus said about asking or praying.

> "But when you pray, enter into your closet, and when you have
> shut the door, pray to your Father which is in secret;
> and your Father which sees in secret will reward you openly."(6)

We have forever misconstrued this verse as somehow suggesting that our prayers can or should be done silently, or in a closet, when this is not what the Lord is saying here at all.

Jesus is saying that when we ask or pray, we should endeavor to go to a private place to do it.

Jesus is using a closet as an example of a place that is without distraction, a place where you can say what you desire without interruption or concern for any others who might see or hear you.

Going to Him in secret is what He sees, and your heart and prayers _spoken_ in secret are what He hears. It is by being in these quiet places and by asking or praying that we not only show our trust in Him, but we initiate and activate the process of moving in and with Him, and then receiving from Him.

The Lord sees these actions in secret.

Notice what else the Word says at the end of the last verse.

"Your Father which sees in secret will reward you openly."

What are we looking for when we ask? Are we just throwing our words out there just to say them? Or are we sincerely asking and looking for answers and results and response/reward in and of and from the asking?

And there it is in the verse above. The Lord says He will reward us openly.

Jesus goes on to say,

> "But when you pray, do not use vain repetitions, as others do: for they
> think that they will be heard for their much speaking. Don't be like them:
> for your Father knows what things you have need of, before you ask Him.
> So after this manner pray: Our Father who is in heaven, Holy is Your
> name. Your kingdom come, Your will be done in earth, as it is in heaven.
> Give us today our daily bread.
>
> And forgive us our trespasses, as we forgive those who trespass against
> us. And lead us not into temptation, but deliver us from evil: for Yours is
> the kingdom, and the power, and the glory, forever. Amen."(7)

Notice that Jesus introduces what we know as the Lord's Prayer by
telling us not to use vain repetitions. Vain repetitions are words that are
said by memory, by rote, out of habit, without consciously realizing
what is being said.

Do we sometimes make our prayers, and maybe especially the Lord's
Prayer, a vain repetition? Do we make it something that is just said,
without consciously realizing all of its marvelous meaning?

Jesus is giving us this very important precursor so that we do not make
this prayer, or any prayer, just words repeated or done solely out of
habit. Jesus is saying that the form and number and repetition of a set of
words doesn't profit, or doesn't help us much at all.

But by asking in earnest, consciously with our own words, from our
hearts and spirit, we can know that our asking is heard and can and will
be far more effective in gaining marvelous answers in our lives.

The Lord's Prayer is a powerful and soothing reaffirmation of Who God
is, and a beautiful message in itself, one that can be very reassuring and
comforting in times of need.

But we still need to make sure that this prayer, along with any and all of
our other asking, doesn't become just a repetition of words said without
thought or understanding in our lives.

What else does Jesus say when He describes praying this prayer?

He says, *"After this manner pray..."(8)*

He is saying that we should meaningfully include the things He is about to tell us in our own asking or praying, but that we should use this only as a guide.

We are to use our own words, and our own 'believing', to make this and any other prayer our very own to God.

He wants us to have and know these things more and more in our lives. He wants us to **own** what we say and all that these words encompass.

He is not asking us to repeat a set prayer, but He is showing us the manner of how we should pray, and how we should ask, from our own heartfelt belief in our Lord and with our own understanding and words.

Here's an example of a prayer "after the manner" of the Lord's Prayer...

> *Our God, Our Father, my God and my Father, Who abides in heaven, far above all things, all principalities and powers, Who created all things by Your great wisdom, Great and Holy and hallowed and honored are You, and Your Name, in this earth, and in my life.*
> *Your Kingdom will come, and even is here now, and I desire that Your will be done, here on earth, in my life, and in my family's life, and in those all around me, as it is done in heaven. Give us this day our daily bread, which is not only food for our bodies, but even more importantly the food of Your Word in our lives, that we might live this life abundantly in You. Thank You Lord Jesus for being the Bread of Life in my life and in my family's life, that we would hear You and Your Word in all things.*
> *And as I walk in the life that You have created for me, and receive of You, please forgive me of any wrong I have done, knowingly or unknowingly, as I make all effort to always forgive those who do wrongfully against me, completely taking away any hard feelings or bitterness I might have and removing it far from me.*

254

Please help me to see temptation coming and help me to avoid it completely, and help me keep far from it, and help me to never accept or consider acting on being tempted, and thank You for always giving me a way out of all temptation so that I will not hurt myself or others.

Please deliver me from any and all evil, protect me from deceit, and from harm, and keep myself and my family from evil and from harm all of our days.

For the Kingdom, and the Glory and the Honor and the Power, and the Majesty, and the Greatness are all Yours; You alone are Lord God Almighty, and I praise You and worship You with all of my whole heart, my whole mind, with all of my soul and all of my strength, and in my life and my family's lives and in the lives of those around me.

You alone are Almighty God forever and ever and ever. You are the great I AM, Who WAS, and IS, and IS to come.

Thank You Lord for all of these things, and for all that You do and are in our lives, and thank You so much for being my/our God and Savior and Lord and King..

In the beautiful and powerful Name of Your Son, Jesus, Amen

(Amen = So be it).

This is just an example of what Jesus was saying, <u>*after the manner of*</u> the Lord's Prayer.

Try saying the Lord's Prayer in your own words. Make it your own. Re-create it in your own life. This will bring not only a new meaning to this prayer for you, but as you do, it will also bring a new level of belief and trust and faith in the Lord into your life and walk!

Oh, and by the way, as concerning praying/asking out loud, have you or anyone else ever prayed the Lord's Prayer silently?

Immediately after Jesus shows us about how to pray the Lord's Prayer, He gives us another key to how to ask.

As Jesus is describing how to pray, He then gives an analogy about a friend who goes to another friend's home at midnight and wakes him up to ask for some bread for his late-night guests who had just arrived.

> *"I say to you, though he will not rise and give it to him because he is his friend, but because of his <u>importunity</u> he will rise, and give him as much as he needs."(9)*

I have always considered this verse to mean that the man who was awakened will give his friend the bread, not because he is his friend, but because he has to go out of his way, at an <u>inopportune</u> time, in order to get up and give the friend the bread.

But this is not what the Word is saying here.

The word Jesus uses is "<u>importunity</u>", which means to be "persistent in asking or even demanding, or to urge, or entreat, or ask repeatedly".

So what this verse is *really* saying is that the friend making the request is being very persistent in waking the other friend up, and letting the friend know that he earnestly desired something, and also what that something was.

It is because of this <u>intentional entreating and requesting,</u> the mans <u>importunity,</u> that the friend got up and gave the man the bread.

The word "tenacity" might also describe this persistence and a "never give up" aspect of importunity and of intentional request. The verse above is saying that having tenacity when making our requests known to God is an effective way to ask, to pray.

At times I think that the Lord wants to see how much we really want something before we can receive it. He sees and likes our tenacity as it relates to Him. It is a reflection of the level of our desire in our asking.

One of Jobs positive traits was that he had tenacity in his integrity, and he just wouldn't give it up.

In the "Initiate Yourself" chapter, we looked at many who initiated themselves, came to Jesus, and received something great in their lives.

They all had a degree of tenacity. One of the characteristics they all shared was a certain "importunity" in their asking.

And they all received what they truly desired.

Jesus is saying here to have tenacity in your asking. Be tenacious. Don't give up. Have a "stick-with-it" mentality if you earnestly desire what you're asking for. Ask even if it's in the middle of the night, like the man desiring bread from his friend. And don't worry, you won't be waking God up. He never slumbers or sleeps. The Father sees and hears, and He answers. Like the friend with the bread.

If we trust the Lord and His Word, we can have a confidence in God and the things of God in our asking.

> "And this is the confidence that we have in Him, that,
> if we ask any thing according to His will, He hears us:
>
> And if we know that He hears us, whatever we ask,
> we know we have the requests that we desired of Him."(10)

This is one of my all-time favorite verses. Do we know, and are we confident that the Lord hears us, and by this answers us?

We will talk about this again later on, but one of the things we can indeed fully have in our walk is this confidence in Him hearing us and answering us!

God showed Job, and through Job shows us that He hears us. He hears our requests and prayers. When Job realized this and then asked, the Lord brought his answers in a beautiful and bountiful way.

Do we know that the words we speak are very important and have great meaning? Do we know that the Lord hears our words?

Job had it in his mind that God would hear nothing he said. But God was listening to *everything* he said.

- ➢ The Lord hears our desires to know Him.
- ➢ He hears our desire to be with Him and in His presence.
- ➢ He hears our thoughts.
- ➢ He hears our desires.
- ➢ He hears and sees every act of Love.
- ➢ He hears every prayer from an open and grateful heart.
- ➢ He hears every thankful heart.
- ➢ He hears every word.

He hears you.

Do you spend time with God? Do you pray? Do you communicate with the Lord and His Holy Spirit? Do you know that God hears you? What do you ask for? Do you ask Him for the understanding of Who He is? Who Jesus is? Who the Holy Spirit is?

Do you ask for His Wisdom in your life? Do you ask for wisdom for your family, and for your friends? How about for your enemies?

If you don't, then it is time!

Taking a related tangent here, a friend of mine asked me once "When do you know to pray for someone's healing?"

When do you know to pray and to ask?

Whole books have been written on this, and the short and long answer of it is...

Always.

Always pray and ask.

Your faith in asking could be the very difference in a person's receiving, whether it is healing or anything else.

All you have to do is trust the Lord and the Holy Spirit and He will guide you as you pray.

Don't worry about, or try to decipher beforehand if it is to be or not. You may not know at the time, and it is not up to us to see it first, but it is up to us to ask, that it may lead to the Holy Spirit's moving in their lives.

Many times, it is only after I have begun to pray that the Holy Spirit shows up and moves in it all in great and amazing ways.

The Lord uses us, and the Spirit of God moves in us and others when we initiate ourselves and ask. We may not know when the Lord will move in someone's life in a cool and miraculous way, but we can have faith that if it is at all possible, it will be done by our God in heaven.

The Word says that we can have what we ask.

So ask. With God, all things are possible. They really are.

The Holy Spirit will lead you to pray in various ways and directions, and it will always be for good in people's lives.

And the Lord and the Holy Spirit will begin to work through you in amazing ways.

I have initiated and have been part of many, many great and awesome answered prayers, without ever knowing beforehand what would happen. People who were in the hospital to die have walked out healed and well. Families are miraculously brought back together. Captives and those who are bound or blinded are truly set free. The enemy abiding in homes is cast out... as the darkness **must** flee when the Light is brought in. Darkness _can't stay_ where the Light of the Lord is!

Peace and relief and healing and Life have been and are brought to many. And God is personally and magnificently glorified!

When the Father, Son and Holy Spirit move, it is always amazing. And it's always worth the asking.

We find that there are two types of situations we can pray for in our lives. There are those things which can and will be changed if we ask and pray, and there are times when we might not receive the answer we are looking for, as there are things that occur and remain as part of our human element and experience,.

How do we know which is which?

Again, we may not know at the time which is which, but the only way we will find out is by asking. The Spirit of God surely knows, and He helps us and guides us when we ask, and then brings to pass those things which can be changed. When we ask in faith, we are doing our part.

Conversely, what if we don't pray? What if we don't ask, especially when the Lord has said over and over for us to ask?

Does this possibly hinder or remove an opportunity for God to move on someone's behalf, and/or hinder or remove an opportunity for our joy and others joy to be full?

Think about this.

If we don't ask, are we actually choosing **not** to do what the Lord has said for us to do? Does this also mean we are choosing **not** to walk in what He has said we can and should do by our asking?

God uses us to bring life and encouragement and even miracles, large and small, to others. He uses our words, and our trust in His words, and in His Name and in His Spirit to accomplish these things.

Do you know that the Father has given a certain amount of faith to you for a reason? Do you know that you already have enough faith needed for these things of God? Do you know that this faith is activated in and by your asking?

This is faith given to you to grow in, to live in, to bring to you and others real joy, and to truly glorify God in.

It is the Father, the Word and the Spirit who actually do the works. He just asks us to ask, and to believe.

> *"Jesus said to him, If you can believe, <u>all things are possible to him who believes.</u>"(11)*

Not only are all things possible with God, but all things are possible to those who believe...

Do we see the answers to our asking every time? Not necessarily. We may not always see the results.

Does the Lord show us the answers to our asking at times? Yes!

Isn't it worth the asking, even if you're not sure of the outcome? Isn't it worth using the amount of faith that you have to possibly make a difference in someone's life, that God may join His power to your portion of faith to heal or deliver, or to give wisdom and/or any number of great God things He brings to someone or into a situation?

Yes. It's worth it.

Every time.

Prayer changes things. 'Asking' changes lives.

And if you can receive it, asking and prayer also effects eternity. It affects lives. Forever.

Jesus says over and over, *"Ask..."*

> *"For every one that asks, receives..."(12)*

There is great power in connecting with God in asking, in prayer.

The Spirit and the Power of God are there.

Asking Fervently

"Elijah was a man with the same passions that we have,
and he prayed earnestly that it might not rain:
and it didn't rain on the earth for three years and six months..."(1)

Let's talk about a fervent prayer for a moment.

Fervent prayer can be described as asking earnestly, with your heart and spirit, in faith, and with intent.

Many times people confuse fervent prayer with asking with emotional intensity. There is a big difference between asking with our emotions, even heartfelt ones, and asking intently or earnestly with trust and confidence in the Lord.

The words 'intense' and 'intent' have two very different meanings.

Asking out of our emotions with <u>intensity</u>, or passionately, are many times be based solely on our feelings, on our own perceptions of what is right or wrong, and what we think should happen according to only us. These emotions can be very strong and even overwhelming to the point of obscuring the truth at times.

Asking fervently or earnestly in faith and with <u>intent</u>, is based on trust. It considers the purpose and the task at hand. Asking in this way comes from knowing the Lord and knowing how to come to the Fathers throne room of grace, with boldness, to ask and receive of Him, knowing that He hears you and will answer you.

James writes about this as pertaining to receiving wisdom in the New Testament,

> *"If any of you lack wisdom, let him ask of God, Who gives to all*
> *men liberally, and upbraids not; and it shall be given him.*
> *But let him ask in faith, nothing wavering. For he that wavers is*
> *like a wave of the sea driven with the wind and tossed.*
> *Let not that man think that he shall receive any thing of the Lord."(2)*

James is saying two very important things here.

First, he is saying that we can receive an abundance of wisdom from God, Who gives to all men, to everyone liberally, and doesn't upbraid, which means He doesn't look at our faults as to whether we deserve to have it or not.

Wisdom is one of the greatest things we can receive from God. We all have the opportunity to receive abundant wisdom from the Lord, as we will see a little later on.

Secondly, James is saying in this verse that if you're not asking in and by faith and trust, then you may be asking by some other means, by something that wavers, such as emotions. Emotions and emotional asking can be easily moved and swayed by feelings and our own perceptions, as mentioned earlier. Asking from a wavering emotional state is not what God is looking for, and as James says, can even be an obstacle or hindrance to our receiving anything from God.

The Father has set it up where we need to ask in faith and in trust, and we need to know that believing and knowing is far more important than feelings or emotional states in order to receive answers to our requests.

This doesn't mean that our emotions are bad, they are not, and are an important part of our nature and our lives. In fact, many times our emotions can actually lead us to the point of going to God and asking.

What we need to realize is that when we get to that point of asking, we need to move out of our emotions, out of an emotional state, put them aside, and get into a pure faith and trust mode, and then go to God, to His throne room of Grace, knowing that He hears us, and knowing He desires to give good things to those who ask Him.

Jesus gives us a perfect and wonderful example of this in John chapter 11. This also is another one of the most iconic and repeated phrases in the Bible.

John is talking about Lazarus' death, and the profound effect it has had on everyone, including Jesus.

John writes in verse 35,

> "Jesus wept."(3)

Jesus Himself was not exempt from emotions, as we may sometimes might think, and as we see here.

Can these emotions be considered some sort of weakness? No.

Jesus had a deep compassion for the people and for the friends of Lazarus and for their loss. Jesus came to earth as a man and also shared our emotions and emotional states. Again, emotions are an integral part of our human nature and experience.

But Jesus also knew how God works and what the Father wanted to do in this situation. Four verses later, in verse 39, Jesus intentionally moves from the emotional compassion He is in, and moves into the realm of the Spirit of God. He then begins to operate fully in God's system of faith and trust. When He does this, He ushers in a great miracle and brings Lazarus back to life.

I would suggest that He may not have done this, or have been able to do this, if He had remained engaged in an emotional state. But by putting aside His emotions, and moving into the place of faith and knowing the ways of God, He was able to do this great miracle by the Spirit of God.

And according to the Word, so can we.

> "Elijah was a man with the same passions as we have, and he prayed earnestly that it might not rain: and it didn't rain on the earth for three years and six months. And after he prayed again it rained, and the earth brought forth her fruit."(4)

This verse says that Elijah was a man just like us. He had the same emotions, feelings, concerns, joys and troubles, as we do., and **his** prayers were answered, and powerfully too!

Elijah knew who his Lord was, knew the power of his God, and how to ask for these things. This was a prayer of faith and of trust, and not wavering.

What this verse is saying is that we too can receive from our asking, just as Elijah did, and if you will, just as Jesus did, and we too can have great results and answers from God when we ask earnestly in trust, knowing our Lord, and knowing how and what our God can do!

It's not fervent or earnest _emotions_ that God hears, it's fervent and earnest _trust_ in Him.

Here's another example.

> *"And one of the crowd said, Master, I have brought to You my son,*
> *who has a dumb Spirit... and often it casts him into the fire and*
> *into the waters to destroy him:*
> *but if You can do anything, have compassion on us, and help us."(5)*

Notice that compassion does have a part to play. It is an emotion, and from the love of God.

And Jesus answered,

> *"If you can believe, all things are possible to him who believes.*
> *And right away the father of the child cried out, and said with tears,*
> *Lord, I believe; help me in my unbelief."(6)*

The man said "I believe", which he did, but then even more importantly he showed his very real and conscious concern about his own level of trust. He was completely honest with the Lord, including in his emotions, and at the same time he showed his earnest desire to believe and trust all the way, even in those circumstances.

The man in this story was saying that he didn't have perfect faith, but Jesus acted on the faith he did have, and his son was healed.

> *"...according as God hath dealt to **every** man the measure of faith."(7)*

Again, keep in mind we don't have to be perfect, or have perfect faith in order to receive the things of God.

We aren't perfect. God knows this. He created us, and gave us a certain amount of faith, and He wants us to use it, for ours and others benefit.

> *"For verily I say to you, if you have faith (trust) as a grain of mustard seed, you can say to this mountain, move to another place; and it shall move; and <u>nothing</u> shall be impossible to you."*(8)

The Lord created us, and He knows that we only need to act on the "measure of faith" He has already given to each one of us in order to receive from Him.

We already have it, and have it within us. We just need to know it, and live in it, and use it and exercise it.

God has given us this faith so that we can, not by our emotions, but by earnest and "intent" faith, and with full confidence, go to Him,,,

...And Ask.

...And Receive.

Availing Much

"If you abide in Me, and My words abide in you,
you shall ask what you will, and it shall be done for you.
In this is my Father glorified, that you bear much fruit;
and by this you will be My disciples."(1)

"By this you will be my disciples..."

Jesus often tied greater works and bearing much fruit together with asking and receiving. Bearing much fruit means doing some thing or things, such as asking, that produce or accomplish results.

The above verse is talking about asking, or praying, so the "fruit" it describes would be the results that are produced when we pray, and receive the answers to our prayers. It is the "works", the good things that are produced and/or accomplished by our asking.

The first part of the verse says that we will be His disciples if we abide in Him and His words abide (live) within us. This is a conditional statement. We will bear much fruit, or as we said earlier, we will produce results, if His Word abides, or lives, within us, and as we abide or live in Him.

Our part is only to make sure that His Word lives within us...

...and that we ask.

The Word then says that we'll be able to ask what we will, and it will be done for us. That's a pretty big statement. But remember we are the sons and daughters of a pretty big (very Big) God.

So what is the purpose of all this asking? The purpose is so that we will bear much fruit, and from this fruit all involved will receive the great rewards which come with it.

The verse also says that one of the great results of us bearing fruit is that the Father is glorified.

How is the Father glorified?

He is glorified when we ask, and when we receive answers. He is glorified when others see or receive of His great works, done through our asking.

"**_By this_** you will be my disciples…"

By what? By us asking and bearing fruit, by us receiving results and answers to our prayers, by us receiving and sharing all that He has for us and for those around us.

For some reason we often feel that our faith, our trust, should only be in our asking.

But in His Word, the Lord says that we actually exercise, or work our faith and trust by knowing that we will also _receive_ what we have asked for!

So according to the chapter verse, we need to not only have faith and trust in our asking, but we also need to have faith and trust in Who He is and in our receiving from Him. By this we will bear much fruit, and will be His disciples, and by this, God is glorified!

In order to bear much fruit we need to know in our hearts that we will receive answers to our requests from the Lord.

> "And this is the confidence that we have in Him, that,
> if we ask anything according to His will, He hears us:
> And if we know that He hears us, whatsoever we ask,
> we know that we have the requests that we desired of Him."(2)

How great is that! And not only can we know this, but this means we can also have absolute _confidence_ in it, and in Him. I love this verse. This is faith and trust, All-in.

Oh and by the way, the benefits of receiving answers from the Lord are completely profound and wholly amazing and will not only bring you great joy but it will also build your faith exponentially…

The Holy Spirit and the Word inside you coupled with excercising/using your faith and asking will not only avail, produce and accomplish much, but it will also grow your faith and your trust in Him as you see the Holy Spirit at work in yours and in others' lives!

So now having heard all of this, how do we find out these things for ourselves?

We will find these things first by learning about and seeking the Lord. We learn and know these things by actually spending time (abiding) in Him, searching and seeking His Words to us, and by going to Him in all things.

By learning and understanding, and by residing in Him, you will start experiencing these things of the Lord for yourself.

You will then find that you will have opportunities to bear fruit, as the Holy Spirit will use you and the Lord's Words inside you to bring life to others around you.

This all comes from the Lord, and the only condition is that we believe and exercise our faith and trust in Him. We are to Ask, and then trust Him for the answers.

Jesus said,

> *"Verily, verily, I say unto you, he that believes on Me, the works that I do he will do also; and greater works than these will he do; because I go unto my Father.*
> *And whatever you shall ask in My name, that will I do, that the Father may be glorified in the Son.*
> *If you shall ask any thing in My name, I will do it."(3)*

Jesus is saying here that if we ask, in His name, He will do it.

Okay, that's strong. As we talked about before, are these just idle words by Jesus?

Or is He actually expecting us to really walk in these things?

269

Let's take a look at that last verse a little more closely.

Jesus says that if we believe, if we trust and know, then we will do even _greater_ works than He did.

So how is this possible? What can possibly be greater than raising someone from the dead? Or what's greater than healing the lame or the blind? Or breaking the chains of bondage? Or freeing people from the captivity or hardship they may be in?

We already know that we'll never be actually greater than the Master, the Son of God, the King of Kings and the Lord of Lords. And nothing can top giving sight to the blind or bringing the dead back to life, and all the other amazing things that He did.

So, what is Jesus saying here?

Jesus is saying that we will indeed be able to do the works that He did, but the "greater" works Jesus is talking about is not doing better or more powerful things than He did, but it is doing the same works in greater **_number_**. He is talking about quantity, saying that we will be able to do more of these works, more in number, with the authority He has given us, in His Name, because He has gone to the Father.

And because He is now with the Father, we have a direct connection to God through Him, and by and through His Spirit, and He is able to do these works through us!

What is the only pre-requisite to all of this? That we truly believe in Him, in the Lord, and in all He can do, with and through us.

> _"And these signs shall follow them that believe;_
> _In my name they will cast out devils; they will speak with_
> _new tongues; They will take up serpents; and if they drink any_
> _deadly thing, it will not hurt them;_
> _they will lay hands on the sick, and they shall recover..."(4)_

And it all comes from knowing Him.

Some folks will say that these works were only for the 12 original disciples. I know this to be untrue from many personal experiences, but as for proof in His Word, we need to look no further than when Jesus sent out a group of seventy men to do these same works.

> *"After these things the Lord chose seventy others, and sent them in two's into every city and place where He would go. Then He said to them, The harvest is truly great, but the laborers are few: pray to the Lord that He would send laborers into His harvest.*
> *Go your way; behold, I send you as lambs among wolves...*
> *And heal the sick that are there, and say to them, the kingdom of God has come near to you."(5)*

> *"And the <u>seventy</u> returned with joy, saying, Lord, even the devils are subject to us through Your name!"(6)*

These 70 were not the original disciples, and yet they did the very works that Jesus did, and were amazed at all they were able to do in Jesus name. They were able to do all that He said they could!

Jesus gave them the authority to do these things, and when they believed in Him and in the power of His Name, they did them.

And He said that we too can do these greater things because He is now with the Father.

He has given us this same authority as believers in Him and in the power of His Name. These 'signs and wonders' have been happening for generations, and continue to happen all over the world today. They've happened with me and with many others all around us; they happen when we seek the Lord and ask, and as the Spirit of God moves and answers.

This is the "bearing much fruit" and "greater works shall you do" that Jesus was talking about.

And by this God is greatly glorified.

Here is another interesting perspective to consider about all this. The original chapter verse that says if we abide in Him, and ask, that we will

271

receive and bear much fruit, and God will be glorified, and that _by this_ we will be His disciples.

So, conversely, doesn't this mean that if we _don't_ abide in Him, and if we _don't_ ask, then we _won't_ bear any fruit; and then if we _don't_ bear any fruit, God will _not_ be glorified, and then also if we _don't_ bear any fruit, and God is not glorified, then we will **not** really be His disciples?

Hmmm. Think about that for a minute.

Jesus was filled with the Spirit beyond measure. He had it all. We do not necessarily have it all, but He also said over and over that we can ask and receive and have access to these things in His Name.

The ability we have to do these things lies in knowing Jesus and in knowing the greatness and authority and power that is in His Name. It is in Who _He_ is, and what _He_ has given to us. All we have to do is believe. And ask. And receive.

> _"You have not chosen Me, but I have chosen you, and have ordained you, that you should go and bring forth fruit, and that your fruit should remain: that whatever you will ask of the Father, in My name, He may give it to you."(7)_

We again see Jesus talking about results, and that the Father is glorified when we ask and receive and bring forth fruit (accomplishments) which come from our asking, in Him.

One of the greatest things about all this is that the Father and the Son and His Spirit do all the works. They always have. All we have to do is avail it by believing and asking...

> _"These things I have spoken unto you in proverbs: but the time will come when I will not speak to you in proverbs, but I will show you plainly of the Father."(8)_

When is that time?

That time is now. He is showing us plainly of the Father, by His Spirit.

272

So is Jesus talking about this "asking" as asking others, or asking your friends (Job), or asking your wife, or your work associates, or your Facebook friends, or your kids, or your Sunday school class these questions?

No.

He's saying go directly to the Lord and the Spirit of God will show you.

Spend more time in the Lord, and ask the Lord about these things and for these things. When this is done with even a tiny grain of faith, of trust, it produces results, small or great and full of wonder, in your life.

Then also comes an amazing rejoicing in God... and rejoicing through and in you. God is glorified, others are blessed by it, and your joy becomes full to overflowing.

> *"But I have called you My friends; for all the things that I have heard of my Father I have made known to you."*(9)

Jesus calls us friends... Don't we spend time with our friends, and when we need something that they are able to provide, don't we ask them?

We are friends of our Lord Jesus and He calls us and desires to show us the things of the Father God. He said that we should ask of the Father by His Spirit through Him and by His name. And we will receive.

In the Word, the Bible, we find that God was greatly glorified when amazing things of God happened to people. These great things were life changing and something those who received couldn't hold in.

These things are still amazing and life changing today, and these "greater" things are still happening all around us!

The effective, fervent prayer of a person who believes, and asks...

...Avails and accomplishes much.

In the Spirit

*"Paul said to them, Have you received the Holy Ghost
since you believed?"(1)*

One of the greatest things I have ever done in my walk with the Lord is to believe the Word, and by doing so, in addition to receiving salvation and the Spirit of God, receiving what the Word says is an additional baptism that is the power of the Spirit of God.

There is nothing like it.

> *"He that believes in me, as the scripture has said, out of his heart shall flow rivers of Living water. (But this He spoke of the Spirit, which they who believe in Him should receive...)"(2)*

The King James Version says 'out of his belly', but the Greek translation of this is "out if his heart", or "his spirit", which clarifies and describes this infilling so very well.

The rivers of living water are words of life from the Lord, in us and through us and powerfully into ours and other's lives. They are tangible elements of truth and life and love which bring the things of God alive and into our lives, and into the lives of others.

When you receive this "infilling", you personally see the things of the Father in a much clearer and much more profound way, and even more is revealed to you as you seek Him.

Notice in the above verse that Jesus says that this is for all who already believe in Him, and that it is something that all believers _should_ receive.

This means that a believer, in order to grow closer to God, ought to, or should take advantage of this, though it is not absolutely necessary to do so.

It is for those who desire more of the Lord.

Many people, even whole generations, have lived their lives without receiving this power of the Holy Spirit, but I can tell you by experience that if you do receive it, it will, for the rest of your days, marvelously enhance and exponentially enliven your entire walk with God.

Many Christian leaders have never experienced this or don't know it well enough to teach and minister on it and to help others to realize all that it encompasses.

Because of this there are many Christians who don't know much about this baptism, and therefore haven't realized what Jesus was saying here. They don't know what John and Paul were talking about to Christians in the lead verse and in the New Testament, and all the good that comes with it.

This is unfortunate for the body of Christ because this baptism, or infilling, is an amazing and a wonderful revealer and magnifier of the things of God.

Many people are told that it was only for the disciples of old, and not for today.

This very same misunderstanding about the Spirit of God happened back in the apostles' day too.

> *"He (Paul) said to them, have you received the Holy Ghost*
> *since you believed?*
> *And they said to him, We have not even heard that there is*
> *any such Holy Ghost."(3)*

Today, many have heard of the Holy Spirit, but have not heard of all that He does and all that we can have, and do, and be, in Him.

The Spirit of God, or Holy Ghost is the third person in the Trinity along with the Father and Jesus.

As we looked at earlier, Jesus said He would send a Comforter in His place to show us all things.

Jesus taught that this is a good thing, and that we should recognize and receive the Holy Spirit, and allow the Lord to show us more of the great and greater things which God has given to us, one of which includes receiving the power of the Spirit of God.

> "But wait for the promise of the Father, which you have heard of from Me...
> For John truly baptized with water; but you will be baptized with the Holy Ghost..."(4)

> "You will receive power after the Holy Ghost has come upon you: and you will be witnesses to Me both in Jerusalem and Judea..., and (everywhere you go) to the uttermost parts of the earth."(5)

These are the words of Jesus to his disciples, but they are also for us and apply to anyone who believes. The Lord wants us to have this additional empowering so that we might understand more, and to be able to share and move in all of the things of God with those around us through the Lords' amazing and magnificent Spirit, and by doing this we spread a greater understanding of God to all the earth!

> "Now when the apostles who were in Jerusalem heard that Samaria had received the Word of God, they sent Peter and John to them: who, when they arrived, prayed for them, that they might receive the Holy Ghost:
> (For as yet the Spirit of God had come upon none of them: they had only been baptized in the name of the Lord Jesus.)
> Then they laid their hands on them, and they received the Holy Ghost"(6)

Notice that these people already believed and had been baptized in the Lord Jesus. They _then_ received the power of the Spirit of God through this subsequent transfer.

Again, it is for anyone who believes.

The Apostle Paul speaks several times about the *"doctrine of baptisms"*(7) in the New Testament. He intentionally uses the plural form, meaning more than one.

We are baptized when we receive the Lord into our lives. It is a truly amazing thing and is the "Hello" we talked about earlier in this book.

At this point of "Hello", we receive the Lord and Savior Jesus Christ into our lives. We receive Jesus and realize His Lordship, and our own spirit is connected with the Father through His Holy Spirit.

This is when we believe that He is, and all that He did, all so that we might know salvation and His new covenant with us, that we might be able to receive the things of the Father into our lives.

We are connected to the Holy Spirit at "Hello", and our spirit is connected to His. We can then live the rest of our lives knowing the Lord's salvation and live a life as unto God.

We are also many times physically baptized in or with water at some point in our lives. This is done after the manner of John the Baptist baptizing those in his day. It was John who baptized Jesus. It is a great symbolic and spiritual event, and one that can be of great promise in and for our lives as well, and as an important milestone we can point to in our Christian walk.

We can also receive at any time this baptism of the Holy Spirit, which is an infilling, or a fulfilling, in and of the Spirit of God. We then receive the power of the Holy Spirit into our lives, and we are connected to the _power_ of the Spirit of God.

We then have the opportunity to learn and receive of the greater things of the Lord that are made available to us, as we seek Him. It brings us to the deeper aspects of the Lord, to greater things that can be realized and understood and activated in our lives through Him.

This again may be foreign to many, but if you initiate yourself and reach further toward and into the things of God, the Lord and Spirit of God Himself will show you of all that He has for you, and all that He is!

This 'infilling' is not intended to heighten your emotions, or make you do crazy things. The purpose is to take you to a deeper, wider, higher understanding and place in the Lord.

277

Once again you don't have to have this baptism in the Spirit for the Lord to hear you. He does that for everyone who believes.

But the clarity and depth and profundity of the Word, and His word to us and you, and the power of God that comes with the baptism in the Spirit of God can and will bring you much nearer to Him. It will vividly show you the way to the answers you are looking for, and it is certainly worth seeking and realizing in your life.

These things concerning the Spirit of God are written in the Word, and brought to us by Jesus and the Holy Spirit, so that we might grow and understand and know the greater things of the Father. As we continue to seek the Lord and His Spirit, we will discover truths such as these which will bring new and profound understanding to us.

The depth and width and height and length of all that the Father has for us are there for us to receive; and are far greater than we can even imagine! And we have just scratched the surface...

Endeavor to seek more about God, more about His Son, and more about His Spirit.

Seek and you will find.

Knock and it will be opened to you.

Ask and you will receive.

And when you do, you will find that asking in and with the infilling and the power of the Spirit of God will avail so much more.

And you will find yourself much nearer to God.

And Be Ye Thankful

"Be worried for nothing; but in everything by prayer and supplication
<u>with thanksgiving</u>, let your requests be made known to God.
And the peace of God, which goes far beyond all understanding,
will keep (defend, maintain, keep safe) your hearts and minds
through Christ Jesus."(1)

One of the biggest keys to being effective in all of our asking and in our subsequent receiving, is being thankful.

Do we see that Job was thankful?

Not until the very end when he realized he could be.

There is one absolute cure for misery. It is being thankful. Misery departs when gratitude and thankfulness are present and realized.

One question that many may contemplate is how can you be thankful when what you're going through is very, very hard?

The answer is that it may not be easy, but it is very possible.

Let's go back to Job.

Is there anything that Job might have been able to be thankful for?

This is where our human nature kicks in and in our commiserating with the man, we feel that Job had nothing to be grateful for at all. Indeed he had lost a large portion of his wealth, which some of us can relate to. And he had lost a portion of his health, which again many of us can relate to at times in our lives.

But in actuality there were many important things he could have been very thankful for.

He could have been grateful for his friends who came to him, even though they gave him a very hard time. He was still alive. He had food.

279

He still had material things, including his house and household (it was only the eldest brothers house that was destroyed), he had his land, and his clothes (he wasn't naked as he had said), he might have been thankful for his wife, he had no broken bones or internal injuries, he had his eyesight, hearing and speech, use of his hands and limbs, and had his bodily functions.

Could Job have been thankful for anything else? If you want to take this a step further, God gave him a very long list of things to be thankful for in Gods first soliloquy. The beauty of the stars, the majesty of the oceans, the clouds above, the greatness of the earth, light and darkness, "the treasures of the snow", flowing waters, lightning and thunder, the glories of the morning, the intricacies of frost and ice, the rain and drops of dew. This first soliloquy very well may have been an additional perspective, from God, to show Job what he could indeed be thankful for.

Could Job have been thankful for all of God's creation in his life? Yes.

Sometimes we feel as if we have to search long and hard for things in our lives to be thankful for, though in truth they are not far from us at all. We too can be very thankful for these things.

> "Whatever things are true, whatever things are honest,
> whatever things are just, whatever things are pure, whatever
> things are lovely, whatever things are of good report; if there be
> any virtue, and if there be any praise, think on these things...
> and the God of peace shall be with you."(2)

Being thankful puts us in an entirely different frame, or state, of mind and more importantly, a different state of "heart" if you will. It brings peace. It takes our minds off of us, and it looks at a bigger picture in and of our lives.

Having this attitude of thankfulness is important too as we seek and knock and ask, as it puts us automatically into a better condition or position in which to ask and receive.

It opens up and clears the channels and the flow to and from our God.

"Let us come before His presence with thanksgiving..."(3)

And let us also remember to be thankful after we have received from the Lord.

"As Jesus entered into a certain village, ten lepers met Him, and stood afar off: And they lifted up their voices, and said, Jesus, Master, have mercy on us.
And when He saw them, He said unto them, Go show yourselves to the priests.
And it came to pass, that as they went, they were healed.
And one of them, when he saw that he was healed, turned back, and with a loud voice glorified God, fell down on his face at Jesus feet, giving Him thanks: even though he was a Samaritan.
And Jesus said, were there not ten cleansed? But where are the other nine? No one else returned to give glory to God, except for this stranger?
And He said to him, Arise, go your way: <u>your faith</u> has made you <u>whole</u>."(4)

There is a big difference between that which the nine received and what the one man who returned to thank the Lord received. The nine were cleansed of the leprosy, which was indeed a great thing in itself, but the man who returned to thank Jesus was "made whole", or made complete, which is a far greater thing. He received healing in not just his body, but in his whole life as well.

We receive more when we're thankful, and it is also evidence of our faith in Him.

Lord, help us with our asking, help us to know that our prayers have been heard, and answered, and help us to be thankful, even as we ask.

"And let the peace of God rule in your hearts, to which you are also called; <u>and be ye thankful</u>."(5)

Let us remember to always be thankful,,, even, and especially, in the hard times.

Wisdom

Ask for Wisdom

"If any of you lack wisdom, let him ask of God,
Who gives to all liberally... and it shall be given to him."(1)

So now that we know how to Seek, Knock and Ask, what do we ask for?

Solomon, the son of King David, asked God for wisdom.

"The LORD appeared to Solomon in a dream by night: and God said,
Ask Me what you would have Me give to you."
And Solomon said... Give me an understanding heart... that I may discern
between good and evil. And it pleased the Lord that Solomon had asked
this.
And God said to him, because you have asked for this, and have not asked
for long life or for riches for yourself, nor have you asked for death to
your enemies; but you've asked for understanding to discern judgment;
Behold, I will give to you according to your words: I will give you a wise
and an understanding heart; wiser than any before you or after you.
And also because of this, I have also given to you the things that you have
not asked for, both riches and honor... And if you will walk in my ways, I
will give you long life."(2)

Because Solomon asked for wisdom and understanding and also for discernment, and did not ask for riches of material wealth or harm to his enemies, God gave him the wisdom he asked for, as well as abundant riches, great honor and long life.

And Solomon is considered to be the wisest man ever.

Solomon himself writes in Proverbs that one of the most important things we can receive is wisdom.

"Wisdom is the principal thing; get wisdom: and get understanding.
Exalt her, and she will promote you: she will bring you to honor when
you embrace her. She will give you an ornament of grace and a crown
of glory will she bring to you."(3)

Solomon also describes the benefits...

"Happy is the man who finds wisdom, and the man that gets understanding.
For the gain of it is better than silver and better than fine gold.
She is more precious than rubies: and all the things that you can desire cannot be compared to her.
Length of days is in her right hand; and in her left hand are riches and honor.
Her ways are pleasant, and all of her paths are peace.
She is a tree of life to those who lay hold upon her: and happy is everyone who retains her and is guided by her."(4)

When you receive wisdom you understand completely the beauty and perfection of what these verses mean!

We talked about wisdom earlier in the Seek chapter, but let's look it again in a little more depth.

What actually is wisdom?

Wisdom simply put is applied understanding. Wisdom personally received and realized is a complete understanding of the nature of a thing as it applies to a given situation. It brings with it a perfect and profound understanding of an idea, a person, a situation, or whatever it is applied to.

Where does wisdom come from?

"Who has put wisdom in the inward parts? Who has given understanding to the heart?"(5)

"For the LORD gives wisdom: out of Him comes knowledge and understanding...[And when you receive it] you will then understand righteousness, and judgment, and equity; and every good path."(6)

Though we would like to think that somehow we generate wisdom from our own wonderful selves, the truth is that wisdom comes only from our Creator, the Lord, and His Holy Spirit.

Wisdom is the application of understanding given to us by the Lord and His Spirit, in moments of time, and is amazing truth and perspective of a particular thing.

What are the clues, or the evidence that something is wisdom? How can you tell when it is wisdom?

> *"Wisdom from above is first pure, then peaceable, gentle, and easy to be entreated, full of mercy and good fruits, without partiality, and without hypocrisy."(7)*

Let's look at this verse.

First, wisdom from God is pure. There is nothing that needs to be added to it. It stands on its own and many times, after it is spoken, it is followed by complete silence, as there is nothing more that needs to be said. It is inherently profound and stands alone in all of its application.

We have all felt or known this wisdom in our lives. We all know those times when something comes to us and we immediately understand the whole of it, and when we speak it, it fits perfectly on its own into a given situation.

Wisdom has been given when we understand or say something and realize it is immediately beyond our selves. At times it seems to come to us, and out of us, out of nowhere. We may think that we have somehow conjured it up out of our own amazingly clever ability or produced it from our wonderfully wise selves, but I would suggest that if we look at it honestly and clearly, we will find that we may not have come up with it at all, but it has come to us as wisdom from the Father by His Spirit through our own spirit.

This can happen even with funny and incidental things, but I notice this most vividly when speaking into people's lives about the things of God and/or when relating or sharing with my children, especially during important events in their lives. In these times, out of my heart and mouth can come these great truths that are exactly right for the given situation, and I sometimes wonder how such a thing was even said.

I then realize that such a perfect illumination could only have come so genuinely and easily from the Father, the Lord, and His Spirit.

These truths are pure. There is nothing we can add to them to make it any better.

They are also peaceful and come across peacefully and easily. There is no strife to be found in them whatsoever. Even though the events surrounding a situation may not be peaceful, and in fact may even be extremely and even wholly chaotic, these truths provide a peace and a knowing and understanding directly into the moment and/or situation.

Wisdom is also gentle, easy to be received, full of good things, and fruitful things. It is exactly right.

I always thought that the statement "*easy to be entreated*" in the verse we are looking at meant 'easy to be received', but the word "entreated" actually means "*easy to ask for.*" This fits ever so well with what we've been talking about in asking God for wisdom and His truths.

Wisdom is easy to ask for.

Wisdom doesn't take sides, is not hypocritical, and it stands on its own. There is no pretending in it at all, it is just perfect, and in it is complete Truth.

> "Behold Lord, You desire truth in the inward parts: and in the hidden part of me You will have me to know wisdom."(8)

The Lord wants us to know and to have wisdom in our lives.

So who can have this wisdom?

Anyone. Anyone who desires it can have it.

How do we get this wisdom?

> "If any of you lack wisdom, let him ask of God, Who gives to all men liberally and upbraids not; and it shall be given him."(9)

God wants us to have wisdom, and He wants to give us His wisdom. The Word says that we can ask for it easily and the Lord will give it to us liberally, or abundantly.

And He won't upbraid, which means He won't rebuke or punish us, or find fault in us asking for it, or for receiving it. The Lord desires for us to have His wisdom, and knows how very important it can be to and for us.

If we desire wisdom, the Word says we can obtain it, and liberally, in great amounts, and as much as we can receive.

And all we have to do is believe, and ask.

The verse continues...

> "But let him ask in faith, nothing wavering. For he who wavers
> is like a wave of the sea driven with the wind and tossed.
> Let not the man that wavers think that he shall receive any thing
> of the Lord."(10)

This verse once again ties asking and receiving, in this case about receiving wisdom, with having faith and trust in the Lord. He is saying that we may not be able to receive if we don't use or exercise our trust in Him.

We all have a certain amount of faith... it doesn't have to be much; we just have to use it.

Seek wisdom and ask the Father and Spirit for it. Ask the Lord what He wants you to see, and you will.

God makes wisdom available to us and gives it to us liberally when we set ourselves to hear and understand, and as we initiate ourselves to know Him.

Ask the Father for wisdom, and He will give it to you...

As much as you can possibly hold.

God's Presence and His Rest

"Come to Me, all of you who labor and are heavy burdened,
and I will give you rest.
Take My yoke upon you, and learn of Me; for I am patient and
humble in heart: and you will find rest for your souls.
For My yoke is easy, and My burden is light."(1)

We've all heard this verse, probably a gazillion times. It truly sounds wonderful, but have we ever really looked at it to see what it says? What is really being expressed here?

The first part is fairly obvious:

"Come to Me, those who are burdened, and I will give you rest."

The Lord is saying I am here for you and if you come to Me, I will give you peace and rest.

We need to seek this rest, and we need to find His Rest. It is similar to His peace we talked about earlier. If we seek it, and seek Him, we will find His rest for our soul.

Much can be written about finding 'rest' in God. It is often the very thing we need, and that we need more of, and more often.

It has much to do with having the Lord as your fortress, as your refuge and strong tower, as a place where you can go and be safe from all the forces and pressures in and of the world.

Know the refuge and rest of God. Rest in His power and strength. Even if you go there for only a moment, or for a time, or for however long,,,

Go there. You will be renewed in all that you do.

"Take My yoke upon you..."

At first glance this may sound as if you are giving up something, or being restricted or bound by something somehow.

But it is not.

His yoke means being connected to, and connecting with the Lord. By doing this, you are not being limited, but you are actually gaining everything.

Having this connection to and with the Lord will bring you into amazing rest.

"And learn of Me"...

The Lord is saying that He wants us to learn of Him, and to know all that He is. This book talks much about this very thing. He knows that this is the means by which we can find the entrance and indeed the way into His presence and His rest.

I think that God sometimes hides meanings behind words that our human pride might consider as not very attractive, or something other than what it truly means, such as meek being weak, or lowly being of low estate. We have to get past our pride to see some expressions as they really are. In the next verse, the original "meek" and "lowly" often distract people and may intentionally obscure the real meaning, maybe even to see if we really want to find out the truth. "Meek" and "lowly" are better expressed and defined as "patient and kind", and "humble in heart" which are excellent attributes. I have replaced "meek and lowly" with these here.

"Learn of Me, for I am patient and kind, and humble in heart, and I will give you the rest for your soul that you are looking for..."

Jesus is patient, and kind, and humble at heart...

"For being connected with Me is easy, and what I have for you is not at all heavy, but it is light."

Give up your heavy burdens for lightness.

"Connect with Me, and learn of Me", the Lord says, "and you will find rest". Not the worlds rest but a much greater rest,,, His Rest.

As part of this rest in God, we draw closer to Him, and He also draws closer to us.

> "Give yourselves to God.
> Resist the devil, and he will flee from you.
>
> <u>Draw near to God, and He will draw near to you.</u>
> Cleanse your hands, and purify your hearts...
> Humble yourselves in the sight of the Lord,
> and He will lift you up."(2)

One thing Job desired was this rest. Did he submit himself to God, draw closer to Him, and humble himself before the Lord?

Not until the very end of the Book.

The beginning part of the verse or action described above is resisting the enemy. Resist that which is evil and anything which is not "good".

This may also include poor attitudes and responses to negative influences that may be present or present themselves to us. These things need to be strongly and earnestly resisted.

There are some prerequisites or conditions that can be learned about and accomplished, but the main thing for us to know, and always keep in mind, is that as we put God first, and as we draw closer to Him, He will indeed draw closer to us.

Ask the Lord what you can do to be nearer to Him... and then go there!

> "But they that wait upon the LORD will renew their strength;
> They will mount up with wings as eagles; they will run, and not
> be weary; and they will walk, and not faint."(3)

We all want to have our strength renewed and to be continually strong.

This verse applies to strength in all aspects of our lives; physically, mentally, emotionally, intellectually and spiritually. This verse says that we can have all of these renewed in our lives by waiting on the Lord.

Okay, well what does it mean to "wait" upon the Lord?

Does it mean to stand by doing nothing in life, never looking in God's direction, waiting and wondering if He will just drop something great on you?

Does it mean for us to just wait for something to happen?

Does it mean for us to continuously be as servants to Him somehow?

Remember Jesus said we are friends and not servants. We'll talk more about that in the next chapter.

Or might it actually mean to actively listen for Him and to be connected with Him and to learn of Him?

There is very real power in connecting with God.

Many times experiencing God is realized and accomplished by "waiting", or just "being" in God's presence. Finding the things of God does not always mean asking the Lord for something, but can also be found by just spending time with and in Him; desiring to be closer to Him.

The Lord knows we can be renewed by spending time with Him and in His presence, and He desires for us to do so.

Being in the presence of the Lord brings not only rest, but renewing and replenishing as well.

> "...when the times of refreshing shall come from the presence of the Lord;"(4)

Endeavor to be in God's presence, and His Spirit will bring His Rest and

His Refreshing.

Sometimes this is all we need in our life, even for a moment. Gods rejuvenating and reviving Spirit is in the personal realization of Him.

> "Be still, and know that I am God..."(5)

So much can be gained by just being quiet before God and spending time in and with the Lord and the Holy Spirit.

> "You will show me the path of life: In Your presence is fullness of joy; at Your right hand are pleasures for evermore."(6)

In His presence there is also fullness of joy...

Spend more time in God's presence. Spend time in the Goodness and Holiness of Who He is. Spend time with the Spirit of the Lord. There you will find rest unto your souls, refreshing and so very much more...

"Lord, I want to know You more. I want to know about You, Your ways, and all that You would reveal to me, so that I may be closer to You. Show me more, and help me to keep my eyes ears and heart open to Your Spirit and all that you have for me, now and all the days of my life. In the name of your Son Jesus, in His Holy name and by Your Holy Spirit Who I am connected to and Who is within me, I pray..."

"God Calling" is a favorite book of mine. It was written by two "listeners" in England in the 1930's. The book reveals much about the Lords presence and His rest. I would suggest this book to anyone looking for a deeper walk in the presence of the Lord, and in the fullness of our Christ.

God said to Moses,

> "My presence shall go with you, and I will give you rest."(7)

His Rest is what He desires for us too.

It is also what He desires for _You_.

As the Lord Sees

"I will instruct you and teach you in the way which you shall go:
I will guide you with My eye..."(1)

The Word says that the Lord will instruct us and teach us and guide us with His eye.

What does this mean, that God will guide us with His eye?

As I was prayerfully considering this, I began to see the verse in a very different way than I ever had. It came to me that God wants us to see things as He sees them. Through His eyes. We are His children, and He desires that we endeavor to see things as He sees them.

As the Lord sees.

Don't we as parents desire that our children have the knowledge that we have, and to see things from our perspective? As we see them? That they might also know the understanding and wisdom that we have, and have found? Don't we spend much of our parenting lives trying to share these perspectives with our children?

So does our Father God desire for us to see these things, the things of Him, that we too might have His understanding and wisdom in our lives.

The above verse goes on to say "don't be like a mule that has no understanding, or as a horse that has to be bridled." It is saying not to be stubborn, not hearing, and turning away from listening to the things of God. If we listen and receive, we can have all the wisdom and all of the understanding that we can desire.

As a young Captain at sea, I had the opportunity to experience many different and amazing things all around the world. I had received many years of the finest training available anywhere, and was well experienced in the leadership role in which I was employed. I was confident in my abilities, and was fair but firm in the discharging of my command duties.

Life at sea is not for most people, and certainly not for the faint at heart. Among others, I had worked with many an old scallywag who had had rough years and had spent much of their lives going from ship to ship, making a living and a life as best they could.

One day, a certain arduous task was required which was not a very desirable one, but which had to be done. The feedback upon delivery of the news was considerable groaning and complaint from the men, as most news of this sort was generally received despite my usual earnest and motivating attitude. I always led by example though, so the crew knew I would also be directly involved.

This particular day, the task did not sit well with one of the old grizzled career deckhands, who decided to express himself very strongly to me after the meeting had broken up. He was visibly upset and proceeded to let me know by getting right in my face, raising his voice, threatening and cursing (of course, like a sailor). I let him vent, and in the middle of his time of ranting, I inwardly asked the Lord to show me what his reaction was really all about, why he was acting this way. These kinds of jobs weren't new to the man, and he had done this type of work for most of his life.

Then almost immediately, in a download of amazing understanding and revealing, I knew all about this man's past, his upbringing, and of the difficult things he had gone through in life. It was as if I could see all that he had been through, and all that had been done to him, which led him to this present state and behavior.

A perfect peace then came over me. I believe that something in my expression must have revealed that I somehow knew, and his expression changed completely. He offered a quiet apology and then went on to carry out what was he was called upon to do. He never came to me in that manner again, and I will always remember it.

This was wisdom from God in an instant and not like anything else that had ever happened to me. The Lord showed me all about this person and his past, and how the Father saw the man, and the love He had for him, which in turn gave me a great compassion for him.

As we know the Lord more, we will begin seeing things more and more in the way God sees them. We will have better direction and will be able to be more clearly guided in our lives, especially as our lives relate to those around us.

> "Henceforth I call you _not_ servants; for the servant doesn't know what his lord does: but I have called you _friends_; for all things that I have heard of my Father I have made known to you."(2)

Jesus is saying here that he does not consider us to be servants, or people who don't know what their Lord is doing, but He calls us His friends. He desires to show us the things of the Father and wants us to be a part of _all_ that He is doing.

Jesus then goes on to say,

> "You have not chosen Me, but I have chosen you, and ordained you, that you should go and bring forth fruit, and that your fruit should remain: and that whatever you ask of the Father in My name, He may give it to you."(3)

The Lord has chosen us to be His friends and for us to be very much a part of His purpose. He has chosen us, and He has even prepared us to bear fruit and to produce results, giving life to ourselves and others.

The more we realize this, the more we will be able to have, be, and do, in Him.

"Lord, help us to see things as You see them. Help us to know and really understand that we are Your friends, not your servants, and that You desire for us to be part of all that you are doing, in You and with You."

Seek the Lord and His wisdom and understanding. His Spirit will comfort and help you with it all, and give you these things.

His Holy Spirit is here to help us find and receive all of these things.

He will even through the Holy Spirit show you what and how to pray, using His words that "abide" within you. This then becomes effective and powerful prayer.

*"But the Comforter, which is the Holy Ghost, whom the Father
will send in my name, He shall teach you all things, and bring
all things to your remembrance, all that I have said to you."(4)*

Some of the most amazing results (fruit) and miracles that have
happened through my asking have come when the Holy Spirit has
reminded me of the words and inferences of Jesus, and His Word, so
that they could be used and applied into each person's particular
situation.

The Father and His Spirit know far more about a given circumstance
than we do. As we ask and allow the Holy Spirit to show us what to say
to a person, or in or into a situation, He brings His Word from within us,
and when we ask according to that Word, His Spirit then goes on to
accomplish and produce great and wonderful results, or works, through
us.

By Him, and through us. And all to His glory!

*"So will My Word be that goes from out of My mouth:
It will not return to Me void, but it will accomplish all that I please,
and it will prosper in the things wherever it is sent."(5)*

His Word doesn't come back empty, but it accomplishes all that it is sent
to do. Whether we see it or not. And we're a part of it all.

It is from the Lord, by His Spirit and it lives within us.

In the next chapters we will look at the importance of asking and
praying for others. But before we go there, I want to add that asking and
praying also applies for ourselves, that we can ask the Lord and pray
and receive from our God those things we need in our lives as well.

This is how I learned about the Lord and healing. He heals miraculously
today, and His Word really does accomplish and prosper and 'bear
much fruit' wherever it goes. It doesn't come back empty, but it returns
full of good, full of life, and full of accomplishment and reward in and
through Him!

The Lord God desires that we would have life, and that we would have it more abundantly. There is so much that we can ask, and receive, and know, and see, of and from Him in our lives.

This ties in so well with all that we are talking about with Job, and about what has been revealed to us in and through Job.

Can we now start to see Job, and the Book of Job, through the eyes of the Lord?

Let the Lord guide you with His Spirit.

Ask to see things as God sees them, and expect to see and receive.

He will show you.

See as God sees.

And you will find that truly amazing things will follow.

And He will guide you with His eye...

Pray
For
Your
Friends

Pray for Your Friends

"And the LORD turned the captivity of Job, when he prayed for his friends: also, the LORD gave Job twice as much as he had before."(1)

Here's another secret. Pray for your friends. Pray for others. Pray for neighbors, family, friends, anyone and everyone. Even those you don't know. Do it, do it, do it. Ask for others wherever and whenever you can.

That was a key to Jobs immediate recovery. Job now knew that God was indeed listening, and when he prayed for his friends, his 'captivity' to his emotions and his outlook completely changed, and the Lord healed him.

This very thing is also a key to situations we find ourselves in, and to our own personal living and thriving as Christians.

The Lord shows us things in the most amazing ways. For a long time while writing this book, I was enduring considerable financial hardship. Prior to this, I was accustomed to finances falling into place on a regular basis and doing well, but for this period of time, it was not that way. Contracts would fall through, which otherwise rarely happened, and nothing seemed to be going right.

I couldn't understand it. Here I am writing this book about going to God, and about Job, and things seemed to be falling apart all around me. I was able to receive the Peace of God, which kept me going and was way past understanding, but it was as if there was something I was missing.

The turning point in Job's life was when God showed Job that he hadn't gone to Him at all. When Job realized this, God gave him all the answers and direction he needed. One of those answers and directions was for Job to pray for his friends.

Then one day it hit me. In the past I had prayed with others often. I had asked the Lord for the answers and for help for them, or for whatever the still quiet voice of the Holy Spirit would put on my heart to pray.

299

Then, as my financial situation and other burdens had become larger, I began to pray for myself and for my situation more and more, and for others less and less. I did this to the point that not only I was completely consumed with my own situation, but I was dwelling more and more in the difficulty of it, asking the Lord only for things for my own desires, and not asking outwardly and openly for my friends or anyone else.

My thoughts had become so self-absorbed and so overwhelming, that at the point when I realized what I had been doing, I tried to think of who I had been praying for, and had to think hard to even come up with any names! I couldn't believe it. I was shocked and humbled and even embarrassed by my own actions and even more so, non-actions.

In this moment of realization, in the instant when I realized the fullness of what I had been doing, I immediately felt a very deep remorse and even sorrow, and with all my heart said, "Forgive me, Lord."

In that same moment I also realized something else. This was the very same reaction that Job had when he realized all that he had *not* done, when he had stopped worshipping God and had stopped praying for others.

I've always known God to be a great and "cool" God, and as He does, He shows us things in marvelous ways and with such great and amazing grace, as only we can truly receive them.

I also believe that there are certain things that we need to see and/or experience in our lives in order to more perfectly know and share in His truths, and this experience, I believe, was one of them.

Even though I was still earnestly worshipping God, I was looking far more at my problems than I was at the nearness of Who He is and the refuge He was in my life. I had surrounded myself with myself, and had stopped asking for anything outside of myself. I found that I had spent far too much time in worry and in defeat, and had rarely taken any friends or anyone else to Him in thought and prayer.

Why had things so easily come my way in the past? Certainly God is good, we are provided for, and His grace was and is involved.

But for me there was also the consideration of not only looking upward, but also reaching outward.

Job had always given of himself to the Lord, to prayer, and to others, prior to his afflictions. When all this happened to him, he had let go of all that he had known, and been, and had done before.

His friends pointed this out to him when they said,

> "Behold, you have instructed many, and you have strengthened the weak hands. Your words have lifted up him that was falling, and you have strengthened their feeble knees.
>
> But now it comes upon you, and you faint; it touches you, and you are troubled..."(2)

I then found that as I began praying for others again, and again trusting Him, my outlook and situation began to turn around as well.

> "Confess your faults one to another, and pray one for another, that _you_ may be healed."(3)

We'll look at this verse closer in the next chapter, of how **we** can be healed through our asking for others, but for now let us realize that the Father wants us to reach outward for and to others, in our actions and in our asking. This is what God showed Job, and as Job acted upon it, the Lord rewarded him openly and greatly.

As we pour out into others' lives, the Lord pours back in to our lives and everyone involved is blessed. Lives are lived to the fullest, and we are rewarded with things we can see and even things we cannot see.

The Lord showed Job that a very important part of his life was praying for his friends.

Through Job, He is also showing this to us.

Pray for your friends.

Asking for Others

"I exhort (suggest and encourage) that supplication, prayers,
intercessions, and giving of thanks, be made for all men;
For kings, and for all that are in authority; that we may lead
a quiet and peaceable life in all godliness and honesty.
For this is good and acceptable in the sight of God..."(1)

What we've looked at, and need to know, is that when we go to the Lord and ask, He hears us. And when He hears us, things happen. Change happens.

Jesus said this over and over during His time here.

Spending time with the Almighty and asking of Him changes things in other people's lives as well as in our own. And if that isn't enough, if we look at it with the larger picture in mind, this asking not only affects ours and others lives in this life, but it also affects ours and others lives in and into eternity. It bears fruit eternally.

Asking for others also gets your mind off yourself and into a much stronger place. Job was completely focused on himself, but as God said later, should have been focused on other things and in other directions.

In the last chapter, we began to look at asking for others, and praying outwardly.

Part of what the Father desires for us is that we would be moving and asking in an outward direction. He desires that we would be pouring ourselves out of ourselves, and reaching outward into others' lives with Him, His Word, and His Spirit. When this happens, everyone involved receives good.

A natural body of water will either become stagnant or dry up if there is no inflow and outflow. It becomes lifeless if there is no movement of it.

Only when there is an inflow and an outflow does a body of water possess the life-giving nutrients and nourishment required to provide all that is good to everything in and around it.

As we pray, as we ask for our friends and for others, we are pouring Living Water and all that is good into others' lives, and the Lord and Holy Spirit in turn renew us by pouring Living Water back into our own spirit, fresh and new, and full of life.

This Living Water is always moving, always refreshing and always life giving.

Asking for others brings wisdom, and peace, healing and comfort, change and deliverance, into other's lives, and into our own lives. It revives and brings life to all involved.

Along these lines, and as we said earlier, one of the greatest things that happens when you pray or ask for others is that when you pray, _you_ also receive from your asking!

James says,

> "Confess your faults one to another, and pray one for another, that **you** may be healed."(2)

Notice that this verse is talking about _two_ people receiving life and benefit and answers from your asking. One is the person being prayed for, and the other is the one doing the asking,,, _You._

This is not a mistake or a typo. James is saying purposely and correctly that as you pray for others, you also receive from the Lord, and the benefits of your asking are truly great! Everyone is blessed and receives when you pray, including you.

I have found this to be true. When asking for others, we too receive the very thing which we are asking for others.

For instance, if we pray strength into someone else's life, we also receive strength. If we pray for the Lord's peace, His love, and joy for others, we can receive these into our lives as well.

So asking for others not only brings answers and God's refreshing to others, but it brings life to us and into our own situations.

When we ask anything of God, we also need to keep in mind the nature of God.

> *"God is a Spirit: and they that worship Him must worship Him in spirit and in truth."(3)*

God's realm is spirit and truth. It is out of this that He gives to us. We need to ask of Him in spirit and in truth.

Things asked in the Spirit of God can then become manifest, or come to pass, in our natural or physical lives.

We also need to remember that "God is Love." Everything that the Lord does is from Who He is, from His Word and from His Love. God not only heals, but He brings all good things to us by and through His Great Love.

Are you asking and praying for others through the Spirit of God, and out of God's love for them?

Here's something that might test that. Jesus also said to not only for us to pray for our friends, but for our enemies too.

How often do we do that...???

How many times in life have you had to be with, or deal in some manner with someone who you consider to be very difficult, or adversarial, or even an enemy? What is your reaction to that adversity?

Do you avoid them and verbally condemn them to yourself, and to others? I believe that this reaction many times can be right at the top of our response list.

> *"But I say unto you, Love your enemies, bless them that curse you, do good to them that hate you, and pray for them which despitefully use you, and persecute you; and you will be the children of your Father which is in heaven."(4)*

Once again Jesus is showing us a greater and better way to face and handle this kind of adversity.

Remember, asking the Lord changes things, people and situations.

Praying for them, with trust in God, can and will change the situation.

The Lord is also saying that by actively being good toward them as well as asking for good for them that we will have the things of God and a greater answer will come. It can sometimes be difficult to do, but asking gives the Lord and His Holy Spirit something to work with.

God works in and through this, and in and through your asking.

He also asks things of us.

> "And when ye stand praying, forgive."(5)

Forgiveness. So much can be written about the greatness and the depth, and also the rewards of forgiveness.

Forgiving someone is truly an amazing thing, and it has nothing to do with the person who is being forgiven.

By forgiving and continuing to pray good into people's lives, no matter how hard it is, over and over if necessary, you will not only release and be released from the bondage that might be affecting you, but you will also move into a place far above or beyond it all, which will in turn bring life and good to you. You will also handle the situation in a much better and stronger way.

Forgiving a person always benefits the person who does the forgiving, not necessarily the person being forgiven.

Give it to God, completely, until change comes. And a change will come...

> "And the prayer of faith (of trust) shall save the sick,
> and the Lord shall revive him; and if he has committed sins,
> they shall be forgiven him."(6)

Asking can bring results in all areas of ours and others lives. Asking can bring salvation, can heal the sick, and can heal relationships.

Asking can bring forgiveness, even eternal forgiveness, rooting out even the deepest bitterness, and can set you, or those who are captive, free from their captivity, whatever it may be.

And then with the answers comes a greater rejoicing in God!

Jesus was always listening to His (and our) Father and to the Spirit of God. The Father worked through Him to accomplish great and amazing things.

Jesus said,

> *"The words that I speak unto you I speak not of myself:*
> *But the words are from the Father Who dwells in me,*
> *and He does the works."(7)*

In this Jesus is revealing to us how God works. He is showing us how God operates, the power of the Lord and how we also can be involved in what He is doing.

If we listen to the Lord via His Holy Spirit, and hear with our hearts, and have His Word within us, we will be able to hear and respond in and with Him on behalf of others. Our prayers will move and flow with the Spirit of God, and we will become effective and bear much fruit as we move in Him.

Let's make this a little more personal. If *you* listen to the Lord and His Holy Spirit, and *you* hear with *your* heart, and have His Word within *you*, *you* will be able to hear and respond in and with Him on behalf of others. *Your* prayers will move and flow with the Spirit of God, and *you* will become very effective, and *you* will bear much fruit as *you* continue to move in Him.

And as you ask and pray for others, all involved will be blessed by it.

Including, and maybe even especially, *You*...

Going
To
God

God's Will

"This is the confidence we have in Him,
that if we ask anything according to His will, He hears us.
And if we know that He hears us, whatsoever we ask,
we know that we have the requests that we have desired of Him."(1)

God hears us.

And if we know this, then we **_know_** we have what we've asked. This says we can be confident in this.

The above verse does not use the word "faith", but uses the word "know".

Do we **_know_** that we can ask Him anything? Do we **_know_** that He hears us? Do we really **_know_** we can have those things which we desire?

The verse also says that we can have confidence in the Lord answering our petitions and requests if we ask according to His will.

So how do we know God's will? What indeed is God's will?

It's a big question and I find that there are two general responses from people when asked.

The first is very similar to the ideology and response of Job's friends. "How can we possibly know God's will?" The underlying assumption in this response is that one can't.

The person saying this usually has not spent much time personally searching out God and easily ends up resigning themselves to the fatalistic perception that they can and will never know. Unless they find out that they actually can ask, and receive, that person will rarely request anything of God.

This outlook generally also may result in a "not really sure" kind of faith in God.

Until that person realizes, by experiencing Him, that God does indeed desire to answer our asking, they may continue to rely on this resigned response and fatalistic approach.

And until they begin to search and to truly know God more, and to ask using the amount of faith that they have, they may not see many of their answers come to pass.

Unfortunately, when nothing happens with their non-requests, it also perpetuates their belief in their original hopeless response of "oh well", and the cycle continues.

Again, Job's friends said that we can never know God's will, and we've believed their "words without knowledge" for a very long time.

What we haven't truly realized is that God showed up at the end of Job to tell them they were very, very wrong. When He did this, He was answering their very questions!

The other response people can have to the "Can we know God's will?" question is that they earnestly consider it and honestly ask themselves, and ask the Lord the questions, and then earnestly and honestly desire and search for the answer.

And that's when God shows up in their lives.

So let's ask the question that many ask, and arises from the beginning chapter verse.

"How can we, or how do we know, His will?"

It is actually fairly simple. The more we know about Him, the more we will know His will. The more we know about anyone, the more we will know their desires, their purposes, and their will.

Do we know God well enough to know what His will is?

God's Word says,

"God has abounded toward us in all wisdom and prudence; <u>having made known to us the mystery of His will</u>, according to His own good pleasure and His purpose..."(2)

This verse says that He has <u>already</u> made His will known to us! This may jog somebody's religion a little bit but we actually can and should already know His will. He's already made it known to us!

As we get to know Him better, we will discover that His will is found in His Word, and through His Spirit.

When you begin taking the time to know God, and to search for Him through what He has said, or in His Word, you will find His will.

You will also begin to find all of the things that God has for you. Jesus has sent the Holy Spirit here to show us all of these things.

You will find that He has given you authority in this earth through the Name of His Son, Jesus. You will find that He has set it up so that His Words and your own words not only are important in our lives but they indeed are powerful, they create, and avail much for and in the lives of those around you.

And you will find out so much more about Him, and what His will is in your life.

In the next chapter I've included a number of actual prayers by Paul and others which are found in His Word and are very much a part of God's will for us.

Let's look at one of those prayers here.

"That God would give you, according to the riches of His glory, to be <u>strengthened with might</u> by His Spirit in your inner man; That Christ may <u>dwell in your heart</u> by faith and that you, being rooted and grounded in love (In God, as God is love), might be able to <u>comprehend with all saints what is the breadth, and length, and depth, and height;</u> And to know <u>the love of Christ</u>, which passes knowledge, <u>that you might be filled with all the fullness of God.</u>"(3)

God wants us to be strengthened, and not only just strengthened, but strengthened _with might_, by His Spirit in our inner man, within us, in the core of our being.

He wants to have Jesus dwelling in our hearts by faith and trust. He knows how valuable and powerful that is in our lives.

He wants us to be rooted and grounded in Him. As a fundamental part of all this He wants us to know for ourselves His love, and the love of His Son which is far beyond all knowledge, beyond anything we can imagine or ask or think.

And God _wants us_ to understand the _breadth, and length, and depth, and height_ of all the things of Him. This is why He sent His Son to us, and why His Son sent His Spirit.

And He wants us not only to know, but to be completely _filled, with all of His fullness!_ That is huge... And the best part is, we can be!

The Lord wants us to know that all of this comes through His power and His Spirit and His Son, and that His greatness works within us and through us.

This is God's will.

God's will also includes many of our own desires, with His desires and purposes for our lives. It is in what we know to be true and right and good according to the Father and the Spirit of God within us.

His will is all the good He has given us. Remember that all good things come from Him. And He turns those things which are not good, or not from Him, into good through His powerful love.

You will also find that when we tie our will to and with the Spirit of God, to His Word, and to His will, it has and brings tremendous power in our lives.

God desires for us to see these things and to know His will more and more. It is God's will that we pray, or ask, not in anger or in doubting, but in spirit and in truth and in faith and trust, and also that we look for the answers!

> *"I will therefore that men pray everywhere, lifting up holy hands,*
> *without wrath and without doubting."(4)*

Jesus said over and over again "Ask, and it will be given you..."

God wants us to learn of Him and receive more of Him, and to know His will. One of the ways we do this is by asking, and receiving.

And as we do this, His will *shall* be done,,,

In our lives,

And in your life,

On earth, as it is in heaven...

The Word

"And <u>the Word</u> was made flesh, and dwelt among us,
(and we saw His glory, the glory as of the only Son of the Father,)
full of grace and truth."(1)

The Word is also His Will.

The Word of God is filled with so many amazing and marvelous truths, and even many more hidden truths. Let's take a look at the above verse a little more closely, in conjunction with the below verse.

"For there are three that bear record in heaven, the Father,
the Word, and the Holy Ghost: and these three are one."(2)

Both of the above verses say that Jesus was and is the Word of God, or God's Word, Who came to us in the form of a man, in the flesh.

Jesus also said,

"I am the way, the truth, and the life: no man comes to the Father,
but by (through) me."(3)

So look at this. when we combine these verses, we find that Jesus is the Word (who came here as a man), and He is also the Way, the Truth, and the Life.

So this means that the Word is also the Way the Truth, and the Life.

Following this progression, the "Word" is the Word of the Way, the Word of Truth and the Word of Life.

Are we in Him? Are we in the Word of Life? Are we in Christ? Are we in Jesus who was the Word made flesh?

In the New Testament, Philippians and Revelations talk about our names being written in the Book of Life. Might this also be the Word of Life? In Jesus? Are we there? Are you there?

313

Knowing the Word of God for yourselves will lead to a much greater ability to move in the Lord and the Spirit of God, and as you "bear much fruit", you will also have a greater joy and fulfillment in your life!

Below are a number of examples of God's will for us found in His Word, or in the "Book of Life" if you will. One way to assist in your asking is to insert your name (or 'I', 'me' and 'my'), or the name of whoever you are praying for, into the "___" places in the verses. By doing this you will be joining with the Word and His Will and making your asking much more direct and personal. You will also be making His Will your will.

Take one or two of these verses and prayers and make them your own. Ask them from your heart, and in your own words. I think you will find that they will start to become very real and will begin to bear much fruit in yours, and others lives.

"Grace be to _____, and peace, from God our Father, and from the Lord Jesus Christ.

I thank my God always on behalf of _____, for the grace of God which is given to _____ by Jesus Christ; That in everything _____ is/am enriched by Him, in all things spoken, and in all knowledge; Even as the testimony of Christ was confirmed in _____.

So that _____ come(s) behind in no gift; waiting for the coming of our Lord Jesus Christ: Who shall also confirm _____ to the end that _____ may be without blame in the day of our Lord Jesus Christ.

God is faithful, in that _____ was called into the fellowship of His Son Jesus Christ our Lord."

(1 Corinthians 1:3-9)

"Grace be to _____, and peace, from God our Father, and from the Lord Jesus Christ."

"Great is the God and Father of our Lord Jesus Christ, who has blessed _____ with all spiritual blessings in heavenly places in Christ:"

"According as God has chosen _____ to be in His Son before the foundation of the world, that _____ should be holy and without blame before God in love:

Having predestined _____ to adoption by Jesus Christ to Himself, according to the good pleasure of His will,

To the praise of the glory of His grace, where He has accepted _____ into His family.

In that _____ has redemption through His blood, the forgiveness of sins, according to the riches of His grace; In which He has abounded toward _____ in all wisdom and prudence;

Having made known to _____ the mystery of His will, according to His good pleasure: That in the end He might gather together all things in Christ, both which are in heaven, and which are on earth; even in Him:

In that _____ also has obtained an inheritance, being predestined according to His purpose; Who works all things after His own will:

That we should be to the praise of His glory, who has first trusted in Christ.

In that _____ also trusted, after _____ heard the Word of truth, the gospel of our salvation: in that _____ also believed, and was sealed with that holy Spirit of promise, which is the earnest and evidence of our inheritance, until the redemption of each one of us, to the praise of His glory."

(Ephesians 1:2-14)

"I cease not to give thanks for _____, making mention of _____ in my prayers;

That the God of our Lord Jesus Christ, the Father of glory, may give to _____ the spirit of wisdom and revelation in the knowledge of Him:

That the eyes of _____ understanding would be enlightened; that _____ may know the hope of His calling, and the riches of the glory of His inheritance in the saints, and know the exceeding greatness of His power to _____ who believes, according to the working of His mighty power, which He created in Christ, when He raised Him from the dead, and set Him at His own right hand in the heavenly places, far above all principality, and power, and might, and dominion,,,"

(Ephesians 1:16-23)

"For this cause I bow my knees unto God, the Father of our Lord Jesus Christ, from Who the whole family in heaven and earth is named, that He would give _____ according to the riches of His glory, to be strengthened <u>with might</u> by His Spirit in the inner man;

That Christ may dwell in _____ heart by faith and that _____, being rooted and grounded in love, would be able to comprehend with all saints what is the breadth, and length, and depth, and height;

And to know the love of Christ, which passes all knowledge, that _____ might be filled with all the fullness of God.

Now unto Him that is able to do exceeding abundantly above all that we can ask or think, according to His power that works in _____, to Him be the glory in the church by Christ Jesus throughout all ages, world without end. Amen."

(Ephesians 3:14-21)

"That we from now on will not be children, tossed to and fro, and carried around with every wind of doctrine, by the sleight of men, and cunning craftiness, where many lie in wait to deceive;

But speaking the truth in love, that _____ may grow up in the Lord in all things,,,"

(Ephesians 4:14-15)

"Is _____ among you afflicted? Let him pray. Is _____ merry? Let him sing psalms.

Is _____ sick among you? Let him call for the elders of the church; and let them pray over him, anointing him with oil in the name of the Lord:

And the prayer of faith shall save _____, and the Lord shall revive him; and if he has committed sins, they shall be forgiven him.

Confess your faults one to another, and pray one for another, that you may be healed. The effective fervent prayer of a righteous man avails much."

(James 5:13-16)

"Go into all the world, and preach the gospel to every creature. He that believes and is baptized shall be saved; but he that believes not shall not be.

And these signs shall follow _____ who believes; In My (Jesus) name _____ will cast out devils; _____ will speak with new tongues; _____ will take up serpents; and if _____ drink any deadly thing, it shall not hurt them; _____ shall lay hands on the sick, and they shall recover."
(Mark 16:15-18)

"We give thanks to God and the Father of our Lord Jesus Christ, praying always for _____, since we heard of _____ faith in Christ Jesus, and of the love which _____ has toward all the saints,

For the hope which is laid up for _____ in heaven, where _____ heard before in the word of the truth of the gospel; Which is come to _____, and _____ brings forth fruit, as it does also in _____, since the day _____ heard it, and knew the grace of God in truth."
(Colossians 1:3-6)

"For this cause we also do not cease to pray for _____, and desire that _____ might be filled with the knowledge of His will in all wisdom and spiritual understanding;

That _____ might walk worthy of the Lord pleasingly, being fruitful in every good work, and increasing in the knowledge of God; Strengthened with all might, according to His glorious power, unto all patience and longsuffering with joy;

Giving thanks unto the Father, Who hath made _____ to be a partaker of the inheritance of the saints: Who has delivered _____ from the power of darkness, and has translated _____ into the kingdom of His dear Son:

In Whom _____ has redemption through His blood, even the forgiveness of sins:"
(Colossians 1:9-14)

"For by Him were all things created, which are in heaven, and which are in earth, both visible and invisible, whether they be thrones, or dominions, or principalities, or powers: all things were created by Him, and for Him: And He is before all things, and by Him do all things consist."

And He is the head of the body, the church: and Is the beginning, the firstborn from the dead; that in all things He might have preeminence. For it pleased the Father that in Jesus should all fullness (everything) dwell;

And having made peace through the blood of His cross, by Him to reconcile all things to Himself; whether they are things in the earth, or things in heaven.

And _____, who was sometimes alienated and an enemy by wicked works, God has now reconciled through Jesus' death, to present _____ holy and blameless, without reproof and clean in His sight; If _____ continues in the faith, grounded and settled, and is not moved away from the hope of the gospel,,,"

(Colossians 1:16-23)

"We pray always for _____, that our God would count _____ worthy of this calling, and fulfill all the good pleasure of His goodness, and the work of faith with power:

"That the name of our Lord Jesus Christ may be glorified in _____, and _____ in Him, according to the grace of our God and the Lord Jesus Christ."

(2 Thessalonians 1:11-12)

And these are just a few. There are many other prayers you can ask for yourself and others throughout the Word of God, and the rewards will be great when you find them and ask them.

> *"Abide in Me, and I in you... He that abides in Me,*
> *and I in him, will bring forth much fruit..."(4)*

Abide means to live within. As we live within Him and He and His Word live within us, we can ask of Him, and receive in Him, which in turn produces much in the Kingdom of God.

It is God's will to have the fullness of the things of Him with us, and within us. It is for our benefit, and for each of us to experience throughout our lives. He desires that we produce much through Him, and through His Word, and through His Spirit, to the Glory of the Father.

His Word is His will,,, and His will is in His desire for us.

318

Our Will

*"If you abide in Me, and My words abide in you,
you will ask what you will, and it shall be done for you."(1)*

As we have looked at, God gives, and has even already given His will to us.

It is now up to us to take *our* will, and do something with it; and receive all that He has for us!

It takes *our* will to get to know Him, His Word, and His Spirit.

It takes *our* will to desire to know more deeply and more strongly Who He is.

It takes *our* will to trust God.

To really have trust and confidence in God is a decision each one of us must make personally in order to truly follow Him. Remember that faith and trust are both very much involved in our asking and in having our prayers answered.

If it was important when Jesus was here on earth as a man, then it is just as important if not more so with us now.

It takes *our* will to open our hearts and to open up our voices and ask.

It takes *our* will to "initiate ourselves". It is *our* will which initiates, or moves us to action.

It takes *our* will to desire to be effective and to do the things that avail much. It takes *our* will to ask, and to earnestly desire to ask effectively, and to trust Him in that He will provide answers, in order to accomplish much.

The Lord doesn't do *our* things for us. We must use *our* will, *our* desire, *our* energy and *our* efforts to prepare *our*selves for all that He has for us!

319

We have to <u>exercise</u> **our** will, use and direct it in order that His will may be accomplished in our lives.

From all that we have looked at, if we are not using our will, by asking, then we are not using what the Lord has given to us to create and affect good in our lives and in the lives of others all around us.

Use **your will** to seek Him. As you do, you will find the Lord, and He will use you in profound and wonderful ways.

Our will, and our words, in conjunction with God's Spirit and God's will (along with knowing the authority of Jesus Name) are all extremely powerful, and can, and will, move mountains in ours and others' lives.

We looked at this verse in James earlier.

> *"The effective fervent prayer of a righteous man avails much."(2)*

Asking effectively and asking fervently, by using your will, activates and brings to pass things that are made available and produce much. The effective and fervent prayer of a man or woman, using their will to ask and receive, accomplishes much.

Let's look at what this type of prayer is <u>not</u>. An earnest and fervent prayer is <u>not</u> a casual prayer. It is <u>not</u> "going through the motions" praying. It is <u>not</u> an "I hope they feel better because I'm saying something" words. It is <u>not</u> an emotional plea, and it is <u>not</u> a wish, or sending good thoughts (if that is even possible) to someone.

A **fervent** prayer is one which is focused and specific and diligently asked with and in line with God's Word and in the Holy Spirit. It is one that is asked with faith and trust knowing that he (or she) is heard by the Lord, and knowing also by faith and trust that they indeed will have the things which they've asked.

An **effective** prayer is listening to the Spirit of God and using His Word, combined with our own words and His love in order to produce results.

Spending time with the Father and Son (The Word) and with His Holy Spirit can help our asking be much more effective. As we do this, we will learn and find out more about His will and His ways, and we'll be more able to move with our will in His and in Him.

Use the Word of God in your asking. It is His will. The chapter before this is filled with examples, and so is the whole Bible. And so is the Holy Spirit. They are Jesus' words. Get to know His will, and His Word will come to you and for you.

Remember to keep the channels to God open, as we looked at earlier. As much as you can, remove any obstacles that might hinder your asking.

> *"If My people, which are called by My name, shall humble themselves and pray, and seek My face, and turn from their wicked ways; then I will hear from heaven, and I will forgive their sin, and I will heal their land."(3)*

This verse talks about being humble as we come to God. Excessive personal pride can be an obstacle to prayer and a hindrance to keeping the channels to God open. Though it may sound conflicting, it is quite possible to be both humble *and* bold and strong, in our asking.

This verse is also talking about humbling ourselves __to__ pray. Sometimes pride can hinder or prevent us from even asking in the first place. We need to be able to have control over what hinders us and put pride or whatever holds us back aside, away from us, and we will find ourselves in a heart position, or attitude, or altitude, where we can then easily go to God, and ask and receive.

In short, use *your will* to be humble. That means putting others first. Always remove the "self" obstacle, and being contrite or humble before the Lord will help keep the channel clear.

Also make sure to take any envy, or strife or bitterness out of the way, and completely remove it from the equation, so that you have peace and the love of God as much as possible in all of your asking.

Use your will to ask, from your trust in God, asking more from your faith than out of emotions, and the Lord will honor your efforts.

Make it *your will* to ask for things that are in God's realm. Differentiate between the things of God and what may be desires of lust or greed or irrelevant desires. When considering what God's will is, it can be important to distinguish between what God would have for us, as a loving Father, and what our own worldly desires might have if we don't have Him first in our lives.

Jesus is our great example in this. Those things which He asked, we can also have, and nothing will be impossible, nothing will be unattainable in and with and through Him.

Jesus was always listening and asking of the Father. By the Spirit of God He was able to discern people's hearts, and was able to present the argument and the solution with wisdom between worldly things and the things of God.

An example of this was when the Pharisees tried to trick Jesus by asking Him if tribute money should be given in honor of Caesar.

Jesus asked that a coin be given Him. He then gave a marvelously profound answer.

> *"And He said to them, whose image is on this coin?*
> *They said to him, Cæsar's.*
> *Then He said to them, Give to Cæsar the things that are Cæsar's;*
> *and give to God the things that are God's."(4)*

Asking within all that is in God's realm and His will, as Jesus did, and not necessarily for what the world has, or is, or does or desires, is a good guide to making our prayers more effective, and also bears much fruit.

The Lord certainly desires that we would use His wisdom, and prosper in our lives, even financially, and we can pray that accordingly, but He also desires, and I believe even more so, that we would grow in our Spirit lives, and then when we do, our perspectives will start to align more and more with all that is good and right and true in Him.

Again, all of this is found in knowing the Father, His Word and His Spirit.

Use *your will* to pray in the Spirit of God. And remember that the Holy Spirit is always there, and there to help us in our asking.

> *"The Spirit also helps our infirmities: for we don't know what*
> *we should pray for as we ought to:*
> *but the Spirit itself makes intercession for us..."(5)*

This first part of this verse is saying that we don't always know how or what we should pray for as we should. This "not knowing" how to ask is being referred to here as "our infirmity". It says that because we don't always know what or how to ask, the Holy Spirit is there to help us with our asking, so that we can know we are asking in Him.

The second part of the verse says that the Spirit of God will join you and assist and intercede for and with you in your asking. And if you know that the Spirit of God is helping you, you can know that your prayers are certainly being heard by God.

Agreeing with others in your asking can add to your prayers being more effective as well.

Jesus said,

> *"Verily I say to you, that whatever you will bind on earth will be*
> *bound in heaven:*
> *And whatever you will loose on earth will be loosed in heaven.*
> *Again I say to you, that if two of you will agree on earth as touching*
> *any thing they ask, it shall be done for them of my Father which is in*
> *heaven.*
> *For where two or three are gathered together in my name, there I am*
> *with them, in the midst."(6)*

Let's take a look at these verses, in reverse order.

"Where two or three are gathered together in My Name, there I am with them, in the midst."

I often start my prayers with this. If we know that the Lord is there with us when we agree and ask, as He says, our asking takes on a whole new meaning.

Know that He is there, with you and among you when you ask. What and how would you ask with Jesus standing right next to you?

Know that He is; and ask.

"If two will agree (using their will) about anything they ask, it shall be done for them by our Father in heaven."

This is talking about asking in unity and agreement with one another. Make unity a part of your asking. In it is strength and power, and along with trust, it too produces much.

The expression "One can put a thousand to flight but two can put ten thousand to flight" comes from God's Word and means that we can have exponentially more power in agreement and asking in unity. It is a bold statement, but Jesus is saying for us to know that unity is powerful, and that we should use it, and then experience the results and answers!

Many times people will ask you or someone else for prayer. We generally default to saying that we will "keep them in our prayers", or "pray for them", at some point in the future.

In doing this we are deferring our asking for some incidental time, if at all. Though this is done with good intentions, it takes away from the unity that is available at that moment. Will we actually remember to pray in the future? And if so, will we be in agreement with them at the same time, whenever and if ever we do? Most likely not.

If you pray with someone at the moment they ask for prayer, you will find that your asking becomes much more effective, and answers will come more often. It is at that time when you both are in agreement and in unity, and as you agree with them, in the moment of their asking, you are agreeing according to the Word of God, and this connection in faith and prayer does indeed produce and avail much.

Also, I have found that when praying for someone, ask the person's name and use their name as you pray. By personalizing your request, your prayer becomes much more specific, which will also increase the persons faith and connection (unity), and you will find that your asking becomes more effective by this as well.

"If you bind anything here, it is done in heaven, and if you loose anything here, it is done in heaven."

Binding and loosing. This is referring to the power of our asking and power of prayer in binding the enemy from doing harm and loosing those who are bound from the bonds of the enemy. And when you do it, especially in unity, there is much power in it. And then consider it done.

Let's see something else about using our will. As I was writing this chapter, there came a new understanding about this next verse.

> *"If you abide in me, and my words abide in you,*
> *you <u>will ask what you will</u>, and it shall be done for you."*(7)

"You will ask <u>what you will</u>..."

It always seemed to me that this was just somehow a good observation or suggestion of a general prayer for something.

Then a different meaning was revealed.

The word *"will"* here in the Greek is "thelos, or "theleos" which means to *choose* or *prefer*, to *desire* or *intend, to determine, to be inclined to*, or *to list.*

What this means is that Jesus is not saying to just ask generally or vaguely about something. He is saying that if we abide in Him and His Word lives within us, we can ask specifically *"what you will"*.

What is *your will* to have happen in the matter? What do you desire to have happen, what outcome would you want to see, specifically?

This verse is saying for us to ask *our specific will* in a given situation.

What do we desire to see happen in a given situation or circumstance, or in ours or someone's life?

What specifically do we desire, that it shall be done for us?

Jesus showed us this very thing in a number of instances. In the following example, He asks the two blind men what they desired to receive; what they were *specifically* requesting.

> *"Two blind men were sitting by the side of the road,*
> *and when they heard that Jesus was passing by, they cried out,*
> *saying, "Have mercy on us, O Lord, Son of David."*
> *The crowd rebuked them, saying that they should keep quiet:*
> *but they cried out even more.*
> *Then Jesus stood still, and called them, and said, what is your will*
> *that I do for you?*
> *They said to him, "Lord, that our eyes may be opened".*
> *So Jesus had compassion on them, and touched their eyes:*
> *and their eyes immediately received sight."(8)*

Let's look a little closer at this. Did Jesus not have any idea of what the men wanted? Was He oblivious to their plight? Did He not know they were blind?

Of course, He knew the whole time that they were blind and what they needed. Through the Father and the Spirit Jesus knew all that was going on with them in their lives. He knew perfectly of their faith in Him and why they were calling to Him.

He was leading them to ask *specifically* for what they wanted because He knew that when they asked specifically, and in trust, that they would receive.

So He asked them what they wanted, they told Him, and He gave, and they received that which they had asked for.

Many people I know have this 'happily ever after' and "Watch over us Lord," kind of prayer, which is very sweet, and sounds nice, but is not very specific at all, and quite possibly not very effective, as God is already "watching over us" and wants us to live happily ever after and those sorts of things.

So by being specific we give much more depth and meaning to and in our asking. And our words have power in Him.

If we know that our words have power in Him, we can do this.

*"Let your requests - **be made known** - to God."(9)*

What is your will in the matter? What are you specifically praying to have happen? What are you specifically requesting, asking or desiring to have happen?

Again, consider making a prayerful "theleos" intent or even preference when you ask. So many times, if and when we pray, we pray only very general prayers and are not specific at all in our asking. What exactly do you want to see happen in a given situation? If we can have confidence in Him then we can be specific! God is big enough to handle this. Ask of the Lord specifically!

Using our will to be effective in asking also means asking the Holy Spirit what you should pray for and/or what in His Word you should use in your asking.

The Spirit of God knows exactly what needs to be spoken into or over a situation. He helps us and many times even gives us the words to speak.

You may be surprised when the Spirit connection inside you brings a specific scripture to mind that by the Holy Spirit fits the scenario or situation perfectly. Remember His words abide in us, and when these words are spoken or prayed into a situation, they produce amazing results, bearing much fruit.

We desire for **our will** to be united with **God's will**, and we desire to bring our requests according to His will. Tie your will together with and in God's will, and the Word says you'll have whatever you desire.

Here is the rest of the verse from the last page.

> *"Be careful (anxious) for nothing; but in everything by prayer and supplication, with thanksgiving, let your requests be made known to God."(10)*

Don't worry, at all. Ask with thanksgiving, and let your requests specifically be made known unto God.

And be thankful through it all.

Jesus came to do and to show us that by our faith/trust, and by our will, and by His Will and Spirit, we would be able to do great things, even the things He did, both for ourselves and for others. He came to show us the way, and then sent the Spirit of God not only to Comfort us, and to show us Who God was, but also to show us that we can ask and receive by and through Him, with the great and powerful authority in His name that He has given us.

And in doing so, our prayers will be answered and our joy will be full and filled to overflowing!

> *"For all the promises of God in Him are yes, and in Him Amen (So be it), to the glory of God..."(11)*

When your prayers are answered, a number of things happen.

First, whoever you've prayed for receives all that is good, and greater works are accomplished.

Secondly, everyone involved is wholly and completely blessed and in awe of it all.

Thirdly, you, through the Spirit of God, have borne much fruit, and your faith has grown exponentially, which brings you even more confidence in the things of the Lord, which in turn grows your desire to do more.

Fourthly, your joy is filled, and you understand what it means to have the true 'fullness of joy' that Jesus talked about.

And fifthly, and foremost, God is glorified.

It's all part of the plan, and part of the great reward.

And it all starts with you using *your* will to ask in Him.

> *"Let your light so shine before men,*
> *that they may see your good works,*
> *and glorify your Father which is in heaven."(12)*

These good works, or results, or "fruit", are the things that bring glory to God.

When we, by our will, choose to <u>believe</u>, and to <u>ask</u>, and to <u>receive</u>,,,

Then we and others are gloriously blessed...

And God is fully, and truly,

Glorified.

Going to God

"Ask, and you shall receive, that your joy may be full."(1)

Unlike Job and his reactions during his ordeal, we need to be going to God all the time.

As we talked about before, realizing God's greatness, and understanding that the Lord and His Holy Spirit are with us is a great place to start.

And we do have a part to play. Our part is to ask, and to believe in Him, and to receive. That's it. The Father, Son and Holy Spirit do the rest. It's a relationship like no other.

Here are a number of other things we can ask the Lord for. This is by no means an all-inclusive list, but is only meant as initial suggestions for you to consider. Please feel free to add to these as much as you'd like, as asking from your heart is what the Lord hears.

Again, ask the Lord for wisdom. Ask to know Him more, and ask how to spend more time with Him, and how to be in His presence. Ask to know more about His Spirit, and how the Spirit works in your life.

Ask for the Father's guidance. Pray that you would know God's will and His Words more and more, and that you and others would grow in wisdom and understanding of the things of the Lord in your lives. Ask to know Him and His Spirit more deeply and more clearly and profoundly.

Ask specific things for your family. Pray for your wife or your husband. Asking in unity with your spouse is a powerful benefit of marriage, "where two agree as touching any thing..." Asking to be in unity with your spouse in prayer will also bear much fruit.

Ask for good health for your family, and for their protection, and that they would grow stronger in the good things and the great things of the Lord. Pray for wisdom and discernment for your children.

Pray **with** your children.

Ask to find out more about God's refuge and His throne-room of grace.

Ask to go there. Knock, and open the Door.

Ask the big questions. He hears and answers and I believe He loves the big questions. As well as the little ones.

Pray for unbelievers, especially in your family or your sphere of influence. Ask that other believers would come across their paths and they would find and receive more of the Lord. Ask that the Holy Spirit would move mightily in their lives, and for the rest of their lives.

"Continue in prayer, and watch in the same with thanksgiving..."(2)

A soft spoken friend of mine prayed for 25 years that her husband would receive the Lord, that he would realize the great "Hello". It took time, but when it happened, she, with much joy, said that it was worth every moment of her asking!

"Praying always with all prayer with humble asking in the Spirit, and watching with all perseverance and supplication for all saints..."(3)

Pray that those around you, and that those ministering to you in Christ would hear from the Spirit of God and be renewed and refreshed in their hearts to the things of God. Pray that they would receive further revelation from and of the Lord and ask for their spiritual and physical development and protection, and for their families too.

Ask for strength for Christians in other countries who may be suffering under, in many instances, life and death persecution, that they would be strengthened with might by the Holy Spirit and that they would know the words to say and when to say them.

Pray the same thing for those of faith in our country who are being persecuted for their beliefs. Pray that their enemies would see, and realize and receive the Lord in their lives.

Ask for the Spirit of God to prepare hearts to receive Him.

Ask for the protection of those fighting for us, and protecting us.

Pray for those spreading the Good News around the world that they would have boldness and strength and wisdom and supernatural protection in their lives. Ask that they would have favor with man, and with God, in all that they're doing.

Ask for healing for others. Ask not only for physical healing, but also for healing for the broken hearted.

Ask for healing and sound minds.

Ask for people and people's spirits to be moved.

Pray for miracles.

Ask that blinders be removed from people's eyes and ears that they might see and hear. Ask for chains of bondage to be broken.

Pray that darkness would be revealed by the light, and that those in darkness would come to the light.

Ask for peace in yours and others' lives. Ask the Lord for strength and vision, to see as He sees, and ask for laborers to go out into the harvest of the Lord.

> "I encourage you, first of all, that supplications, prayers, intercessions, and giving of thanks, be made for all men; For kings, and for all that are in authority; That we may lead a quiet and peaceable life in all godliness and honesty..."(4)

Ask for wisdom for our leaders that they would make wise decisions that we may live in peace. Ask that they would have and use wisdom and truth and have boldness in their decision-making.

Pray for the health of our country and for wise and earnest leaders to rise up and be elected and that they would serve truthfully and valiantly. Pray for strength and protection for them as they lead.

Ask that your country's leaders would turn to the things of God, and away from poor decisions and lost and wrong directions.

Pray that they would unite strongly in the good things of God and under the banner of the Lord. Pray that these people would see the truth and that the truth would set them free. Ask that the Holy Spirit would move in the lives of those in authority and guide them that they and we might live in all Godliness and honesty.

> *"Rejoicing in hope; patient in tribulation;*
> *continuing instant in prayer;*
> *Distributing to the needs of saints; given to hospitality..."(5)*

Continuing instant in prayer?

There really aren't any words that accurately express the joy you have when the things you've asked for come to pass. It is amazing, truly and genuinely spectacular in your life. Your faith skyrockets, and is built up exponentially more and more every time. You realize the greatness of God and personally know the profound joy Jesus talked about.

You then want to do more of it and become ready to "ask" anytime. You will find that you will want to be ready to move in the Spirit of the Lord in a moment's notice, even continually.

Experiencing the Lord and His Spirit more and more leads you to desire to become instant in prayer, and then you begin living that way.

Pray to become quick to ask, and instant in your asking and then instant in your listening.

Learn to be in the mindset to ask the Lord for the things of Him in any situation, even if you don't feel you have time to do so. The asking in itself may only take a moment, but it also may affect eternity for others.

And it will always be worth it.

Pray for refugees and those families without homes that they would find peaceful protection and habitations.

Ask that those who have been abused will find peace and then to live and love a good life again, and be able to know true love, the truest of which is the Love of God.

Ask that those without food will be fed, and then help feed them.

Ask for marriages and friendships and relationships to be healed and made whole. Pray for strength and wisdom for all those involved.

Ask for the truth to come to light and be shown and understood as you pray for others. Ask for the realization of forgiveness, and pray that others would understand and receive the strength and all of the rewards that forgiveness will bring in their lives.

> *"That Christ may dwell in your hearts by faith; that you,*
> *being rooted and grounded in love,*
> *may be able to comprehend with all saints*
> *what is the breadth, and length, and depth, and height;*
> *And to know the love of Christ which is far beyond human knowledge,*
> *that you might be filled with all the fullness of God."(6)*

Ask to know more of God. Ask to see the things of the Lord.

Ask to find the depth of the Love of Christ.

Ask to know the hope of the Lords calling in you, in and for others.

Pray for abundant life, and for further understanding of the Lord in yours and in others' lives.

Thank the Father and the Son for being with you, His Spirit within you, and His truth and life living in and through you.

Initiate yourself. Ask for downloads, the revelations of the Father, the Son and the Spirit of God in yours and others lives.

Ask these things from your heart, from your spirit and from love. Ask specific requests. This may take time to begin doing, at least initially, but will become much easier and will avail and produce much as you do it more and more.

Pray for boldness, even as the original disciples did.

Ask for the impossible.

Don't shy away from praying for things that don't appear do-able, for **all** things are truly possible with God, including and especially things that appear to be impossible. Many times this is where you will find the most profound answers and greatest reward!

Pray for strength and protection. For you and those around you.

Pray for peace, and comfort for those in need, and for those the Lord directs you to pray for.

Pray for your enemies.

> "Do good to them that hate you, and pray for them which despitefully use and persecute you;"(7)

> "Bless those who persecute you: bless, and curse not."(8)

Pray for those who persecute you, and those who spitefully use you.

Bless them and don't curse them. Ask for goodness to come into their lives and ask that they would see the truth and the things (of God) which will turn them from their ways. The Lord said you will be blessed in doing this.

Pray for a deeper and more profound way to praise and worship God.

Learn to rejoice more and more and always. Ask that joy and an abundance of hope would come into yours and other's lives. Rejoice in that hope. Encourage others with your words. Find joy in rejoicing.

Rejoice evermore.

Give. Give to others. Give to others from the Holy Spirit you have within you. Give of yourself.

Ask that others be filled with the Spirit and Life of God. Live that Life to the fullest and share it. Others will share it with others and that's when these rewards grow exponentially.

Ask for those who need answers from God to come across your path, and then have the boldness to ask for their needs with and for them.

Ask to hear from the Holy Spirit before and as you pray. And then expect to hear the answers.

Ask that you would be filled with all the fullness of God.

> *"Be worried for nothing; but in everything by prayer and asking, and with thanksgiving, let your requests be made known unto God. And the peace of God, which passes all understanding, will preserve your heart and mind through Christ Jesus."(9)*

As we've looked at, Paul gives an excellent overview of our asking here. He says for us not to be anxious or worried, and only to have trust, knowing the power of God in your life, and to pray and ask with thanksgiving. As you do this the peace of God and the Lord of Peace will come to you and will be with you, and you will have that Peace.

Pray for faith. Pray to see and be shown and to know that God answers your requests.

Ask what He would have you do.

Be open and conscious as to how the Spirit of God may be leading you, in your asking and when He is moving through you into others' lives.

As we said, Jesus was filled and always in "tune" with the Spirit, praying and hearing and healing and giving life from the Father.

Ask for this, and how to be tuned in more and more, that you might give or share or show life to others from the Lord.

Jesus healed a number of blind men who came across His path. We see that He healed each of them in very different ways.

With some He touched their eyes. In one case He took a man out of the town, spit on his eyes and put His hands on them. In another He told a man to go his way and that his trust had made him whole. To another Jesus made a mud ball from spit and dust and put it on the man's eyes.

In the end they all were healed, yet they were all healed in different ways. There was no set formula or format for Jesus in what He did, how He moved, and how the Spirit moved through Him.

We need to also understand that there is no set formula or format for us in how He moves through us either. Be open and ready for the Lord and the Spirit of God to move in many amazing ways with and through you.

Also know that there is no set formula in how we pray.

Again, we don't have to have "perfect" prayers. What God considers a perfect prayer is when the heart of the person praying is earnest and the asking is done in faith and trust in Him.

I've suggested a number of things to make your asking more effective, but know that the most important, and the only true prayer, is one from your heart to God.

Job said, *"If I had called, and God had answered me..."(10)*

But he never called. He never sought, knocked or asked. He never went to God with any of it.

But we have every opportunity to do so.

> *"For the eyes of the Lord are over the righteous (those who are seeking and have their hearts toward God), and His ears are open to their prayers."(11)*

Spend time in and with the Father, His Word, and His Holy Spirit,,,

And Ask.

"Ask and it shall be given you..."(12)

And your Father in Heaven will hear,,,

And He will be with you,,,

And He will answer you!

The Secret

"Draw near to God, and He will draw near to you."

James 4:8

The Secret

"One thing have I desired of the LORD, that will I seek after;
that I may dwell in the house of the LORD all the days of my life,
to behold the beauty of the LORD, and to inquire in His temple.
For in the time of trouble He shall hide me in His pavilion:
in the secret of His tabernacle He shall hide me
and He shall set me up upon a rock."(1)

Remember how we talked about a mystery? The great thing about a mystery is that the clues, and the answers, are there all along.

We have seen that there are many secrets hidden in the Book of Job.

The number one revealed mystery of the Secret of Job is that the Lord wants us to learn about Him, to have a great and meaningful relationship with Him, to know Him and trust Him and to go to Him with everything in our lives, and for all of our lives.

Job had a perfect heart toward God. Because of this, God had an expectation of him, that when things went wrong, Job would come immediately to Him, his Father God, as his Rock, his Shelter, his Strong Tower, his Fortress, and as his Lord.

And even though he had a diligent worship of God, it also turns out that Job also had a limited understanding of Who his God was. When things fell apart, he in turn made some very wrong assumptions and decisions about God and ended up *not* going to His Father for any help at all. He even turned and blamed God for all that happened.

Do we also have a limited understanding of Who our God is and do we do this as well?

Do we hide from Him, and not go to Him because we don't know Him well enough?

Do we worship Him from afar, not endeavoring to know Him more?

Are we, too, afraid to know Him more, and thereby we don't seek Him?

Are we too set in our "Christian" ways, in our religious routines, not wanting to go any further into Him, not wanting to transition into the next level of life in Him?

Or do we know Him as our Friend, and know that He is always there to help us, guide us, and to be with us?

It is my belief that if Job had gone directly to God, the Father would have delivered him from his afflictions and immediately given him all of the good things that he eventually ended up with, and his ordeal wouldn't have been nearly as long, if at all.

And in the end, when God showed him the truth, we see that Job realized what he had done, and/or not done, and he deeply regretted his actions.

The Great Irony of the Book of Job is that God reveals perfectly, through Job and his friends, our very own human nature.

- ➤ We react to the events of Job in exactly the same way that Job did.

- ➤ We have responded to the afflictions of Job by wholly commiserating with him, and even agonizing with him.

- ➤ And we too indirectly blamed God, while even continuing to recognize His greatness.

Job, in turn, is constantly accusing God of wrongdoing, and creating his own 'pachad' fear. He blames God, when God is not causing any of his torment at all.

How often do we blame God, especially for bad things that happen in our lives? How often do we just guess about God, and not try to find out the truth?

How often do we think God punishes us? How often do we accuse or judge someone else when we really know very little about them or about the circumstances before us?

Job's friends are constantly accusing Job of doing something wrong and believe that God is punishing Job for something he did or is doing, and they are trying to set him straight.

God strongly shows us in the end of the Book of Job, that Job, and Job's friend's perceptions about the Father, about punishment, and about the character of God, are all very wrong.

God then shows Job the truth about His real nature, which Job then realizes, and then he deeply regrets and repents for not having realized Who his God *really* is.

God is revealing to us through Job that we don't have to remain in a dry routine, in a state of limited understanding of Him, and that we can go further and further, deeper and deeper, and higher and higher into all that He is and all that He has for us.

Which is His purpose, and His will, for us and in us.

God had an expectation of Job, and I also believe that the Lord has an expectation of us. He desires that we would know Who He is. He has sent His Son and His very own Spirit for the express purpose of showing us more about Him, to show us Who He is and Who He can be in our lives, so that we indeed can have life, and life more abundantly in Him!

Another revealed secret of Job is that God has shown us, right in the middle of His Word by direct comparison with Job and David, a greater and better way to handle, and react to, and overcome adversity in our lives.

The Lord created us, and knows what will benefit us, and is showing us by His grace how to find peace and comfort and rest and strength and healing and life, in our daily lives, especially during the adverse times and seasons that are inherent in our lives here on earth.

King David, in Psalms, said over and over that God is our refuge and our strength.

Job decided not to go there, until the end, after God showed him he could, and led him there.

Let us get to know that place, that refuge, that strong tower in Him, and go there often for protection, peace, and rest, especially when all around us is crazy and when we need it most.

We also see that the things of God are revealed to us in a very personal way by His Spirit.

Not only do we have the opportunity to know who the Father is, and Who His Son Jesus is, but we also have the opportunity to know Who the Holy Spirit is and how He moves and lives and works with us and in us and through us.

Jesus heard from the Father, and He, by the Spirit of God, moved with the power of the Holy Spirit. So can we also hear from the Lord, by His Spirit Who lives within each of us, and can also move with and in Him.

For generations we have not seen or known what God was trying to tell us through Job, and we, because of our very nature, have never really tried to look further than the apparent, face value events.

We can now see things from the Fathers perspective in all of this. We can now see and know that He desires us to "see as He sees."

Jesus said over and over that if we ask, it **will** be given, that if we seek, we **will** find, and that if we knock, it **will** indeed be opened for us and to us. Not that it might be, but that it ***will be***.

Let's come to that realization in our lives, and come to know and experience the things of the Lord more deeply and personally and profoundly, as much as we can, as often as we can, even all the time.

I would offer that Job was originally living in a place of not knowing God, and certainly not to the fullest. But in the end the Lord showed him, and He is showing us, that we can come to Him and have the most marvelous 'knowing' relationship with Him.

344

God showed Job that he indeed could come to Him with everything.

The Lord has intended that we might live this way as well and to have life more abundantly, and joy in our lives.

Jesus was the nature and character of God, and He came to show us that we don't have to fear God, and that we can come to Him with anything and everything.

> "...let your requests be made known to God, and the peace of God, which is far beyond understanding... shall keep you and shall be with you."(2)

Let's get to know that peace.

> "And they shall call his name Emmanuel, which is interpreted, God with us."(3)

Let us also know that our great and wonderful and powerful God is with us.

Always.

The Lord and His Spirit and His Word teach us, and show us, and give us a lifetime of opportunities to know Him.

What are we going to do with all that He has provided for us and all He is revealing to us?

What is by far the most powerful force in the world?

The Father, Son (the Word) and Holy Spirit of God.

Three in One, and One in Three.

What is the second most powerful?

Believe it or not, it's our own words and heart/spirit!

We need to learn how to use our words and our requests to bring life to our lives, ourselves and to others.

We've only scratched the surface of the depths of the fullness of God that He has for us, and all that we can do in and through Him.

The Lord says for us to ask, and receive, that our joy would be full. That you would ask, and that you receive, that *your* joy would be full!

Have you built your trust and used your will and has your faith been developed to the point of having great expectations of the things of God happening in your life?

You can do it! The Lord *wants* you to!

May we all endeavor to grow to a higher and deeper understanding of all of the things of our God, that we may be filled with all the fullness of Him in all things.

God was there the whole time listening and waiting for Job to come to Him.

He, and His Son, and His Holy Spirit are still here,,,

Listening and waiting...

For you.

Bibliography

I.   The Secret of Job

Everyone Loves a Secret
1. Luke 8:10
The Past
1. Colossians 2:8
So what is the Purpose of Job?
1. Romans 15:4

II.   Part I – God (and Satan)

There Was a Man in the Land of Uz...
1. Job 1:1
2. Deuteronomy 6:13
3. Matthew 4:10
4. Romans 3:23
5. Job 1:4-5
6. Job 1:3
7. Job 4:3-4
The Adversary
1. Job 1:6
2. Luke 10:18
3. CS Lewis "The Screwtape Letters"
4. Genesis 3:13
5. John 10:10
6. John 8:44
7. James 2:19
8. Revelations 12:10
9. 1 Peter 5:8
The Challenge
1. Job 1:8
2. Job 1:7
3. Job 1:8
4. Job 1:9-10
5. I John 4:16
6. Job 1:11
7. Job 1:12
8. Job 1:21
9. Job 1:22
10. Job 2:3
11. Job 2:10

        12. Job 2:10
        13. Job 2:12
        14. Job 2:13
    Job's Integrity
        1. Job 2:3

III. **Part II – Job**

    Job
        1. Job 3:1
        2. Job 3:3-10
        3. Job 3:3
        4. Job 3:11, 20-21
        5. Job 3:25
        6. Job 6:2-4
        7. Job 19:8-11
        8. Job 10:1
        9. Job 9:4-10

IV. **Part III – Job's Friends**

    Eliphaz, Bildad, Zophar and Elihu
        1. Job 2:11
        2. Job 4:2
        3. Job 4:3-5
        4. Job 4:7-9
        5. Job 5:8-17
        6. Job 6:25-28
        7. Job 8:2-6
        8. Job 11:3-6
        9. Job 16:2-4
        10. Job 37:14-22
        11. Matthew 12:36
        12. Job 38:2
    Iyyob – Persecuted One
        1. Job 16:2-3
        2. Job 19:2
        3. Job 11:2-5
        4. Job 8:6
        5. Job 22:5
        6. Job 16:2-3
        7. Job 19:2
        8. Job 17:2

2. Job 1:8
3. Job 3:1
Job's Choice
   1. Job 19:21
   2. Job 7:11
   3. Job 4:4
Relationship
   1. Matthew 11:28
   2. Job 1:4-5
   3. Job 13:20-22
   4. Matthew 11:29
Job's Fear
   1. Job 9:34-35
   2. Job 3:25
   3. 2 Corinthians 10:4
   4. 2 Corinthians 10:5 – The Amplified Bible
Don't Blame God
   1. Job 9:16-17
   2. 1 Thessalonians 5:21
   3. Matthew 12:25
   4. John 14:9
   5. Luke 9:55-56
   6. Hebrews 12:5-7
   7. James 1:16-17
   8. Matthew 13:36-43
   9. Isaiah 57:1
   10. 1 Corinthians 13:12
   11. Job 40:2
   12. Job 40:8
God's Grace
   1. Ephesians 2:8
   2. Ephesians 2:5-9
   3. Acts 20:32
Mercy and Grace
   1. Hebrews 4:16
   2. Psalms 86:15
   3. Psalms 145:8-9
   4. Psalms 136:1
   5. Lamentations 3:22-23
   6. Romans 12:19
   7. Luke 9:51-56
   8. Matthew 5:44-45

5. Acts 4:24
6. Psalm 57:1
7. Psalm 62:6-8
8. Psalm 91:1-2

Trust God
1. Hebrews 11:6
2. Hebrews 11:1
3. Romans 1:17
4. Hebrews 11:6
5. Hebrews 11:1
6. Matthew 8:10
7. Romans 4:20
8. Matthew 9:29
9. Luke 8:48
10. Mark 11:22
11. Mark 11:22
12. John 10:10

The Power of God
1. 1 Corinthians 2:5
2. 2 Timothy 1:7
3. Luke 4:18-19
4. 1 Corinthians 4:20
5. 1 Corinthians 2:4-5
6. John 14:10
7. Mark 16:15-18
8. Acts 3:6-8
9. Ephesians 1:17-19
10. Ephesians 1:20-23
11. Ephesians 3:20
12. Colossians 1:9-11
13. 2 Thessalonians 1:11-12
14. 2 Timothy 3:1-5
15. Ephesians 6:10

The Patience of God
1. James 1:4
2. Romans 5:3-4
3. James 5:10-11

Praise
1. Psalm 9:1
2. Psalm 146:2
3. Job 1:20
4. Psalm 34:1-4

Peace
1. Philippians 4:7
2. Luke 10:38-42
3. Psalm 34:14
4. Colossians 3:15
5. 1 Corinthians 14:33
6. Revelations 13:18
7. Romans 1:7
8. Romans 15:33
9. John 14:27

God Rewards
1. Hebrews 11:6
2. John 6:29
3. Matthew 16:15
4. Job 11:7
5. Matthew 7:7

Desire
1. Proverbs 18:1
2. Proverbs 3:13-18
3. Proverbs 2:2-5
4. Isaiah 58:6-11
5. John 16:24

XII.   Knock

Knock
1. Matthew 7:7-8
2. Hebrews 4:16
3. Exodus 17:5-6
4. Matthew 7:11
5. Mathew 7:8

XIII.   Ask

You Have Not Because You Ask Not
1. James 4:2-3
2. Job 19:7
3. Job 30:19-20
4. Job 9:34-35
5. Job 13:20-22
6. Revelations 3:20-21
7. 1 Peter 5:7
8. John 16:24

Jonah
1. Jonah 2:1
2. Jonah 1:10-12
3. Jonah 1:16
4. Jonah 2:3
5. Jonah 2:5
6. Jonah 2:1
7. Jonah 2:7
8. Jonah 2:10

Ask
1. Mat 7:7-8
2. Mat 7:11
3. 1 John 4:7-8
4. 2 Timothy 1:7
5. Matthew 18:19
6. Matthew 7:7-8
7. Matthew 21:22
8. John 16:23-24

Asking Effectively
1. James 5:16
2. Philippians 4:6
3. Genesis 1:3
4. Psalms 54:2
5. Mark 11:23
6. Matthew 6:6
7. Matthew 6:7-13
8. Matthew 6:9
9. Luke 11:8
10. 1 John 5:14-15
11. Mark 9:23
12. Matthew 7:8

Asking Fervently
1. James 5:17
2. James 1:5-7
3. John 11:35
4. James 5:17-18
5. Mark 9:17, 22
6. Mark 9:23-24
7. Romans 12:3
8. Matthew 17:20

Availing Much
1. John 15:7-8

2. 1 John 5:14
3. John 14:12-14
4. Mark 16:17-18
5. Luke 10:1-3, 9
6. Luke 10:17
7. John 15:16
8. John 16:25
9. John 15:15

In The Spirit
1. Acts 19:2
2. John 7:38-39
3. Acts 19:2
4. Acts 1:4-5
5. Acts 1:8
6. Acts 8:14-17
7. Hebrews 6:2

And Be Ye Thankful
1. Philippians 4:6-7
2. Philippians 4:8-9
3. Psalm 95:2
4. Luke 17:12-19
5. Colossians 3:15

XIV.   Wisdom

Ask for Wisdom
1. James 1:5
2. 1 Kings 3:5,9-14
3. Proverbs 4:7-9
4. Proverbs 3:13-18
5. Job 38:36
6. Proverbs 2:6,9
7. James 3:17
8. Psalms 51:6
9. James 1:5
10. James 1:6-7

God's Presence and His Rest
1. Matthew 11:28-30
2. James 4: 7-8,10
3. Isaiah 40:31
4. Acts 3:19
5. Psalms 46:10
6. Psalms 16:11

7.   Exodus 33:14
As the Lord Sees
   1.   Psalms 32:8
   2.   John 15:15
   3.   John 15:16
   4.   John 14:26
   5.   Isaiah 55:11

XV.   Pray for Your Friends

Pray for your Friends
   1.   Job 42:10
   2.   Job 4:3-5
   3.   James 5:16
Asking for Others
   1.   I Timothy 2:1-3
   2.   James 5:16
   3.   John 4:24
   4.   Matthew 5:44-45
   5.   Mark 11:25
   6.   James 5:15
   7.   John 14:10

XVI.   Going to God

God's Will
   1.   1 John 5:14-15
   2.   Ephesians 1:8-9
   3.   Ephesians 3:16-19
   4.   1 Timothy 2:8
The Word
   1.   John 1:14
   2.   1 John 5:7
   3.   John 14:6
   4.   John 15:4-5
Our Will
   1.   John 15:7
   2.   James 5:16
   3.   2 Chronicles 7:14
   4.   Matthew 22:20-21
   5.   Romans 8:26
   6.   Matthew 18:18-20
   7.   John 15:7

www.ingramcontent.com/pod-product-compliance
Lightning Source LLC
Chambersburg PA
CBHW072133090426
42739CB00013B/3180